THE EARLY
SOCIOLOGY
OF RELIGION

Printed and bound in Great Britain by
Antony Rowe Ltd, Chippenham, Wiltshire

THE EARLY SOCIOLOGY OF RELIGION

Edited by
Bryan S. Turner

Volume IX
Primitive Religion
Robert H. Lowie

ROUTLEDGE/THOEMMES PRESS

© Routledge/Thoemmes Press 1997

Published in 1997 by

Routledge/Thoemmes Press
11 New Fetter Lane
London EC4P 4EE

The Early Sociology of Religion
9 Volumes: ISBN 0 415 14447 7

Routledge/Thoemmes Press is a joint imprint
of Routledge and Thoemmes Antiquarian Books Ltd.

British Library Cataloguing in Publication Data
A CIP record of this series is available
on request from the British Library

Library of Congress Cataloguing in Publication Data
The early sociology of religion / edited by Bryan S. Turner.
p.   cm.
Includes bibliographical references.
1. Religion and sociology.   I. Turner, Bryan S.
BL60.E19 1996   96-11408
306.6—dc20

ISBN 0-415-14447-7

Publisher's Note

These reprints are taken from original copies of each book.
In many cases the condition of those originals is not perfect,
the paper, often handmade, having suffered over time and
the copy from such things as inconsistent printing pressures
resulting in faint text, show-through from one side of a leaf
to the other, the filling in of some characters, and the break
up of type. The publisher has gone to great lengths to ensure
the quality of these reprints but points out that certain
characteristics of the original copies will, of necessity, be
apparent in reprints thereof.

PRIMITIVE RELIGION

PRIMITIVE RELIGION

BY

ROBERT H. LOWIE, Ph. D.

ASSOCIATE PROFESSOR OF ANTHROPOLOGY, UNIVERSITY OF CALIFORNIA;
AUTHOR OF ' *Primitive Society* '

LONDON
GEORGE ROUTLEDGE AND SONS, Ltd.
BROADWAY HOUSE : 68-74, CARTER LANE, E.C.
1925.

Printed in Great Britain by MACKAYS LTD., Chatham.

PREFACE

THIS work does not purport to be a handbook of either the theories broached on the subject of primitive religion or of the ethnographic data described in hundreds of accessible monographs. My purpose is to provide an introduction to further study in which other than the traditional topics shall assume a place of honor. On the other hand I have taken pains to reduce to a minimum the discussion of theories that have been more than amply treated by previous writers.

The mode of approach will be found to differ fundamentally from that of my book on *Primitive Society*. The reason lies in the quite different status of the two subjects at the present time. In the field of primitive sociology it seemed desirable to marshal the evidence against the indefensible neglect of historical considerations that persists in some quarters. In the study of comparative religion it is the psychological point of view that requires emphasis; and however important history may be for an elucidation of psychology, its part is ancillary. By consistently stressing the psychological aspects of primitive religion I hope to have contributed something to a closer alliance of two sister sciences that too frequently have pursued their paths in mutual neglect.

Several friends have been good enough to read or listen to portions of the book—above all, Dr. Leslie Spier and Mrs. Erna Gunther Spier of the University of Washington; Professors A. L. Kroeber and Erasmo Buceta of the University of California; Mr. E. W. Gifford of the same institution; and my friends Mr. Donald B. Clark and Dr. Jaime de Angulo y Mayo. I take this opportunity to thank them for their encouragement and their comments. To Mr. Gifford I am also indebted for the orthography of proper names in Mariner's account, which is brought into accord with approved Tongan usage and thus comes closer to phonetic spelling.

My manuscript was completed when I received a copy of Father Wilhelm Koppers's book on the Fuegians. It was no longer possible to utilize it as I should otherwise have done, but I took pains to incorporate some of the interesting data presented there and to include the work in my bibliography. On the other hand, a paper on some basic religious concepts by Dr. John R. Swanton, which is to appear in a forthcoming issue of the *American Anthropologist,* reached me too late to be used in any way, so that I must content myself with this meager reference.

ROBERT H. LOWIE.

BERKELEY, CAL.,
May, 1924.

CONTENTS

PRIMITIVE RELIGION

INTRODUCTION

A work on "Primitive Religion" may well begin with a definition of the terms in its title, for neither unfortunately is unambiguous. The word "primitive" by its etymology suggests "primeval," but when the anthropologist speaks descriptively of "primitive peoples" he means no more—at least, he has no right to mean more—than peoples of a relatively simple culture; or, to be more specific, the illiterate peoples of the world. To be sure, it is impossible to suppress the inference that what is shared by the illiterate peoples of rudest culture in contrast to those possessing a more complex civilization dates back to a relatively great antiquity; but this *is* an inference, not an immediate datum of experience. Moreover, it is certain that, no matter how simple a particular culture may be, it has had a long history. Human civilization may be roughly said to be 100,000 years old. It is inconceivable that any distinct subdivision of mankind, even if separated from others for only one-tenth of that immense span of time, should have remained in an absolutely static condition. There are two cogent reasons to the contrary. First, isolation has never been more than relative when very great periods are considered. In other words, influences from without have everywhere produced *some* changes in custom, belief, and the material arts of life. Secondly, such alterations occur, though more slowly, even in the absence of extraneous stimulation because of the social

results of individual variation, that is, of innovations successfully impressed on each generation by some able individuals of sufficiently powerful personality. Both determinants
of change can be detected in so isolated and so simple a people as the Andaman Islanders of the Bay of Bengal. Their
remoteness did not prevent them from borrowing the device
of the outrigger canoe, presumably from some Malaysian
tribe; and the local variations found within their islands,
both in language and social heritage, prove the occurrence of
novel ideas even in a population ignorant of metals and every
form of husbandry, nay, lacking even the dog and the art of
fire-making. In other words, the Andamanese culture of
fifty years ago is not the culture of their ancestors five hundred years ago, or in still earlier periods; and, so far as direct observation goes, we cannot select any one feature of
their social life as of hoary antiquity. "Primitive," then,
for our purposes shall be devoid of chronological import.

It is far more difficult to explain what shall be designated
by the word "religion." Of course, a formal definition of
religion would be as futile at the outset as a corresponding
definition of consciousness in a textbook of psychology, or
of electricity in a treatise on physics. The rich content of
these comprehensive concepts can be appreciated only *after* a
survey of the relevant data is completed. Yet some circum-
scription of what is to be included is not only possible but
necessary, and it will be convenient to begin by illustrating
the wrong approach to a definition by two extreme instances
gleaned from Fielding's novels. Says Parson Thwackum
in *Tom Jones,*

When I mention religion, I mean the Christian religion; and
not only the Christian religion but the Protestant religion; and
not only the Protestant religion, but the Church of England.

And Parson Adams, in *Joseph Andrews,* is equally explicit:

The first care I always take is of a boy's morals; I had rather he should be a blockhead than an atheist or a Presbyterian.

Why do utterances such as these strike us as ineffably parochial? From one angle it might seem that a man has the right to define his terms as he will, provided only he adhere to the usage once established; and if to embrace the Anglican Church means salvation, while Calvinism spells perdition, then from that particular point of view there is nothing to choose between being a Presbyterian and being an atheist. This position is indeed inexpugnable so long as it is avowedly no more than a personal evaluation; it is shattered as soon as it pretends to give an objective classification of the pertinent data. In this second rôle it recalls that comical classification of some aboriginal language by which male adult members of the tribe are of one gender, while all other persons are lumped in a vast complementary category together with animals, plants, and objects. We require no proof that a boy or a woman or a foreigner is nearer to a tribesman than to a tree or a rock; and so we see at once that it is arbitrary to dichotomize the religious universe after the manner of Fielding's parsons, that such division wrests the phenomena out of their true context and does violence to their true inwardness.

But when once committed to this moderately tolerant attitude, we are still without guidance as to where the line shall be drawn. Working our way backwards from a particular branch of Christianity, we are still able to recognize some kinship between our faith and that of other monotheistic creeds. When we come to Buddhism, with its theoretical atheism, many of us will be inclined to deny that any doctrine dispensing with the notion of a personal deity can fairly be brought under the same heading with familiar religions. Yet William James, our greatest psychologist, has espoused the view that Buddhism, like Emersonian transcendentalism, makes to the individual votary an appeal and evokes a response "in fact indistinguishable from, and in many respects identical with, the best Christian appeal and response." [1] James may conceivably err in this particular judgment, but anthropologically speaking there can be no doubt of the correctness of his test: *if* Buddhism satisfies that part of the Buddhist's nature which corresponds to the devout Christian's longing for acceptance by the deity, then it is a veritable religion, just as polygyny is anthropologically no less a form of marriage than monogamy, and an oral tradition must be reckoned, despite etymology, a specimen of literature. What we should determine is wherein such satisfaction essentially lies. Confronted with beliefs and practices divorced from an organized priesthood, lacking congregational worship and a standardized cosmogony, we must ask not whether this or that objective feature shall be counted as essential but whether the subjective condition of the believers and worshipers corresponds to that of an unequivocally religious frame of mind.

That the mere presence of some objective feature is wholly irrelevant may be illustrated by citing the opening paragraphs of Leibniz's *Metaphysics:*

The conception of God which is the most common and the most full of meaning is expressed well enough in the words: *God is an absolutely perfect being.* The implications, however, of these words fail to receive sufficient consideration. For instance, there are many different kinds of perfection, all of which God possesses, and each one of them pertains to him in the highest degree.

We must also know what perfection is. One thing which can surely be affirmed about it is that those forms or natures which are not susceptible of it to the highest degree, say the nature of numbers or of figures, do not permit of perfection. This is because the number which is the greatest of all (that is, the sum of all the numbers), and likewise the greatest of all figures, imply contradictions. The greatest knowledge, however, and omnipotence contain no impossibility. Consequently power and knowledge do admit of perfection, and in so far as they pertain to God they have no limits.

Whence it follows that God, who possesses supreme and infinite wisdom, acts in the most perfect manner not only metaphysically, but also from the moral standpoint. And with respect to ourselves it can be said that the more we are enlightened and informed in regard to the works of God the more will we be disposed to find them excellent and conforming entirely to that which we might desire.

Is this passage an expression of religious sentiment? Of course it is in thorough harmony with traditional religion, yet it belongs to a different compartment. It shares with monotheistic religion its subject-matter as an artist and a scientist may share a bit of landscape, the one for depiction, the other for a study of the flora. In Leibniz the religious flavor is singularly absent, because his abstract propositions leave the *religious* consciousness cold. Whatever disagreement may exist on the subject, the dominance of the emotional side of consciousness in religion is universally accepted, and where that phase of mental life is in relative abeyance religion must be considered wanting.

It is the insufficient consideration given to the emotional factor of religion that makes it necessary to qualify and revise the views enunciated by the greatest of comparative students in this field. When, in 1871, Edward B. Tylor published the first edition of his *Primitive Culture*, he was above all interested in the problem of evolution. Darwin's *Origin of Species* had begun to stimulate historical thinking in other than biological lines, and the investigator of culture naturally sought to parallel the paleontologist's and embryologist's record by corresponding sequences in industrial arts, social organization and belief. As to the last-mentioned branch of culture, it was clear that if evolution were accepted at all there must have been some stage in the development of man, whether corresponding to a human or prehuman level, at which religion had not yet evolved. Then there inevitably arose the query, whether that stage was represented by any people still living. It was this problem, among others, that Tylor set out to solve. But in order to solve it he was obliged to frame a "minimum definition" of religion. Rejecting as too exclusive, as expressing rather special developments than the basic nature of religion, various current definitions, he found its essence to lie in animism, that is, in "the belief in Spiritual Beings"; and because such a belief had been reported from all adequately described tribes on the face of the globe, Tylor inferred the universality of religion.[2]

What more recent scholars reject is not this conclusion itself, which stands practically unchallenged, but its motivation. In Tylor's discussion the belief in spiritual beings, that is, religion in his sense, is made to arise in response to an *intellectual* need,—the desire of an explanation for the physiological phenomena of life, sleep, dream, and death. This rationalistic bias appears clearly from the very phrases used in referring to primitive animism, which is again and again alluded to as a philosophy, a doctrine, "the theory of dreams," "a perfectly rational and intelligible product of early science," "the theory of souls."[3] It is conceivable that the craving for a causal explanation might lead to the

notion of spirits as suggested by Tylor without the slightest consequent or associated emotional reaction essential to
religion; indeed, not a few examples might be cited of
spiritual beings postulated by primitive tribes for, so far
as one can see, an exclusive satisfaction of their metaphysical demands.

In this way, then, Tylor's formulation is not exacting
enough, for it omits an essential determinant of the phenomenon to be defined. Yet in another sense, meager as it
may appear at first sight, it demands more than is required.
For we have already seen that even a system of belief devoid of animistic conceptions, like Buddhism, may function
as the psychological equivalent of Christianity or any other
of the faiths of Western civilization. What, then, is the
bond that unites beliefs which on the surface are so divergent? The essentially correct answer seems to me to
have been given by Dr. R. R. Marett and Dr. N. Söderblom, the Archbishop of Upsala, and I will try to set forth
in a few words the most significant points involved. In
every society, no matter how simple it may be, there is a
spontaneous division of the sphere of experience into the
ordinary and the extraordinary. Some writers, notably
Lévy-Bruhl, impressed with the fantastic theoretical notions obtaining among unlettered peoples in regard to the
constitution and origin of the universe, have broached the
view that such odd fancies must be rooted in a mental
condition radically different from our own. Yet closer attention to the usages of savage life demonstrates beyond
the possibility of doubt that in grappling with the problems
of everyday life primitive man often employs precisely the
same psychological processes of association, observation,
and inference as our own farmers, engineers, or craftsmen.
When a Hopi Indian in Arizona raises corn where a white

tiller fails, when a Papuan boatwright constructs elaborate
buildings without nails or metal implements, when a Polynesian carves the most esthetic patterns with a shark's tooth,
he is solving his everyday problems not only competently
but with elegance. All these activities, however, though
sometimes curiously associated with (to our mind) irrelevant considerations, belong in the main to what Dr. Marett
would call the *workaday* world, i. e., the domain of reason,
of normal experience, of an empirical correspondence of
cause and effect. But everywhere there is, in addition to
such practical rationalism, a sense of something transcending the expected or natural, a sense of the Extraordinary,
Mysterious, or Supernatural. Certainly that sense is very
frequently, and conceivably might be always, linked with
the recognition of spiritual beings; but to what extent such
a correlation obtains is a matter for empirical inquiry and
should not be prejudged. But even were this association
of spirit-belief with a sense of mystery an invariable phenomenon, it would still be legitimate to argue that it is the
latter which is indispensable to religion, that the belief in
spirits derives its religious value solely from this association
instead of being religious in its own right. The fact that
subjective states indistinguishable from religious ones are
indifferently found with and without animistic notions definitely settles the matter. We shall therefore recognize as
the differentia of religion what Drs. Marett and Goldenweiser have called "supernaturalism." [4]

Reverting to the problem that engaged Tylor's attention,
we shall say: Religion is verily a universal feature of human culture, not because all societies foster a belief in
spirits, but because all recognize in some form or other
awe-inspiring, extraordinary manifestations of reality.
The present treatise is accordingly dedicated to the discus-

sion of those cultural phenomena of the simpler societies which center about or are somehow connected with the sense of mystery or weirdness. Owing to the many ramifications of such supernaturalism, this definition leads not to a rigid exclusion but merely to a somewhat different appraisal of features commonly treated under the head of religion.

For the colorless terms employed above Dr. Söderblom substitutes the concept of the Holy or the Sacred. It is undoubtedly true that in a great many instances that which is set over in contrast to everyday experience is invested with a halo of sanctity that justifies the use of the terms cited. However, if I correctly interpret the data, the Supernatural is Janus-headed, and its more sinister aspect is not adequately rendered by our word "holy" with its traditional connotations. I therefore prefer to use noncommittal expressions when groping for a *minimum* definition of religion, though I am the last to deny the great frequency with which the Extraordinary or Supernatural assumes the aspect of the Holy.

In studying alien religions the same precaution must be observed as in the study of comparative linguistics. Pioneer investigators of primitive languages were wont to pattern their descriptions on the Latin grammar. Indeed, many of us were taught English grammar on the same plan,—obliged to recite the non-existent datives and accusatives of nouns and the equally chimerical imperfect subjunctives of verbs. Gradually, however, philologists came to realize that Latin grammar, thus used, was a Procrustean bed and that each tongue must be viewed according to its own genius. The application is obvious. When we approach an alien faith, we have no right to impose our received categories. Because *our* sacred Book contains an account of cosmogony, it does not follow that a given primitive cosmogony comes within the scope of religion. Though immortality has played an enormous part in the history of Christianity, it need not occupy the center of the stage in other forms of belief.

The only legitimate mode of approach will then correspond to the modern linguist's: considering each religion from the point of view of its votaries, let us ascertain what are their concepts of the Supernatural, how they are interrelated and weighted with reference to one another. For reasons of space it is manifestly impracticable to sketch more than a limited number of distinct aboriginal religions, even were it possible to gain a sympathetic insight into the essentials of many more. Hence, I have made a selection of four representative samples.

I begin with the Crow Indians of eastern Montana because I am here able to offer the results of personal inquiries in the field; and because this tribe exemplifies one particular conception of the Extraordinary, a conception, moreover, typical of many other North American aborigines.

From this group of Plains Indian hunters I pass to the horticultural Ekoi of Kamerun and Southern Nigeria because these West Africans represent a wholly different attitude toward the Supernatural and neatly set off some of the features that distinguish Old World from New World belief and ritual.

The Bukaua and their neighbors, the Jabim and Tami, about the shores of Huon Gulf, New Guinea, while sharing some of the African notions, exhibit and stress still other methods of reaction toward the Extraordinary and exhibit one form of widespread ceremonial with great clarity.

Finally, the Polynesians display an incomparable elaboration of what exists in germ not only among the Bukaua but, in a wider sense, in the primitive world at large.

In all four cases my choice has been determined in part by the availability of ample and trustworthy material.

Lest there be any misunderstanding on the subject, I take pains to point out that the general statements made in these synthetic sketches will not be found in that form in the descriptive monographs laid under contribution,—not even when these happen to be by myself. What I have tried to do is to saturate myself with the material and to interpret it as far as possible from the natives' point of view; and in this attempt I have sometimes turned the observers' data inside out. That accordingly a subjective element attaches to these pictures, is undeniable: to be forewarned is to be forearmed. Nevertheless, the compensatory advantages seem to me sufficient to justify the undertaking from a pedagogical, and not merely from a pedagogical, point of view.

REFERENCES

All titles are fully quoted in the terminal Bibliography, where authors are listed alphabetically and their several publications chronologically; titles of the same author are distinguished by letters. The chapter references cite the author's name if he is represented by a single title; his name and the date if two or more papers or books are listed; and if there are two in the same year, the letter is added. The pages are set off by colons. *Examples.* James: 34. Tylor, 1877: I, 424. Lowie, 1915 (a) : 62.

[1] James: 34.
[2] Tylor, 1913: I, 424.
[3] Tylor, 1913: I, 440, 447; id., 1881: 371.
[4] Marett, 11, 101-121. Goldenweiser, 1922: 231.

Part I: Synthetic Sketches

CHAPTER I

CROW RELIGION [1]

THE VISION

As a young Crow Indian approached adolescence, he could not fail to observe the differences among his tribesmen in point of social position. Though hereditary distinctions of rank were wholly lacking, some individuals were regarded with far more respect than others, possibly because of their wealth and wisdom but especially because of their great exploits in war. When a father wanted his newborn babe named, Bell-rock would be summoned to dub it after one of his own deeds of valor; and he might receive a horse by way of compensation. At the time of the great Sun festival brave men—and only such—were entertained with that prized delicacy, buffalo tongues. Warriors about to raid a hostile camp would go to Sore-tail for instructions, and when they returned laden with spoils the choicest of the booty went to Sore-tail's lodge till he ranked as the wealthiest Crow within the memory of man. Why had he become rich while Small-back remained horseless except for the little nag a generous brave had in sheer pity donated to him? Why was Bell-rock the greatest of all chiefs and Yellow-crane rated a good-for-nothing poltroon? The young man knew, for from a boy he had had the answer dinned into his ears: to become great, to make sure of success in any of life's critical situations, one must gain the blessing of some supernatural power. A few favored persons were lucky enough to be visited by the spirits in their sleep or in some other way that involved no effort; but the majority had to earn their vision through pain and hardship. The ambitious warrior, the mourner filled with the lust for vengeance, the spurned lover, and the youth chafing from a sense of his family's poverty, must mortify their flesh and thus rouse the compassion of the supernatural powers.

The procedure was fairly fixed. A would-be visionary would go to a lonely spot, preferably to the summit of a mountain. Naked except for a breechclout and the buffalo robe to cover him at night, he abstained from food and drink for four days or more if necessary, wailing and invoking the spirits. Usually some form of bodily torture or disfigurement was practised as an offering to the supernatural beings. Most commonly, perhaps, men would hack off a finger joint of the left hand, so that during the period of my visits to the Crow (1907-1916) I saw few old men with left hands intact. The Sun was generally the being supplicated, and the following may serve as an example of a typical prayer:

Hallo, Old Man, I am poor! You see me, give me something good. Give me long life; grant that I may own a horse, that I capture a gun, that I strike a blow against the enemy! Let me become a chief, let me own plenty of property!

But although the Sun was called, he rarely appeared. The actual visitants are occasionally connected with the Sun as his messengers or symbols, but in general they are conceived as in no way related to him. According to a usual pattern, they present themselves in human guise but before they leave their true nature is revealed, either by the words of their song or their re-transformation or by some special instruction. The visitant adopts the suppliant as his child and proceeds to give him specific directions. If martial glory is sought, the spirit may give a dramatic performance of combat, himself equipped in sharply defined fashion, defying the hostile darts and laying low the enemy. The implication is that if the spirit's newly adopted child shall scrupulously imitate his patron's appearance and follow any special admonitions conveyed to him, he will gain his ends.

An illustration or two of visions actually reported by my informants will make the matter clearer.

When Medicine-crow was a young man, he fasted for four days, offered a finger joint to the Sun, and prayed for horses. A young man and a young woman suddenly came towards him, each holding a hoop with feathers in one hand and a hoop with strawberries in the other. The woman said, "We have come here to let him hear something." While Medicine-crow was wondering what she had in mind, her companion went to the other side of the ridge and soon reappeared, driving a herd of horses. The woman followed suit, also returning with horses. Both wore crowns of a certain kind. One of them said, "I have shown you all these horses. I am the sacred Tobacco. I want you to join the Tobacco society with these crowns." The young woman told him not to allow guns at the tobacco planting.

As a result of this experience Medicine-crow not only came to own a great many horses but also founded a new chapter of the great ceremonial organization known as the Tobacco society, making all his followers wear such crowns as had been revealed to him and forbidding the use of firearms in connection with the ritual.

While Medicine-crow's experience is typical of communications that lead to ceremonial prominence and wealth, that

of Scratches-face represents a popular form of war vision.
He, too, fasted and cut off a finger joint, which he offered
to a mythical character called Old-woman's-grandson, who
is sometimes identified with the Morning-star. This was
the prayer uttered on this occasion:

Old-woman's-grandson, I give you this (joint), give me
something good in exchange. . . . I am poor, give me a good
horse. I want to strike one of the enemies and . . . I want to
marry a good-natured woman. I want a tent of my own to
live in.

After his sacrifice he heard footsteps but could not see any
one. He fell asleep and heard a voice: "What are you
doing? You wanted him to come. Now he has come."
Then he saw six men riding horses, one of them seated on
a bobtail, and this one said, "You have been poor, so I'll
give you what you want . . . I am going to run." The
trees around there suddenly turned into enemies and began
to shoot at the horsemen, who rode away but returned un-
scathed. The rider of the bobtail said to Scratches-face,
"If you want to fight all the people on the earth, do as I
do, and you will be able to fight for three or four days and
yet not be shot." The horsemen began to ride east . . .
The enemies attacked them once more, but the rider of the
bobtail knocked them down with a spear. A storm came
up (explained as the Thunder), and hailstones big as a fist
knocked down the enemies.

In consequence of his blessing Scratches-face struck and
killed an enemy without ever getting wounded. He also
obtained horses and married a good-tempered and indus-
trious woman.

The character of a vision could determine the whole of
a man's career. If he was promised invulnerability, as in

the case of Scratches-face, his confidence in the supernatural patron's aid might lead him to snap his fingers at
danger and to establish a reputation for reckless daring.
If, on the other hand, the visitant demonstrated the use
of some medicinal herb, the seer would set up as a practitioner in some branch of medicine and, if fortune favored
him, might become rich from his patients' fees. Medicine-
crow, through a variety of revelations, was equally famous
as a leader in war and in ritualistic activity.

A keen sense for melodramatic tension and climax is
sometimes displayed by the narrator of such experiences.
More particularly, there is a desire to stress the demonstration of the vision's potency. Just as in the conversion
stories familiar to our culture a sharp cleavage is made to
divide the convert's sinful existence before his regeneration
from his virtuous mode of life when reborn, so the Crow
loves to contrast his destitute condition or lack of distinction before his revelation with the material benefits or exalted position that followed. Says One-blue-bead:

When I was a boy, I was poor. I saw war parties come back
with leaders in front and having a procession. I used to envy
them and made up my mind to fast and become like them.
When I saw the vision I got what I had longed for. . . . I
killed eight enemies.

Similarly, Gray-bull in narrating his grandfather's experience is careful to point out that until then his hero had
achieved nothing in war, was indeed the butt of his joking
relatives' mirth because he had never taken part in raids;
after the revelation, however, he charged a group of en-
trenched enemies, wrested a gun from one, a bow from
another, and escaped unhurt. *"The people then knew his
medicine to be true."* Again, Sore-tail is represented as the

poorest of all Crow Indians before going out for a vision,—
so poor that he was even without a horse to ride; after his
revelation he became the wealthiest man in the tribe, owning a herd of from seventy to a hundred horses.

Some dreams are rated equivalent to a vision, apparently
because of the profound impression they create. Religious
value is also attached to the dreams of the officers of the
Tobacco society before the planting of this sacred plant,
and the site of the garden is chosen accordingly. Very
commonly a dream in which the conventional symbols of
the seasons figure is interpreted as a promise that the
dreamer shall live in safety until the next return of the
division of the year seen: the leaves turning yellow, for
instance, would indicate a lease of life at least until autumn.
In dreams as in visions the craving for demonstration is
clear. Little-rump said that he often dreamt indoors or
outdoors, night or day, and that he generally heard songs:
"Some of them I consider sacred. When I hear a song and
have good luck immediately after that, then I consider the
song sacred."

The Visionary's Good Faith

At this point a query naturally obtrudes itself on the lay-
man that is likely to be raised by almost every account of
primitive religion. Is there not in all these reports of
spiritual adventures a deliberate attempt to deceive? What
prevents a man from returning to camp with a lying tale
of wondrous happenings in order to gain honor and pelf?
Is it not the old story of an unscrupulous priesthood hood-
winking the stupid mob into blind submission?

Few questions of theoretic import can be so decisively
answered as the one here propounded; and the answer is

negative. To turn first of all to the Crow, there neither exists nor ever existed a priesthood whose selfish interests might be served by the maintenance of traditional usage. Any Crow, no matter how humble his status, might seek a vision on a perfect plane of equality with the remainder of his people. As for the veracity of the accounts, not a few of the Indians admit their failure to receive a communication. Thus, one witness repeatedly tried to get a vision, but without success. His retrospective comment is interesting: "All who had visions became well-to-do; I was destined to be poor, that is why I had no visions." This view of the vision leads to another consideration. Manifestly distinction in wealth or war or anything else must be rare; the really potent supernatural experiences must therefore be correspondingly rare, and the natives fully realized the fact. Hence they were by no means prone to being duped. When an untried captain claimed an inspiration that would enable him to kill a hostile camp and return with raided horses, he was by no means sure of an enthusiastic response; indeed, he often found difficulty in rallying men to his standards. Only by the test of success could the validity of his claim be established to the satisfaction of the tribe at large. The varying reactions to the report of a vision are well illustrated in a legendary tale, which may be cited in abstract. An Indian was nearly blind, so that he and his wife became quite destitute. Then the Moon appeared unbidden and showed the woman where horses could be captured. Because of her husband's condition, the visionary invited four braves to undertake the expedition on his behalf. Two of them declined, arguing that if the poor couple had really had a spiritual blessing they would not be reduced to their present penury. The other pair accepted the invitation: "Though they are poor, it may come true." Of course their confidence was justified by ensuing events, and the doubting Thomases were put to scorn. But on the basis of Crow psychology, one attitude could be as abundantly propped up with evidence as the other. Sometimes a vision was deceptive; sometimes it was only partly prophetic; and no man was wise before the event. Hence the two skeptics, apart from the author's sympathy with his characters, were hardly culpable. On the other hand, the two other warriors cannot be accused of undue credulity, for one of the strongest holds of the vision on the native mind is precisely that it can raise up the abased.

To revert to the visionary's frame of mind, his whole conduct bears the stamp of sincerity. He gashes and disfigures himself to earn the coveted revelation, yet confesses his disappointment and tries again. He observes with mincing care the regulations laid down by his monitor, however disturbing to his personal comfort. Even in recent times he will abstain from some delicacy in order to maintain a quite irrational taboo imposed at the time of his fast. He will unwrap the memento of his sacred experience with every sign of profound emotion and sentimental regard. He will recount the happenings not merely to impress a crowd of gaping outsiders but in the bosom of his family. His essential truthfulness is beyond cavil. As a half-sophisticated convert to Catholicism once told me, "When you listen to the old men telling their experiences, you have just *got* to believe them."

Psychological Analysis of the Vision

But though the visionary's good faith is vindicated, this hardly solves the psychological problem. It leaves us in the dark as to what really happened when Scratches-face's trees turned into enemies and attacked the mysterious horsemen, for we shall hardly believe with some early missionaries that such shapes and sounds are conjured up by the devil. A wholly adequate interpretation is indeed impossible, but we can at least formulate some conception of these weird happenings.

In the first place, let it be noted that in the majority of cases there is either a prolonged fast with abstention from drink or at least a condition of unusual nervous strain. Under these abnormal circumstances, physiological and psychological, the critical sense may well fall into abeyance, leaving the field clear for dream fantasies. The phenomenon involved is, in other words, generically that of a hallucination. Its particular character is molded by a variety of causes.

There is obviously some correspondence between the need felt by the petitioner and the blessing vouchsafed to him. The vision of a grief-crazed father thirsting to avenge his son's death at the hands of the Cheyenne cannot be identical with that of a youthful aspirant to military renown; and different again must be the experience of the poverty-stricken man praying for relief from his distress. A certain scope will still remain for individual fancy. Thus, in the last-mentioned contingency, desire may be satisfied in more than one way: a man may become wealthy through raiding a hostile camp or by administering a newly revealed herb to rheumatics or by initiating people into a ceremonial secret divulged to him. Obviously a very important fact in the hallucination is the fulfillment through auto-suggestion of the visionary's wishes: it embodies a promise that he shall attain his heart's desire. But clearly the wish alone does not suffice: Little-rump fails again and again while

Medicine-crow as regularly succeeds. That is to say, we must assume that some people experience visions because of a temperamental predisposition, which their envious copyists lack.

Individual peculiarities may manifest themselves in other ways. Though in accordance with customary usage I have hitherto spoken of "visions," visual images are by no means the only ones reported. (Apart from the speeches of the beings seen, voices are heard and other forms of auditory sensation occur.) Motor imagery is sometimes prominent, as when the Stars appearing to an Indian throw arrows, one of which comes wiggling back. Again, a peculiar susceptibility to kinesthetic and tactile impressions is displayed by a number of persons, all of whom pretend to harbor animals of some sort inside their bodies. Thus, Muskrat asserts that once while she was half awake she felt things running all over; lifting her blanket, she caught sight of two weasels looking at her, and on another occasion a weasel came to her neck, causing a curious sensation, and then entered her stomach.

This subject of sensory types requires further investigation and will be treated under another head. Here it suffices to point out that the experiences of the Crow Indians under the abnormal conditions of the vision-quest reflect individual differences in mental constitution parallel to those found among ourselves.

But though the visions were determined by individual psychology and by individual exigency or desire, they are very far from being wholly intelligible on that basis. Both in a general way and in detail the social atmosphere distinctive of Crow culture and specifically Crow conceptions affect the texture of the hallucinations. As for general purport, the frequency of military visions corresponds pre-

cisely to the high regard in which these Indians hold bravery, and it is only natural that those deeds conventionally
rated as preëminently brave, such as the capture of a gun
or the touching of an enemy, should figure conspicuously.

This influence of tribal idealism seems plausible enough.
But what shall we say when one faster after another states
that he gained his end on the *fourth* day? This is of
course incredible as a coincidence. Unless there is a more
or less unconscious reinterpretation of the experience to fit
a tribal norm, the sameness must be due to the overpowering influence of the mystic number of the Crow, which
might actually lead to a postponement of the thrill sought
until the fourth day. In either case cultural suggestion
operates as the dynamic agent. Another significant feature
is the acquisition of a sacred song. Were this restricted to
a few people, we should not be warranted in singling out
this feature from other auditory hallucinations. But when
practically every visionary mentions the singing of some
song, we are plainly dealing with an accepted model. The
faster hears a song because *that* is an integral part of a
trance: again the cultural tradition predetermines his experience. Equally common is the faster's adoption by the apparition; and here once more it is inconceivable to suppose
that dozens of visionaries would independently of one another hear themselves greeted with the reassuring words,
"I will adopt you as my child." To turn to a particular
category of revelations, those imparting invulnerability, a
frequent incident is the transformation of trees or rocks
into enemies, who vainly shoot at the vicariously invulnerable spirit being. This type of experience occurs not only
in the narratives of recent visions but also in traditional
tales, and nothing can be more obvious than the suggestion
exercised on the individual faster's imagery by the cultural

pattern. He sees and hears not merely what any faster, say in British Columbia or South Africa, would see and hear under like conditions of physiological exhaustion and under the urge of generally human desires, but what the social tradition of the Crow tribe imperatively suggests.

Before leaving the psychological characterization of the Crow vision, still another factor, though less frequently in operation, should be mentioned. In the Sun Dance, which will be described below, the principal performer was not always able to secure the coveted communication unaided. In that case the master of ceremonies resorted to what can only be described as hypnotism. He made the faster dance before an effigy suspended in the rear of the lodge and rivet his gaze on this figure, while the conductor of the rite himself was chanting a song. After a while the doll was seen to paint its face black in token of a promise that the visionary should do likewise as the sign of having killed an enemy. Suddenly the dancer fell down in a swoon, his eyes still fixed on the doll.

The phenomenon of the Crow vision is thus not wholly mysterious on the assumption of good faith, but can be described in familiar psychological terms, such as individual variability, suggestion, and hypnotism.

PRIESTHOOD AND LAITY

Since any tribesman might become a shaman, to use a convenient Siberian term, that is, might acquire a spiritual communication, regardless of his antecedents or preparatory training, there was no priestly caste but a fairly large number of people with visionary experiences. The greater or lesser dignity of these depended solely on the pragmatic test of their efficacy. Thus there were several distinct Sun

Dance effigies, but because one of them had proved especially potent in bringing about the destruction of enemies it came to take precedence of all the rest, while another was interpreted as based on a pretended revelation because its use was accompanied by the death of the chief dancer's wife. Again, there is the historic case of Wraps-up-his-tail who declared in 1887 that he had received power to drive the whites out of the country with the aid of a magic sword. He failed, hence One-blue-bead thinks that his vision was partly false; in part it was true because Indians had seen the "prophet" cut down pines by a wave of his sword.

Corresponding, then, to the cogency of their demonstration was the rank informally assumed by the visionaries. Men conspicuously fortunate in war parties would come to be regarded as favorites of some powerful being and as themselves "extraordinary" (*maxpé*). Yet even they were not generic intermediaries between the laity and the Supernatural but had functions definitely circumscribed by the character of their visions. For example, among physicians some were specialists for childbirth cases, while some devoted themselves exclusively to the doctoring of wounds. Of visionaries blessed with non-therapeutic gifts, some could defy missiles, others could locate a hostile camp, still others were inspired to found a new ritualistic body or to introduce a new type of shield decoration.

Given this religious separatism, there was no universally acknowledged set of dogmas nor any ecclesiastical organization that handed down laws for the guidance of the religious consciousness. No one insisted that a Crow should believe in the creation myth or subscribe to some accepted conception of the hereafter; nor did a youth require any external prompting to go out in search of a vision. The

functions of the shaman, in other words, however important for the public weal, were in their essence private. The
Sun Dance pledger, the parents of a sick child, the ambitious brave, all hired a renowned shamanistic specialist
according to the exigencies of the occasion. In such cases
the shaman naturally assumed complete control as well as
complete responsibility.

But the relationship between a shaman and his client was
not a purely commercial one. In many cases there was a
transfer of power from the original visionary to the man
seeking his aid. A revelation could be shared provided
proper compensation was offered, and thus the considerable
number of people not favored by a direct message from
the spirits could at least share in its blessings through a
go-between. Thus, a man might impart to others the gift
of invulnerability by teaching them what to wear and what
songs to sing in battle; another who had seen a vision of
horses might send out warriors instead of going himself
to capture them. If the client succeeded in his ventures, a
definitely sentimental relationship was established between
him and the shaman; just as the latter had been adopted
by his supernatural patron, so he in turn made a "son" of
his protégé. Sometimes the adopted person would at first
receive a sacred symbol of the primary revelation, but was
subsequently empowered to gain a vision of his own.
Thus, Flat-head-woman prevailed upon the owners of a
sacred arrow bundle to prepare a replica for him, and for
some time they would send him out on raids in accordance
with their inspirations. But later they bade him get visions
of his own, and consequently he saw a grass stalk flying
through the air, with the implication that he should set out
for the spot where it alighted. Thereafter he had various
revelations and came to send out warriors on his own au-

thority. In this instance a principle is applied that finds
still clearer expression among the closely related Hidatsa
Indians of North Dakota: the sacred token of a revelation
may itself become the stimulation for new visions.

Another similarity between the two sister tribes may be
cited as of psychological interest. As a rule, the property
rights involved in a vision not only can be bought, but they
cannot be conveyed in any other way. A ceremonial mode
of painting the face was purchased by a Crow informant
from his own mother; and among the Hidatsa certain hereditary bundles must be bought by the children from their
father. It is plausible to apply to such cases the principle
of rationalization. The notion that a visionary could sell
a share in his "patent" was manifestly of material benefit
to him, and in the more or less conscious recognition of this
fact lay the basis of the usage. But when the rule had
once been firmly established it acquired a sacrosanctity
through the mere force of conservatism and was applied as
rigorously to the nearest blood-kin as to outsiders.

The powerful shamans, then, were not official representatives of religion acting on behalf of the whole community,
but fortunate visionaries who, with small groups of followers, formed diminutive congregational units independent of
one another, though tied together by an unformulated common world-view. Under these conditions there was nothing to prevent animosities from bursting forth between
rival shamans, each relying on the support of his spiritual
patron. Several feuds of varying degrees of intensity are
recollected, and I have myself known one of the principals
in the most dramatic of all, Big-ox, a man generally reputed
to have smitten his adversary with blindness. Big-ox had
seduced a tribesman's wife, and the wronged man asked
White-thigh to avenge the grievance by means of his super-

natural power, of which a sacred rock was the chief symbol, while Big-ox relied on the support of the Thunder. The next time Big-ox went on the warpath he failed because the other shaman had prayed against him. For a while each of the two medicine-men thwarted the other's undertakings; finally Big-ox cursed his rival and made him blind, but White-thigh retaliated by making Big-ox lose all his next of kin, so that he was obliged to wander from one camp to another in his old age. In these contests it is of course at bottom not the human competitors but their supernatural monitors that are pitted against each other, as when in a mythological tale the hero overcomes the Morning-star's beneficiary through the aid of friendly birds.

Supernatural Beings

But who are these mysterious beings that appear to favored believers? And why did I not begin the account of Crow religion with a systematic exposition of the native pantheon? The postponement of this task was not due to inadvertency: I have relegated the individual spirits to the background because in my view of the Crow religious consciousness that is where they belong.

The Crow Indian approached the universe with a sincere humility that contrasted sharply with his personal pride towards fellow-tribesmen. He evinced that sense of absolute dependence on something not himself, which Schleiermacher and Feuerbach postulate as the root of the religious sentiment. By himself man was nothing, but somewhere in the world there were mysterious beings greater than he, by whose good-will he might rise. The significant fact to an individual was that during a spell of ecstasy he had come into contact with something supernatural, and that something was his God while everything else sank into a relatively subordinate position. Other men had gods of their own who perchance figured prominently in tribal myth or were intimately linked with an important ritual; that might matter to them, but not to him. For *his* religious consciousness the chicken-hawk or bear through whose instructions he had cured a dying child or come unhurt out of battle was the primary religious fact. The emotional thrill of his vision, reënforced by its tried potency, gave the apparition a unique value beside which everything else faded into nothingness. Even the trivial feather or claw shown by the visitant partook of the awe-inspiring quality of its revealer, or rather of the occasion on which it was revealed. It is easy to speak of the veneration extended to such badges of the individual's covenant with the supernatural as fetishism, but that label with its popular meaning is monstrously inadequate to express the psychology of the situation. For to the Indian the material object is nothing apart from its sacred associations; and the sacredness lies not in the preëstablished glory of the particular spirit but in the affective correlate of the vision. That is to say, the Thunderbird is not first revered as divine and then sheds the luster of his godhead upon the accompanying circumstances, but his appearance under special emotional conditions constitutes his apotheosis, which extends to the whole experience. Never shall I forget how an Indian once prodded my curiosity by offering to show me "the greatest thing in the world"; how he reverently uncovered one cloth wrapper after another; and how at length there lay exposed a simple bunch of feathers,—a mere nothing to the alien onlooker but to the owner a badge of his covenant with the supernatural world.

In short, the central fact of Crow religion is not a generic

orship of Nature or of some dominant natural force, but
t1 : extraordinary subjective emotional experience with all
its ramifications.

This statement, however, requires modification with reference to one striking phenomenon in the universe. The
Sun was to a marked degree the recipient of offerings and
the object of supplication. Before setting out on a raid,
men would vow to give him eagle feathers or fox skins;
the hide of an albino buffalo was invariably consecrated
to the Sun with a prayer for longevity and wealth; and to
erect a little booth for sweating oneself was considered a
ritual in his honor. It is therefore not at all remarkable
that the Sun should be the first being normally addressed
by the seeker of a vision. The remarkable thing is rather
that he so rarely came. "Sometimes," said White-arm,
"the Sun himself appeared to the visionary, but mostly
animals came. These I do not think are related to the Sun
at all. When men are praying, the Sun is first thought of,
but generally other beings appear." The only plausible
explanation for this anomaly that occurs to me is that Sun
worship and vision concepts may belong to two distinct
compartments or layers of Crow belief. Nothing is more
characteristic of the Crow than a deficiency in systematic
thinking: it was possible for the Crow mind to be deeply
influenced by two quite distinct idea-systems without attempting to bring them into harmony. Nevertheless, in
relatively recent times the need may have been felt for
somehow correlating the two, with the result observed: the
Sun was supplicated for a revelation, but because of his
comparatively recent association with the vision he could
not normally oust the older type of visitants from their
position of vantage. And as regards any individual Crow,

this personal patron remained a more important factor in his religious life than the Sun himself.

The Sun, to be sure, means more to a greater number of persons than any one other spirit; he approaches more nearly than any other our notion of a Supreme Being. Yet what astonishing conceptions cluster about him, and in what chaos is Crow theology concerning the most elementary definition of his identity! The most trustworthy witnesses cannot agree as to whether he is identical with Old-Man-Coyote, the hero of Crow folklore; nay, in a single cosmogonic myth there is constant vacillation on this point. Now Old-Man-Coyote is in many episodes of his cycle a typical trickster, wallowing in grossness and buffoonery. Consequently the fact that the identification is not definitely spurned is in itself significant. My own impression, given for what it may be worth, is that originally the two figures were distinct and that, possibly because of their familiarity with the legendary character of Old-Man-Coyote, the Crow unconsciously tried to give greater sharpness to the vague outlines of the solar deity by merging it into the better-known individuality.

Yet even if the Sun be wholly dissociated from Old-Man-Coyote, he remains an odd sort of supreme being. In fact, he is not really supreme at all: there is nothing to preclude his being worsted by Morning-star or the human hero of a traditional tale. Again, he looms as the creator by having some birds dive into the sea for the submerged earth and by fashioning human beings out of mud; but he is not the source of *all* being. Apart from the cryptic Old-Man-Coyote, the sacred Tobacco (usually identified with a star) and the sacred Rock appear as entities of explicitly independent origin. Finally, from an ethical point of view, he is sometimes benignant but also turns malevolent towards the whole tribe when his mistress is seduced by a boy hero, and is even represented as boiling and eating the flesh of brave warriors.

If the Sun is a shadowy and inconsistent deity, this applies with even greater force to other spirits. Morning-star, for example, is commonly identified with Old-woman's-grandson, the child of the Sun and an Indian maiden. He rids the world of various monsters, triumphing through his father's aid, and is ultimately translated to the sky. Possibly because of his solar lineage some Indians regularly prayed to him, yet others vigorously denied that he was ever addressed by suppliants! As a further sample of Crow consistency may be cited one informant's statement that Sun and Morning-star were pitted against each other in a trial of strength and that Morning-star's protégés vicariously won the game.

The Thunder, commonly identified with a species of eagle, doubtless made a deep impression on the Crow mind and was the patron of several natives even during the last few decades. Yet in one myth this powerful deity requires a human hunter's assistance to slay his traditional enemy, a water-monster; and he is defied with impunity by an Indian named Big-iron, who has been adopted by a spirit in the guise of an aged man.

It is useless to proceed with this enumeration. Evidently a diversified host of beings, whether identified with natural forces or with the apparitions of visions or with what not, may function as deities. But there is no systematization, no coördination or subordination that has fixed validity: the spirits seem to move in a variety of distinct universes, and their religious importance varies with the individual Crow. Gray-bull's grandfather was once visited by two birds, which turned into a man and a woman but after giving him instructions retransformed themselves into birds. These were not conceived as messengers or servants of some deity: they were themselves possessed of mysterious potency and capable of making their adopted son invulnerable. Why should the pragmatic beneficiary fret over their possible inferiority to other beings?

It may not be superfluous to add that while among the motley throng of spiritual patrons who bless the Crow Indians ghosts occasionally occur, these are indeed associated with the whirlwind and the owl but never with the surviving souls of deceased relatives. Ancestor-worship in any form is totally lacking.

RITUAL

There were numerous ritualistic observances, some of relatively simple private character, others elaborated into complex public festivals. The definite procedure followed when a revelation is sought is of course itself ritualistic, but the altogether unique significance of the vision appears as soon as we examine a representative set of rites.

To begin with a relatively simple type, that associated with the sweat-lodge. The ancient Crow did not resort to this form of vapor bath for mere pastime or even for purely therapeutic purposes. It was considered a sacred thing, and the little dome-shaped structure of willows might be erected only by one who had secured an appropriate revelation or had purchased the privilege from a visionary of this type. Nay, even those entitled to build a sweat-lodge would, according to one authority, put it up solely after special spiritual counsel to that effect. The sweat-lodge was most commonly conceived as an offering to the

Sun and linked with prayers in the form of a conditional pledge. A man afflicted with disease might pray, "My father's kinsman (the usual mode of addressing the Sun), if I recover, I will erect a sweat-lodge"; and corresponding vows were uttered by a warrior eager to obtain booty on a new raid or to strike a blow against the enemy. Since four is the ceremonial number, it is customary to undergo the sweating in four successive doses. Rocks heated for hours outside the little hut are carried to a central pit, then the willow structure is covered with blankets so as to become pitch-dark, and one of the inmates, all of whom are practically naked, pours water on the red-hot rocks. For several minutes the celebrants sweat, then the blanket at one side is raised, allowing them to cool off before the second sweating process. Each time more water is poured on than before, causing more and more vapor and proportionately greater perspiration. Each stage is also associated with a prayer formula. Medicine-crow, for example, may have dreamt of the snow on the ground, an image interpreted to mean that he and his kin shall live to see the winter season. He announces his dream and the other sweaters thank him, hoping that they also shall reach that point of time. Others announce their respective dreams when the cover is lifted, and after the final airing all dash to the nearest stream and plunge into its waters.

Passing to the more complex ceremonialism of the Tobacco society, we find that the whole procedure is dominated by the vision-concept. The tobacco in question is a species of *Nicotiana,* but not that smoked by these Indians; in other words, it is raised for exclusively religious purposes. It is planted on behalf of the entire tribe, but while every Crow in some measure shares in the benefits of the performances the right to plant is restricted to persons duly initiated into the Tobacco organization. This originated in a vision and the subsequent adoption of co-celebrants by the original visionary. But in course of time there were supplementary revelations, and accordingly at least over twenty distinct chapters sprang into existence, each embracing the person blessed by a new vision and the people of either sex whom he allowed to participate through adoption. Though the immediate benefits were purely gain in social standing, the Indians down to the most recent times have been willing to pay heavy fees for the privilege of initiation. In the adoption ceremonies I witnessed in 1910 and 1911 the novices' kinswomen were seen staggering under the load of goods offered to the sponsor's chapter in partial payment of the new member's debt. The tyro is instructed for several months in the songs given him and is finally led in solemn procession to a specially constructed lodge, where for hours he and others dance the Tobacco dance, gently swaying their bodies and executing characteristic movements with their arms. Immediately after the dance or on the following morning the novice takes a vapor bath together with his song instructors, and finally he is permitted to take from the members of the adopting chapter some packages of the precious seed as well as other sacred objects. For some of these, as well as for certain highly specialized ritualistic privileges, additional fees are paid. One informant, for example, gave a horse for the right of sitting next to the door. Exorbitant prices were also paid for the more important prerogative of erecting the adoption lodge.

The above is the merest sketch of a highly interesting performance, diversified by the recounting of military exploits and a short dramatic representation of how a warrior coming home from a successful expedition reports the victory, describes the Crow tobacco garden seen on his return trip, and prophesies an abundant crop.

After the acquisition of his seed the novice becomes a full-fledged member entitled to share in the next spring planting. First his seed will be mixed with various ingredients by the official Mixer of his chapter, then all the members of the society proceed to the garden site dreamed by one of the Mixers and plant their seed, each in his allotted space. The procession to the garden follows a traditional style: the members walk abreast, carrying their sacred objects in bags and preceded by a woman who carries a holy otter skin, but in one locality on the strength of a vision this emblem has been changed to a crane. After four stops with ceremonial songs and smoking the members entrust their bags to swift runners, who race to the site and deposit the sacred sacks there. The ground is prepared by burning (nowadays by plowing), then the seeds are dropped into holes dug for them, songs are sung, and the members dance and eat before dispersing. After the ceremony people are wont to lie at the garden in hope of a revelation and are likely to hear Tobacco songs.

The planting is followed by several inspections of the tobacco and at last the seeds are harvested with relatively little ceremony.

An examination of the Tobacco ritual demonstrates with great clearness the importance of the vision. From the institution of the order in the beginning to the tiniest variation in procedure within recent years everything is interpreted as the result of visionary experiences; the membership comprises the visionaries and those to whom by a sort of apostolic succession they have transmitted their powers; even the site of the planting is not chosen without supernatural sanction. On the other hand, the data illustrate equally well the dominance of the basic Crow values. People want to join either for general human benefits—to gain recovery from illness or rise from poverty—or for the simple hankering after social prominence; and to secure the latter end they cheerfully render material sacrifices of property.

If the vision looms large in the Tobacco ceremonies, it is all-important in the Sun Dance. The Crow performed this festival ostensibly from a single motive, the desire for revenge. If a tribesman had suffered the loss of a son or brother at the hands of the Dakota and could not shake off his grief, he would pledge a performance of the Sun Dance. Since his purpose was revenge, he naturally sought the indispensable prerequisite for a successful military venture, a vision. That could be procured with greatest likelihood of success by erecting the Sun Dance lodge with the aid of the whole tribe and dancing before a sacred doll till he saw the image of a bleeding enemy. There were several dolls, each the result of a vision by its owner or one of his predecessors, and the pledger chose one of them to instruct him and become the high-priest of the performance. As soon as the mourner beheld a vision promising the death of an enemy, the ritual abruptly terminated, for that vision was the avowed be-all and end-all of the performance, though a vast number of additional but theoretically extraneous features made it a spectacle of interest to the onlookers. Even these unessential performances revolved in large part about the vision-concept. Thus, many young men considered the occasion a proper one for seeking a revelation on their own account and would undergo the usual austerities publicly for purely individual ends.

The vision is thus the factor that integrates the whole of Crow ritualism; and it is interesting to see that as an ex-

planatory principle it is extended to other tribes. The
closely related Hidatsa were observed to lack the Tobacco
ceremony and to have a Sacred Pipe ritual originally unknown to the Crow. Crow philosophy formulates the facts
by declaring that when the sister tribes parted their leaders
had two distinct revelations, one seeing the Tobacco, the
other the Pipe.

Dogma and World-view

Crow religion does not obligate its votaries to accept a
fixed set of tenets concerning the phenomena of the universe. A man would not be denounced as a heretic because he rejected the current theory of creation, and in the
absence of an official pronunciamento on the subject there
is nothing to prevent a number of varying versions. When
we recollect that the cosmogonic tale of the earth-divers
is found from the Atlantic to the Pacific, it seems a likely
supposition that the Crow did not originate the essence of
their creation story but borrowed it from another tribe,
possibly not many centuries ago. Whether it superseded
an earlier conception or was adopted in the absence of any
creation myth, the theory of an alien origin bears witness
to the trifling part relevant ideas play in the religious life
of the people.

What applies to cosmogony holds in even greater degree
for conceptions of the hereafter. Like other peoples, primitive and civilized, the Crow believe in a survival of the soul,
but the subject is of no emotional interest to the majority
of these Indians and has hardly exercised their imaginations
at all. Such notions as are current can be traced to the
accounts of men who are believed to have died but who returned to consciousness. The general upshot of such re-

ports is that the spirits of the dead are encamped like Indians but are better off than the living. They send back
people who for some reason offend them or, it may be,
from sheer caprice. One narrative associates the spirit
land with the west. In no case are the departed souls associated with one of the more or less established deities, such
as the Sun or the Thunderbird; and never is there the faintest suggestion that the deeds of this world must be accounted
for in another or that the good shall be separated from the
wicked.

This leads to the consideration of how religion and ethics
are related among the Crow. It would certainly be strange
if two such fundamental aspects of culture remained wholly
unconnected, yet their relationship is of an extremely tenuous sort. The Sun, as dissociated from Old-Man-Coyote,
does not play the part of a divine lawgiver nor could he
serve as a uniform paragon of virtue from the aboriginal
point of view. Old-Man-Coyote is indeed the founder of
many customs and the instructor in such arts as fire-making
and stone technique; but he does not lay down elements of
the tribal ethics, which in fact he flagrantly violates, as
when he marries his own daughters or gains access to his
mother-in-law.

Ethical imperatives are sometimes issued by the beings
who appear to visionaries. In order, however, to appraise
such edicts at their true value it is necessary to recall their
setting. The most frequent desire on the visionary's part
is social distinction, which in itself tends to preclude anti-social behavior. When a warrior is bidden to kill an enemy
or to protect the women and children of his camp, he is
told to do what promotes his own as well as the tribal interest. There is indeed the interesting legendary case of
the benevolent Dwarf who indignantly withdraws protec-

tion from the camp tyrant he had taken under his wing: " 'Try to benefit your people,' I said to him. 'Take away and possess their desirable property,' I did not say. 'Kill them continually,' I did not say." But no such loving-kindness towards the people at large is manifested when in other instances, traditional or historic, the spirit supports a favorite regardless of the merits of the case, as in the stories of shamanistic rivalry.

In one sense, it is true, definite, stringent rules of conduct are laid down by the visitant. A man owning a certain kind of shield must shift its position according to the sun's movements. The custodian of a sacred arrow must not knock off the snow from his lodge,—he must gently scrape it. Gray-bull is told not to eat bird's eggs, and Muskrat must not allow any one to bump against her. Dire consequences would flow from disregard of these injunctions, even when transgression, as in the instance last cited, is independent of the visionary's volition.

Subjectively these utterly capricious commandments were undoubtedly among the most important principles of individual conduct; and I am convinced that the reaction to a breach of this personal code psychologically comes closer to what we call sin than anything else in Crow life. But this purely personal and potentially anti-social morality is manifestly unconnected with anything normally included under the heading of ethics. The Crow did have a clear-cut code for social conduct, and this may be said to be almost wholly dissociated from religious sanctions.

To summarize the foregoing, Crow religion is not a dogmatic faith; it imposes no doctrines, cosmological or eschatological; it does not prescribe rules of conduct that possess general validity. It seems subjectivism raised to the highest power.

But this extreme individualism is after all only theoretical. The individual Crow is indeed free from the dictates of a priesthood, but he is in the grip of a more potent, precisely because it is a more subtle, leadership. The stock of ideas and emotions characteristic of his social group fashions his whole cosmic outlook as it fashions the very pattern of his vision. There are certain conceptions which from a child he receives as unchallengeable, even though they are not formulated as so many propositions; and while they may in themselves be completely devoid of religious value they inevitably frame and tincture whatever acquires such value. To give a positive definition of what Dr. Thurnwald calls the primitive *Denkart* (mode of thinking) or *Geistesverfassung* (mental constitution) [2] is not so easy as to sense it from such concrete exhibitions as are yielded by the visionary experiences. Negatively, it seems easy enough to contrast it with our modern world-view, to define it as an eminently irrational one, that is, one that does not involve the checking of associations by the spirit of critical inquiry. No woman has ever been known to handle a Sun Dance doll, hence Pretty-enemy, who disobeyed the rule, must die or suffer the loss of some dear relative as an automatic punishment. A horseman seen in a vision escapes from the enemy, hence the visionary will be invulnerable. To draw a representation of one's enemy and puncture the heart is to injure the man figured. These are all actual illustrations of how the Crow mind applies the principle of causality. The implicit philosophy of reality, imbibed with the mother's milk, limits and predetermines the individual's religious views, just as the social standards current in his community predetermine his life-values and the wishes he seeks to fulfill through religion. In contrast with this body of received notions and ideals the scope for individual creativeness seems, from an outsider's point of view, pitiably meager. Thus even the most extreme subjectivism may merge in abject servility, not to the authority of a personal dictatorship, but to the impersonal, though none the less real, dominance of folk-belief and folk-usage.

REFERENCES

[1] The account given above is based on the author's own researches. Most of the data will be found in the following publications: Lowie, 1915; id., 1919; id., 1922. The reader may also be referred to the author's contributions to Parsons, 1922: 17-43.

[2] Thurnwald: 296.

CHAPTER II

EKOI RELIGION [1]

SORCERY

WHEN several well-known men have died in succession in an Ekoi village, suspicion is naturally aroused that they are the victims of black magic, and some friendless woman may be pounced upon as the probable culprit. Illness, when not traceable to the anger of offended spirits, is likewise derived from the practices of witch or wizard. An unsuccessful hunter lays his bad luck to the charge of sorcery and seeks to break the spell by a rite of conciliation. Prospective mothers shield themselves from the inroads of sorcerers by special charms, and childless women similarly lift the bane of sterility. Towns are abandoned for fear of a half-witted woman's curse.

What seems strangest in the relevant notions of the aborigines is the maniacal dread that even the next of kin may practice sorcery in disguise. Chief Nenkui accuses his own daughter of afflicting him with blindness by touching his eye, a husband charges his wife with bewitching her own children, a grandmother is hounded into suicide by the persistent suspicion that she has killed her son's offspring.

These strange obsessions are fostered by a deep-rooted belief in shape-shifting. Who can recognize a witch when she assumes the form of a bat or owl, and, seated on the roof of a house, sucks out her sleeping victim's heart? Such animals or birds are the sorcerer's familiar spirits and can be exorcised and extracted from his body by a qualified priest.

33

There are other cases of metamorphosis that may or may not be coupled with evil magic. Every man has two souls, one of them dwelling constantly in the body, the other capable of being sent forth to possess some wild animal in the bush. A man need merely drink of the magic potion transmitted in his family as the means for turning into the hereditary animal linked with his kin group. Here, too, there is chance for clandestine wickedness. One man will destroy his neighbor's goats or cows as a were-leopard, while another drags people under water in the convenient disguise of a crocodile.

Sorcerers assemble at night in a sort of witches' sabbath, dance a few feet above ground, simultaneously growing to gigantic stature, and jointly plot the death of a victim. They are invisible to ordinary mortals, but those endowed with "four eyes" have seen them celebrating in the moonlight and may bring them to confess.

It is essential to understand the hysterical fear of evil magic that haunts the Ekoi in order to judge fairly the treatment meted out to its practitioners. From the aboriginal point of view, sorcerers are prospective or actual murderers insidiously destroying their neighbors, nay, their own blood. Small wonder, then, that those convicted of such malpractice receive scant consideration and are summarily put out of the way. It is rather to the credit of the natives that instead of resorting to lynch law they usually conform to the juridical standards established among them, determining guilt by the orderly processes of divination and the ordeal.

The diviner must be sought, for while affliction is perhaps most frequently the result of sorcery, other causes have to be reckoned with, such as the wrath of neglected ancestral spirits. In order to become established as a specialist in divination, a novice must be initiated by a master. The charm consists of two pairs of strings, each composed of four "shells," in reality the dried seed-coverings of a sacred tree. These are laid side by side on either hand of the diviner, and each pair must fall in exactly the reverse manner of the other to secure certainty, otherwise the process is repeated. There are other elements of the diviner's stock-in-trade,—the egg of a bush fowl, the quill and tail of a porcupine, white chalk for good luck, a boar's tooth to ward off evil influences, the small horns of a duikerbok because that animal has "four eyes," that is, can discern phantom shapes that remain unseen by normal mortals. The total number of ways in which the shells can fall is considerable, and each has its own interpretation by the diviner's code. Thus, one shell turned upward while the rest face in the reverse way designates a young man, three shells up and the rest down indicate food, and so forth.

For final ordination of a tyro the old expert chews the leaves and bark of various sacred trees, spitting small quantities into the shells, which are placed high up in the roof-thatch, where they may hold communion with Obassi Osaw, one of the two great tribal deities. After a while they are removed and buried at a cross-road to talk with ghosts and with Obassi Nsi, the second great god. Some days later the new diviner digs them up again and is set up as a fully trained member of the profession, entitled to the traditional fee of threepence in kind and threepence in money.

But the mere declaration of the diviner, while presumptive evidence of guilt, does not convict without a formal ordeal, administered either by pouring boiling palm oil on the suspect's hands or, more commonly, by giving him a potion made from a poisonous wild bean. On the native theory the innocently accused will not take harm in either case, while the guilty sorcerer is supposed to die. The drink is certainly likely to cause intense anguish when of the standard consistency, but an excessive or a deficient dose merely produces vomiting, and if the bean has been previously boiled the same result is effected with pain but without fatal consequences. All this naturally places the alleged criminal at the mercy of the officials in charge.

Highly interesting is the psychological condition of the people concerned in these proceedings. Though personal animosity naturally must be supposed to have often asserted itself in accusations and trials of witchcraft, the evidence for the general good faith of the plaintiffs is quite convincing. Mr. Talbot, a district commissioner to whom we are indebted for an excellent account of the Ekoi, gives even Nenkui a relatively good character, though in his hysterical fear of sorcery this chief seems to have decimated his people, driving two of his own wives and his own children into undergoing the bean ordeal and inflicting untold misery on his subjects at large. Not less significant is the mental state of the defendants. Our authority graphically describes the profound distress of a poor woman charged with the murder of the grandchildren she had eagerly longed for, and the reactions of another accused of having killed her own children: "I ate the . . . bean, so that, if I were a witch and had killed the children, I might die also, for I did not want to live if I had harmed my little ones." In this utterance there is no longer the complete self-assurance of offended innocence. Under the hectoring suggestion of the chief and her whole social environment the accused is no longer certain of herself and solves the mental conflict by willingly submitting to the ordeal. In this connection reported cases of confession also demand attention. It is easy enough to understand that a woman unable to bear the physical agony of the boiling oil should end the torture by admitting her guilt. But how can we account for the story of a chief's son

who declared that he and his father had turned into crocodiles in order to kill two women crossing a river? Or the
confession of a mother that she had killed one of her own infants as well as her sister? Or the wife who owned to preventing a sore on her husband's ankle from healing because
every night a snake issued from her mouth to lick the
wound?

In order both to understand the underlying mental operations and to ward off a prematurely condemnatory verdict
on the benighted people who can entertain a belief in witchcraft at all, it is desirable to turn to our own past. Not in
the so-called Dark Ages, but in the centuries following "the
revival of learning" the belief in black magic gained ascendancy to a point never known before or since and led to the
death of thousands of victims, not through the ebullition of
popular wrath but by the solemn machinery of duly constituted legal authorities. Barely five generations separate us
from the time when a maidservant—the contemporary of
Hume, Kant, Voltaire, and Goethe—was burnt at Glarus,
Switzerland, in 1782, for bewitching a child. Let any one
inclined to pass judgment on the cruelty of the Ekoi read
the official account of the witch-trial at Zug in 1737, by
which half-a-dozen poor women, ranging in age from twen-
ty-eight to seventy, were executed or fiendishly tortured to
death on the accusation of a demented girl of seventeen, who
professed herself to have held intercourse with the devil
since the age of four.[2] There is nothing among the Ekoi
even remotely approaching in brutality and senselessness the
treatment of Kathri Gill, one of the victims of the law on
this occasion. After she had been flogged, racked, and confined for days in a cell that neither permitted her to stand
upright nor to lie at full length, refusing all the time to
confess her dealings with Satan, new incriminating evidence

was discovered. She had eked out a livelihood as a peddler
and her stock-in-trade was found to include a bag of white
powder and a box containing some salve. Could anything
be more obvious than that the powder was the poison with
which she summoned hailstorms and destroyed cattle? Or
that the salve was smeared on her broomstick in preparation
for her diabolic flights? Her assertion that the substances
were nothing but oatmeal and butter were rejected by the
court. Nevertheless the executioner was ordered to test the
supposed poison by feeding it to a dog. The experiment
failed to reveal any harmful consequences. Thereupon the
half-witted accuser declared that God had naturally protected the innocent beast from harm. In vain Kathri Gill
offered to partake of all the substances herself. Her petition was denied and the process of torturing her was resumed. It is essential to note that the accuser herself,
though apparently immune from torture by virtue of her
great service to the State, reaped no material benefits
from her allegations: she merely had the satisfaction of
being executed with the sword instead of perishing by
fire.

In the trial of Zug, as in most of the Ekoi cases, the element of rapacity is completely lacking as a motive for the
prosecution: the Swiss victims were uniformly poor women,
and on the other hand it is not likely that Nenkui's daughter
had any property that the chief, her father, lacked. Nor in
the light of our detailed information can the desire for revenge have played a prominent part in either set of cases.
In both areas we meet with the phenomenon of self-accusa-
tion, which at first blush may seem especially enigmatic. But
in any of our large cities to-day the report of a sensational
crime leads forthwith to a volley of wholly imaginary and
often demonstrably false confessions, which the police auto-

matically disregard. The psychological explanation is doubtless the one offered by Dr. Stoll. There are in every society
individuals to whom the suggestion of any idea immediately
produces a sense of reality, so that they are quite incapable
of distinguishing what they have merely thought or heard
from what they have experienced as eyewitnesses. Given
the firm folk-belief in sorcery, given—even without any special vindictiveness—that emotional ambivalence towards the
most closely related kin which psycho-analysts describe, the
mental processes involved in either European or Ekoi society, however obscure in detail, are at least intelligible in
principle. A stray wave of resentment against a husband
may lead to a momentary wish to bewitch him; in the absence of scientific principles of causation any accident that
may befall him will inevitably be associated with that wish;
and the recollection may produce a definite sense of guilt.
This feeling is naturally reënforced by the notions prevalent
in the social environment; nay, it may be not merely stimu-
lated but awakened by the accusation. The charge of sorcery
strikes a resonant key when it brings into consciousness sentiments of hitherto latent animosity or coincides with a
transient mood of bitterness. But even apart from such
potent affective agencies, the mere dominance of a set of beliefs, backed by all the received authorities of the tribe, suffices not merely to convince the fear-ridden mob but to shake
the defendant's faith in his own innocence. What Sumner
writes of European conditions is equally applicable to West
Africa:

Many perfectly sound-minded and innocent women could not
be sure that they were not witches. They had had dreams suggested by the popular notions, or had suffered from nervous af-
fections which fell in with the popular superstitions.[3]

The Ekoi phenomena can be rightly evaluated only when we align them with their European parallels. If they illustrate the disheartening impotence of human reason in the face of prestige suggestion, they constitute at the same time a cogent if unflattering proof of the psychic unity of mankind.

Ghosts

The magical machinations of neighbors possessed by familiar spirits are not the only weird phenomena that darken the Ekoi's existence. The deceased, too, may become a menace; for an evil ghost will smite a passer-by in the face, causing fatal lock-jaw, and even one's own forbears may avenge neglect by sending illness. A very considerable portion of Ekoi religion centers in the conceptions of ghosts and the ritual practiced to avert or nullify their anger.

According to native psychology, the soul of a person is somehow connected with his breath and leaves him when he expires. Diminutive so long as it dwells within his breast, it becomes rarefied on his death so as to expand to the size and form of his body. But in this condition it remains invisible to all but the "four-eyed" who have the gift of perceiving spirits. The shadow cast by a live man is also regarded as the shape of the soul. There is evidently some confusion in the mind of the Ekoi, for while he is capable of declaring that every man has but one soul he quite definitely describes how a second soul can be sent into the bush to possess an elephant, crocodile, buffalo, or what not. Similar contradiction confronts us regarding the immortality of the soul: it is said to be indestructible, yet in the folk-tales ghosts are slain and recover not by their inherent spiritual quality (ghosts require food like mortals) but through the external application of some magically potent medicine.

It is not only the bush-soul that can go forth in search of new fields of activity. In trances the souls of men, and more frequently of women, fly away to visit remote places; and the fully initiated members of the secret society known as Egbo can summon the shadow forms of living men known to be far away.

Animals, trees, rocks, weapons, and household utensils as well as human beings are credited with souls, and when food dedicated to the spirits remains unaltered to the sight it is because the supernatural beings are capable of sucking out the "astral" essence of the offering.

Normally the souls of the dead descend underground to join the great Earth deity, Nsi, and only return to this world in exceptional cases. But some spirits, either because the persons associated with them died a violent death or from some special cause, roam about for an indefinite period, entering the towns for several hours after midnight. Special locations are haunted by the ghosts, among them two lakes shunned by the natives, who would not even track game in the vicinity for fear of arousing the vengeance of the snakes and crocodiles credited with the guardianship of these sacred waters.

Ghosts are by no means all bad, and it is even asserted that evil ones are usually accompanied by more benevolent spirits to prevent mischief. The folk-tales likewise yield testimony to the kindly sentiments of which the departed are capable, for sometimes they befriend visitors and bestow valuable powers upon them. Nevertheless the dominant note in the native attitude towards these spirits is fear. The Ekoi are afraid of the dark because they do not wish to encounter ghosts. Ghosts sometimes eat human beings. Even the newly deceased have to buy food from older ghosts with the decorative scars on their bodies. People take pains to exclude ghosts by wearing amulets or keeping lamps lit or by burning spices; and they go to great trouble to conciliate them.

Even the ancestral spirits cannot be depended upon, for they send disease when they feel neglected. "I do not know," said the head priest of one of the numerous cults, "if ghosts can do harm to the living, but I always sacrifice yams and plantains to my father's spirit so that I may not fall sick, and to ask him to protect my farms. About once a year, too, generally when it is time to cut 'bush' for our farms, I sacrifice to my mother, for we know that ghosts are hungry just as we are." Similar offerings are presented to the ancestors at funerals, at the building of a new house, or after a return from a victorious raid. In cases of illness the diviner determines not merely whether the cause be sorcery or the spirits of the patient's forbears, but whether the paternal or the maternal kin are responsible, and proceeds to call the names of all individual ancestors till the identity of the disease-giver is ascertained. When the operator has discovered what the offended ghost demands, his client goes before the town, pours out the required libation, deposits the food, and prays as follows: "Here is what you asked of me. Do not let me be sick any more."

Such observances suggest ancestor-worship, but it should be noted that ghosts other than ancestors are also propitiated, that in fact the entrance to every Ekoi town is framed with offerings to the ghosts at large, in the hope of keeping them from coming in. Moreover, the whole series of rites and beliefs about ghosts, though tremendously important, by no means exhausts the totality of Ekoi religion.

Mysterious Potency

Mr. Talbot writes:

The term "Njomm," is so elusive as to defy definition, but as far as may be gathered from the vague conception of the Ekoi, it includes all uncomprehended, mysterious forces of Nature.

It is apparently applied both substantively and as an adjective and corresponds fairly closely to the Crow word *maxpé*. Our authority translates it by what seems to be a West African pidgin English expression, but I see no reason for unnecessarily introducing such terms and shall try to cover the underlying idea by such unexceptionable English words as "mysterious," "supernatural," "weird," and, when hard put to it, shall fall back upon the classical Ekoi *njomm*. Let us examine the range of application of the concept.

It has already been pointed out that when ghosts are killed in the folk-tales they fail to revive by any inherent spiritual attribute of theirs. What resuscitates them is the rubbing on of a mysterious substance with revival power, so that the Lame Boy who functions as the good fairy of Ekoi folklore succeeds in bringing to life an infant hero by clandestinely applying the same device used by the ghosts among themselves. Similarly what makes ghosts invisible in a particular story is the application of some weird black material together with a relevant wish formula; when a spying human outcast possesses himself of the same substance and utters the same charm he, too, becomes endowed with supernatural powers and is capable of preventing the ghosts from feasting. To cite another instance of supernatural power vested in what we consider an inanimate object, chalk is capable of bringing good luck to mortals whose bodies are marked with it, and accordingly it is rubbed over a newborn infant. Again, a tree with magical properties seems to be sacred to every town, and among trees the cotton tree is the one most feared. Specifically, it is addressed in prayer and presented with a gift when an Ekoi desires to revenge himself upon an enemy. He will then call aloud the victim's name, and the tree may consummate his wish by seizing and imprisoning the enemy's child. As recently as 1908 a man accused his own brother of having tried to imprison their sister in a tree.

Since everything that exists, including manufactured articles, has a soul, it would hardly do to separate personal from impersonal manifestations of mysterious power; yet in some cases the personal aspect seems to dwindle away, while in others we are clearly dealing, to all intents and purposes, with individual beings wielding superhuman potency. When the ghosts are said to have been resuscitated by the black *njomm,* the personal quality is certainly not in the foreground of the native's consciousness. Not so when a hunter leaving for the chase makes the customary sacrifice to his *njomm* or breaks his spell of ill-luck by a prayer; nor when a *njomm* is first invoked to smite a tribesman with disaster and in more relenting mood adjured to lift the curse. The impression derived from a careful reading of the evidence— and, indeed, supported by our authority himself—is that the Ekoi mind places in one category both personal and impersonal manifestations of extraordinary power. The difference between the two is at all events often far from well-defined: the supernatural power seems indeed personal, yet unindividualized; it is a personification of the votary's wish but a blindly mechanical personification. Mïam, for example, the oldest *njomm,* protects villages from theft; but he or it is so remorseless a guardian that even a person who innocently tastes a single plantain without the owner's permission must die.

However this may be, it seems clear that while there is an indefinite number of mysteriously potent agencies, many of them are concentrated into personal form and their effigies represent the focus for so many distinct cults, some familial, others local, still others linked with clubs or fraternities. The personal character of these supernatural agencies is also suggested by an important analogy with ghosts: disease, when not caused by sorcery, is the result either of offended *njomm* or of neglected ancestors; and since witchcraft is itself an effect of possession, we may say that disease is traced to the agency of spiritual beings and that the *njomm* as spirits quite naturally figure among pathogenic instruments. Now to say this is essentially equivalent to charging the votaries of the disease-causing *njomm* with sorcery; and in some cases there is explicit statement to that effect. For example, the members of the Mfepp cult use their power exclusively to injure others, whether they be tribal enemies or townspeople who have aroused their resentment, such as dilatory debtors. Similarly, those connected with the Nsann *njomm* are powerful poisoners and can destroy their enemies by lightning. That is to say, the salient fear of evil magic has been connected by the Ekoi mind with the concept of extraordinary power. This association, however, has not uniformly been interpreted in a fashion detrimental to human interests,—quite the contrary, indeed, has taken place. As Talbot points out, irrespective of local differences the protection against witchcraft ranks as the foremost attribute of dominant *njomm*. For example, the destructive agency of Nsann can be overcome by the power of Eja. Here we have an epitome of what is most essential in the whole matter. Sorcery is so overshadowing an influence in native life that the operation of mysterious power is very largely made to hinge on the cause and the prevention of witchcraft.

GODS

Ekoi theology is in a sense dualistic: while there is a host of supernatural beings, two take precedence in all ceremonies or prayers, even when these are primarily associated with ancestors or other divine powers. These two major deities are Osaw and Nsi, the former associated with the sky, the latter with the earth. Both are at present conceived as male, but Mr. Talbot finds some hints of the formerly feminine character of Nsi. Between them these two deities, when originally living together, made all things in the world, but later they agreed to separate and took up their abode in the heavens and under the earth, respectively. Osaw is cruel; sometimes he sends too much rain, at others not enough; then again he will terrify and kill human beings with thunder and lightning. Nsi, on the other hand, is benevolent and ripens the crops. All witchcraft and all bad *njomm* are interpreted as having been sent by Osaw, while all good mystic power is traced to Nsi.

Sometimes people pray to the latter to destroy Ojje (sorcery), for it is well known that no witchcraft can stand against his might.

All of this smacks of Manichæan philosophy, but nothing is more remote from the Ekoi mind than the conception of a cosmic conflict between good and evil, with the fate of mankind as a possible stake. Nsi and Osaw are not to be set at loggerheads by so paltry a point of difference as their respective attitudes towards humanity. They are the best of friends, and Nsi orders people to make offerings to his celestial counterpart. However, the benevolent Earth deity is regarded as the stronger, and of the emblems found in most of the native habitations by far the majority are sacred to Nsi.

The above is the notion of these deities entertained in abstract discussion, but it is by no means strictly borne out by the spontaneous evidence of the folk-tales in which Osaw and Nsi play a part. The "good" Nsi no less than the malevolent Osaw is pictured as cruelly discriminating against an inoffensive but unloved son and plotting his death; and what is at least equally remarkable, this supreme god against whom no sorcery can prevail is on occasion completely thwarted in his wicked designs. Still stranger is the tale of how Nsi, after having been bribed into sending Lamb to his destruction, is duped and himself killed by a falling tree. It is also interesting to find Lamb warning Nsi of a great *njomm!* After all this, it is not surprising that Nsi should at times fear Osaw, irrespective of his theoretical superiority; and here another discrepancy must be noted: while in philosophical exposition the Ekoi represents his two chief deities as closely allied by bonds of friendship, they appear, at least in two myths, as bitter enemies. Needless to say, it is no profound ethical difference that divides them, but the purely personal grievance suffered by Osaw's children at Nsi's hands. Sometimes it almost appears as though Osaw and Nsi have exchanged parts in folklore, for while Nsi may indulge in wanton cruelty, Osaw is capable of benevolence, as in giving water to mankind, who had formerly been obliged to do without. But such loving-kindness is episodic, and the god conforms more nearly to his norm when he chastises Lame Boy for his Promethean theft of fire or envies Tortoise's wisdom. As for his supernatural potency, Osaw, like his terrestrial compeer, may be outwitted by adversaries and even slain by the son whom he had unnaturally sought to destroy.

In short, the two great deities of the Ekoi are no more consistently conceived than the Sun or Old-Man-Coyote of the Crow. Neither is uniformly good; and, however powerful they may be, somewhere in the universe there are stores of mystic potency they have never tapped and which can be used to frustrate their designs.

Compared with other peoples, the Ekoi pay little attention to celestial phenomena; even the Sun, though addressed in daily prayer at sunrise, merely serves as an intermediary between the supplicant and the two main deities. One other spirit, however, must be singled out from the host of *njomm*,—the goddess Nimm, who appears in the triple form of woman, snake, and crocodile. She is the guardian of farms and crops, and figures above all as the women's deity. Her priestesses are famed for their skill in divination, and their sorority, from which men are rigorously excluded, is invested with such a halo of superstition by the natives that it ranks as the equal of the Egbo, the great men's organization. Nimm will avenge wrongs to her followers, and when a man is seized by a crocodile it may be in answer to an abused wife's petition. Every eighth day is a rest-day in honor of Nimm, and if any woman should venture to break the rule and farm her plot, her labors would be destroyed by the beasts that are the goddess's slaves. As might be anticipated from her animal associations, Nimm is a cruel deity; when the great yam festival is held in her honor, she craves offerings in compensation for the fertilization of the land, and any man entering the water during a period of seven days is slain as a sacrifice to the goddess.

Ritual

Some of the most characteristic features of Ekoi ritualism have already been mentioned incidentally in the preceding account. In contrast to anything reported for the Crow, there is an elaborate procedure of divination and a tendency to pacify the spirits by bloody offerings, usually of such domesticated animals as goats and cows, but sometimes even of human beings. Other elements of West African ceremonialism are not so foreign to Plains Indian usage. Thus, when we learn of the pot, the queerly shaped pieces of carved wood, the sacred knife, and the white feathers cherished by every Nimm-worshiper in a special shrine in her room, we are reminded of the miscellaneous assemblage of sacred objects often united in a Crow medicine-bundle.

Still more reminiscent of the Plains, though rather different in both spirit and details, are the more or less dramatic performances of the numerous Ekoi societies, some of them executed in the course of the funeral rites in honor of a deceased man by his fellow-members, others as part of the normal business of these organizations or by way of entertainment. Even the children have clubs which practice public performances, and the mingling of sportive and religious aspects in these ceremonies is well illustrated by an experience of Mr. Talbot. A group of children appeared in a pageant before him, hoping to be rewarded for their pains with some small coin. As is customary in corresponding processions of the adult, one participant had his face concealed with cloth, and the British spectator innocently pulled off the covering, which seemed to handicap the little player. At once the children uttered a cry of protest, while the mummer covered his face with his hands and "the elders hastened up to rearrange the veils about him, volubly explaining that the face of the 'image' must never be seen by his companions."

Among the men's organizations the Egbo takes precedence. It is a fraternity subdivided into at least seven grades with increasing entrance fees. There is a head priest for the whole order, with lesser chiefs for the various grades and other functionaries. Every village has its Egbo house; indeed, the first thing on moving to a new site is to erect a shed to mark the site of the permanent club lodge. In the interior there are carved pillars and a long cut stone sacred to Nimm. The ritual, which is imperfectly known to science, is extremely intricate, involving many distinct cults and diverse sacrificial observances. The utmost mystery was formerly maintained in the performance of certain ceremonies, and intruders, even though by mere chance, might be flogged to death or otherwise dispatched. In spite of this secrecy, or rather as part and parcel of the correlated terrorization of outsiders, there were spectacular public performances, at which each degree exhibited distinctive dances, tunes, and costumes. At least one chief performer, evidently designed to impersonate a supernatural being, appeared in a long garment furnished with eye-holes, robing him from crown to toe, and usually topped by a mask. The player was accompanied by one or more assistants, some of whom were generally prepared to beat spectators or those who had offended the fraternity. The Egbo is charged with political and judicial functions of the utmost importance to the tribe, but for our purpose only the ceremonial associations are considered here, and even they in the most summary fashion.

Comparison of Ekoi and Crow Religion

The essence of Crow religion was found in the visionary experience. That of the Ekoi is not so easily summarized. On the intellectual side, at least, it is difficult to derive the main features from any one source of origin. That there is in the individual consciousness an overpowering sense of the extraordinary, sometimes more, sometimes less clearly individualized, is true enough; but this hardly suffices for a characterization when we recall that this very same recognition of the supernatural has led to such divergent results among the Crow. What seems to set off the faith of the Ekoi most sharply is not this or that type of practice, this or that form of belief, but an emotional undertone that somehow penetrates the whole of their religion. Theirs is

a land full of mystery and terror, of magic plants, of rivers of good and ill fortune, of trees and rocks ever lowering to engulf unwary wayfarers; where the terror of witchcraft stalks abroad, and where, against this dread, the most devoted love or faithful service counts as naught.

This somberness of outlook we should seek in vain among the Crow.

When from such general impressions we turn to concrete elements, a fact of the utmost significance confronts us. Most of the phenomena that occur in either tribe are also found in the other, *but they are quite differently weighted.* For example, the individual psychic experience that looms so large in Crow life is not lacking among the Ekoi. Wraiths of dead friends appear in the dark to warn of danger or to demand offerings. In the dead of night men see some of their acquaintances holding solemn conclave and suddenly assuming the shapes of ducks and elephants. At the jeopardy of her life a woman confesses having a snake familiar, which appears to her in her sleep. A person mysteriously linked with the Oji tree will suddenly hear it calling and must set out post-haste by night or day to respond to the summons, regardless of circumstances, as when a warder deliriously leaves his post to dash into the bush: "To-night I was very tired and lay down on my bed. In my sleep my tree began to call 'Oji, Oji.' I woke and still heard it call. So I started up to run out into the night. It always calls about the time of the new yams, sometimes earlier, sometimes later. When they tried to stop me it called louder and louder. So I fought them to get away and go to my tree." It would be foolish to deny that such experiences may be of the utmost importance to the individual. Nevertheless it remains true that they are far from having the universal and pivotal, because socially standardized, significance attaching to them in the Plains of North America.

On the other hand, such a phenomenon as divination is not wholly absent among the Crow, for occasionally a warrior will read his fate by examining the blood of a badger mixed with that of a buffalo; but the procedure figures so rarely that in my general account it was possible to ignore it completely. Evil magic was certainly practiced by some of the Crow, but it was not often leveled against a tribesman, let alone a relative, hence that abiding terror of sorcery even in the midst of the Ekoi family circle has no parallel in Crow society. Furthermore, Crow sorcery is practically always linked with the favoritism displayed by the tutelary spirit acquired in a vision, so that its associations are quite different from those of its equivalent in West Africa. Similarly, the belief in ghosts bears a quite different character in the two areas: it exists, indeed, among the Crow, but with only an infrequent religious association based on the sporadic

appearance of ghosts in visions; among the Ekoi it constitutes one of the most obtrusive phases of their adjustment
to the supernatural.

The result of this brief comparison is an important one.
Merely to catalog the occurrence of such and such beliefs
and observances is a futile enterprise. When we know that
a tribe practices witchcraft, believes in ghosts, recognizes the
mysterious potency resident in inanimate nature, or, it may
be, the supremacy of some one supernatural being, we know
precisely nothing concerning the religion of the people concerned. Everything depends on the interdependence of the
several departments of supernaturalism, on the emotional
weighting that attaches to each and every one of them.

REFERENCES

[1] This sketch is based on Talbot: 13-88, 165-202, 230-241, et passim.

[2] Stoll: 385-389, 397-430.

[3] Sumner: 119.

CHAPTER III

BUKAUA RELIGION [1]

MAGIC

SORCERY does not play as devastating a part in the Huon
Gulf littoral of New Guinea as in West Africa, yet the
belief in its reality is sufficiently strong. Though there
is no evidence that the dread of its practitioners invades
the intimacy of the family circle, outsiders are potential
agents of evil, and the natives cautiously remove any
material that might furnish them a starting-point for their
malpractices. But among the Bukaua and their congeners
witchcraft, however important, is only one special manifestation of a more general system of ideas, the faith in
magic; and this system is founded on a triple conception,—
the notion that desired ends can be attained by vicarious
action at a distance, the belief in the efficacy of a prescribed
though irrelevant conduct, and a dependence on the supernatural potency of certain traditional formulas. How these
ideas are interlaced in the operations of daily life can easily
be illustrated by a variety of examples.

A number of magicians specialize in regulating the
weather. Theirs is a lucrative profession, for people are
eager to bribe a wizard into stopping excessive rainfall or
ending a season of drought. His stock-in-trade consists
essentially of two coconut cups and a great multitude of
little stones; from two species of vine growing in the depths
of the forest he squeezes enough sap to make a cup half
full, then stone after stone is thrown into it till the fluid

overflows its container: the more it overflows, the greater
will be the precipitation. Thunder is produced by shaking
the stones together with fragments of the tough skull of
a certain fish in one of the cups, after which a hollow sound
is made by striking a palm trunk, while lightning is simu-
lated by tearing a strip of pandanus leaf. The two vessels
are covered and left in the woods. If the wizard is hired
to make the rain cease, he fetches his cups and dries them
on a stage over his camp-fire.

So far there is the characteristic belief in "imitative
magic," i. e., the belief that a desired effect can be produced
by the simple device of imitating it under convenient conditions: as the sap overflows the vessel, so the longed-for
rain will flow from the firmament; as the contents evaporate,
so the moisture will disappear from the atmosphere. But
this is far from being the whole story. Over his cups the
wizard must mutter a magic formula:

The cuttle-fish was devoured by the shark, whose inside
turned quite black. The hen and the cassowary were traveling
in a boat, but the cassowary, angered because people despised
him, destroyed the boat. The hen flew into a village, which was
called "Hen," and a giant tortoise carried the cassowary to
Buso; when it got to the big grassy plain of Bahom, the cassowary turned into a rock, which is still standing there.

Obviously this pointless tale bears no clear relation to
the magician's purpose, and the same irrelevancy appears
in the conduct prescribed for him: until the rain falls he
must refrain from work and betel-chewing; on the other
hand, he is obliged to rub his hair with black earth, dotting
his forehead and nose, and must take a daily bath in the
sea at dawn while extending his hands over the water and
calling the rain. It is by fulfilling the triple set of condi-

tions,—by using imitative magical practices, by reciting a mystic form of words, and by following a ritual mode of conduct,—that the wizard makes sure of gaining his ends.

A similar combination of observances precedes and accompanies the holding of a pig market. Swine form the most highly esteemed article of property, and their public sale is linked with a good deal of solemnity. The inaugurators of the celebration provide a large number of well-fattened pigs and invite prospective buyers, who feel honored by the summons. In order to guarantee high prices and a peaceful gathering and to avert the premature death of the pigs selected for the market, the owners resort to magical practices of a somewhat involved character. A series of little stones represent the pigs' vital organs; others, varying in color, designate correspondingly colored pigs. The sellers or their agents must submit to a rigid diet, all food except roasted taro being tabooed. In a double bowl filled with water are kept a snake and a fish, and on their safety, insured by the celebrants' fast, depends that of the pigs. The vital force of snake and fish are communicated to the stones representing the pigs' organs and are in turn fostered by the presence of herbs credited with high nutritive value. Less transparent is the practice of setting up a stone idol between two clay representations of boars' tusks for the purpose of luring buyers who own valuables worth acquiring in trade, or the clandestine blowing of little shells to make the guests amass plenty of these desirable media of exchange. On the other hand, for the preservation of law and order the procedure is again based on an intelligible enough association of ideas: a bit of root is burnt and the ashes are secretly sprinkled over the site of the gathering, so that they may impart their coolness to the foot of a buyer who should be fired with anger. The charm recited on this occasion over the double bowl is somewhat less cryptic in its application than the one cited above:

A man and his cousin, named Gasi and Anu, wished to hold a pig market; they conferred about the swine and fattened the young pigs until they were big in order to prepare for a feast. Before that they cooked several little pigs and ate them; then the man himself turned into a pig and made a litter. His cousin went, constantly looking for him and saying, "Cousin, what are you doing?" He answered: "Go, look for our wives and bid them come to fetch the little pig." They carried it away, kept it till it was big enough and gave birth to plenty of pigs, so there were a great many. Then he said, "Cousin, let us not wait any longer, but hasten to arrange a pig market after two rainy seasons." They acted accordingly. There were a great many pigs. They made a new clearing and entertained each other, and the people brought boars' tusks and swine there.

In short, the pig-seller uses the same pattern as the rainmaker,—vicarious magical procedure, ritualistic abstinence, and a mystic spell.

This pattern is equally discernible in the machinations of the death-dealing sorcerer, which combine the processes of imitative with those of "contagious" magic, that is, center in the bewitching of some object once intimately connected with the enemy. The profession is usually followed by puny, deformed men, who inherit the technique from their fathers but only begin practice after a period of apprenticeship and a trial of their competence. A wizard is powerless unless he can secure some object, however small, that has been in contact with his enemy; a remnant of his victim's meal, the spittle he has expectorated in coughing, the paint he has used to daub his hair, will suffice, and to obtain any one of these stealth and trickery are employed. But the price of success is once more a prescribed form of con-

duct, both positive and negative: the magician must not
bathe nor drink anything except coconut juice nor eat any
but roasted dishes; and he is obliged to consume what others
shun,—certain species of onions, some bitter fruits, a slightly
poisonous plant. The fragment secured is wrapped up in
leaves, tied together, and suspended in the depths of the
forest. It is the victim's soul itself that is thus bound by
proxy, and its owner must inevitably fall sick. As soon as
the disease takes a serious turn, the patient's kin determine
the sorcerer's identity and pay him to desist from his purpose. If he has not been hired by persons of greater consequence and regards the fee as adequate, he will readily
grant the request, breathe on some leaves, murmur a spell
over them and send them to the sick man, while he himself
will go into the woods and nullify his previous acts by
putting the package into water. This leads to the patient's
recovery. Should he remain ill, the fault is laid to the
charge of another sorcerer or, if *his* conciliation likewise
fails to produce results, to that of evil spirits. But the
magician may refuse the gifts offered, retire to the forest,
and there put his package into glowing ashes while muttering his spell: "As the fire slowly consumes this package,
so shall disease destroy the sick man." Then the patient
must die, but his death will be avenged by his relatives
unless the crafty wizard seeks safety in flight.

The examples cited sufficiently indicate the nature of
Bukaua magic. Its specific object naturally varies, embracing in fact almost the whole range of native activities.
Magic is used to insure a haul of fish, to acquire the min-
strel's art, to fascinate women, to cause a famine. In virtually every instance the recital of a formula—either a
prayer addressed to the ancestral spirits or a snatch of a
tale as in the quoted spells—is linked with a certain mode

of procedure; and in the cases most fully reported the practitioner is under obligation to observe certain taboos and some positive fixed form of conduct.

SOULS AND SPIRITS

According to Bukaua psychology, the soul (*katu*) leaves the body to lead an independent existence during sleep, and the same applies to fainting-spells; when a person awakes from sleep or swoon, his soul has come back. Death, too, liberates the soul, which becomes a spirit (*balum* or *ngalau*) capable of assuming any shape and most frequently tending to malevolence. The souls of the deceased reside in the underworld, whose entrance lies towards the east. Very little attention is paid to their mode of life there, which in general is pictured as similar to existence in this world. The kindred Jabim display a like indifference but are slightly more explicit: they represent the ghosts as haunting the woods at night but retiring at dawn. Neither tribe has the slightest conception of other-worldly reward and punishment.

Although Herr Lehner, our authority, sometimes seems to imply that all spirits are derived from the souls of the deceased, this does not appear from his concrete description of the host of *balum* beings. It is true that certain bodily afflictions are traced to the action of spirits wishing to avenge their neglect by the living, or to inflict penalties for a breach of tribal custom. But when in the enumeration of spiritual beings the local and village spirits are singled out as the ancestors of the villagers, the question naturally arises whether the others should not be conceived as beings dissociated from the idea of ever having tenanted a human body.

However this may be, a variety of supernatural persons are believed to affect the life of the natives, and so far from being confined to the above-mentioned resting-place in the underworld they haunt beach and stream, wood and village. The village spirits, who are to be regarded as preeminently the ancestral ghosts, are invoked in the pig-hunt, in tillage, and on special occasions; they receive offerings either as a bribe to induce favorable action or as a thanksgiving for past services. It would be perilous to excite their wrath by disrespectful behavior. Deference is also shown to the field spirits, who may grant plentiful crops. They are wont to sit on the stumps of trees as sentries warding off danger to the plantation. If the fruits near such a stump grow to exceptional size, this proves the presence of the spirit, and no one may make a noise in the vicinity, let alone chop wood from the trunk of the tree.

With these potentially benign figures may be contrasted a series of wholly or predominantly malevolent ones. Bumo infests the bushes along the beach and attacks innocent passers-by, who are seized with fainting-spells on their return to the village. Balum-buauwi haunts the sinister-looking recesses of streams; her specialty is to blight little children carried across the creek by their mothers, for she infects them with the wrinkled appearance of her own countenance. Mothers crossing streams at uncanny-looking fords can only safeguard their infants by murmuring a spell over some rocks and then throwing the stones towards both mouth and source of the watercourse. Many a Bukaua seriously asserts that he has seen this ill-favored spirit and heard her song. Again in the primeval forest there dwell innumerable trolls, whose voices are recognized in the chirping of wood insects. They play all manner of tricks on people, causing dogs to stray from the right track, making wild pigs ferocious, or assuming the shape of snakes to commit depredations in human dwellings. They—especially one of their number named Molo—are inclined to make men mad or epileptic.

Besides the definitely localized beings there are the vagrant demons, most prominently represented by the love spirits (*wasu*). All the love charms now in vogue are derived from a single being of this category, whose story is told as follows. Once upon a time a native seeking shelter from a shower discovered the spirit sitting in the foliage of a big tree. He reported what he had seen and all the villagers hastened to behold the *wasu*. The women became inflamed with passion and forgot their conjugal duties in their infatuation with the spirit. Their husbands, incensed at such conduct, cut down the tree and killed the seducer, who bore the form of a child, was beautifully decorated, and had a sweet-smelling body. One of two netted bags in his possession was found to contain every kind of love charm, and since this event these charms have been used by men in abducting women. Another member of this mysterious group seeks intercourse with men and women, the result being sickness and death.

Owing to the obscurity that envelops the relations of the ancestral spirits to those of other categories among the Bukaua, it may be well to cite some data from the neighboring Tami Islanders as possibly shedding additional light on the beliefs of their fellow-Melanesians.

The Tami rather clearly distinguish the spirits of the departed from supernatural beings of other categories. The latter are numerous and of varied character. There are local spirits, many of them double-faced, haunting ravine and mountain top, secluded rocks, and giant trees. Only the natives of neighboring villages may approach such spots with impunity; all others are liable to suffer punishment, whether in the form of sickness or some mishap in traveling. This type figures prominently in legendary lore. One representative, Tumangon, for example, lures children to accompany him on a voyage and plans to desert them on a lonely islet, but by shrewdly playing on his gluttony they succeed in foiling and destroying the monster. Yet the story of an almost namesake of this ogre's, Tumangon Sumosum, proves that this class of beings is not conceived as wholly malevolent. Rebuffed by village after village when he approaches in the guise of a skeleton, the spirit gratefully rewards a hospitable old man with a bountiful supply of valuable dogs' teeth. Logically the love-spirits would seem to fall into the same class of local spirits as the foregoing, for they, too, haunt definite spots, such as groves and springs; but in the aboriginal scheme they constitute a separate group characterized by their power to seduce young maidens with magic songs or redolent splinters of wood. Their essence is of finer stuff than mortal flesh, and when a young woman in her ardor seizes a spirit before he has had time to "materialize" she crushes him, though ultimately he may be restored from a drop of his blood. A third variety of spirit is called *ding*. Its representatives are body-snatchers and have the power of assuming the shape of a dog or of one of the mourners of a deceased native. They appear in folk-literature as stupid trolls who are always hoodwinked by their human adversaries.

Still another series of supernatural beings are dignified by our authority with the title of "deities." These include the race of *buwun*, who inhabit an otherwise untenanted island and are represented on house planks as having fish-like bodies and human heads. Normally invisible, they assume human form in order to seduce women, who invariably die as a result of their adulterous intercourse with the spirits. Even in quite recent times inexplicable deaths of women have been explained as due to such experiences. Indeed, the *buwun* are generally a dangerous lot, causing earthquakes and epidemics. Nevertheless, there is little attempt to placate them: only when the ravages of disease are especially terrifying they receive the offering of an emaciated pig or a mangy cur.

Strangely enough, there is no consensus of opinion as to whether Anuto, the generally recognized creator, belongs to the *buwun*. Some figure him as occupying a fair island, others picture him sitting on a subterranean cliff, where a turning of his body produces an earthquake; then again he is described as seated on the earth and supporting the sky with his head. At all events, he is definitely the creator of the world and of the first human couple. His is the first portion of food at public banquets and markets, and the presentation of this offering constitutes the whole of his cult; nor can it be regarded as involving much of a sacrifice since aboriginal theory has it that only the soul of the food is partaken by the gods while its material essence may be consumed by their votaries. Sometimes Old Panku, instead of Anuto, is represented as the creator and earthquake-producer. Apparently the inconsistencies in Tami cosmology are in part due to the existence of distinct family traditions, which in the absence of a theologically-minded caste have not been welded into unison.

But all of the aforementioned beings are of relatively subordinate importance as compared with the ancestral spirits or, to be more accurate, the spirits of those forbears personally known to the descendants. They dwell in the underworld, where everything is finer than on this earth, amidst such abundance of fruit that life is far easier than here. Yet it is but a continuation of earthly existence: men work and marry, fall sick and die, when they are transformed into worms or white ants; or as some contend, into goblins of the woods who damage the natives' crops. The spirits are far from hospitable to arriving souls. A favorite practical joke of theirs consists in sending the novices up trees, then suddenly seizing them by their feet and jerking them down so that the rough bark cuts open all their bodies. To prevent such scurvy treatment the kin of the deceased present them with gifts, the souls of which are designed to placate their hosts of the spirit world.

The dead are not confined to their subterranean abode but are able to reappear at any time. This happens most commonly when one of their relatives approaches death; then they assemble to conduct him to his prospective home. However, this conception is not universal, and at times the departing soul is exhorted not to go astray. But though the dead may return to this world, they do not linger here, because it is too cold for them. Some families make a practice of summoning the spirits of recently departed kinsmen, which appear in the shape of snakes and may be consulted as oracles by those conversant with their language, which consists of whistling sounds. Such performances take place only at night and are conducted mainly by women.

It is not superfluous to add that the séances are wholly devoid of any material advantage for the managers, and the same holds for the complementary enterprise of visiting the spirit land. Here, too, women play the most important part and transmit their powers—that is, their magic spells —to their daughters. If any one desires information from a dead relative, he provides the seer with some article used by the person in question, upon which she lies down after rubbing her forehead with ginger and murmuring her magic formula. Then her soul descends to the spirits and secures the required revelation from her deceased kin. The fame acquired by the performance is her sole reward.

The importance of magic that appears in the last-cited performance is equally manifest in the treatment of disease. There is one formula against pains in the chest, another against catarrh, a third against rheumatism. Spirits, who might snatch away the souls of first-born infants, are banished by the singing of special songs. In general, there is a magical rite for restoring a patient's soul when purloined by ghosts. The performer, reciting his spells, chews ginger or the bark of a certain tree, places these substances into a shell, and blows this as an instrument. The blast recalls the soul, while the odor of the ingredients drives away the spirits.

In this connection it remains to explain some interesting points of Tami psychological theory. The natives recognize two souls, a "long" and a "short" one, both occupying the abdomen. The long soul leaves the body during sleep and also permanently just before death, when it announces the impending event to relatives who happen to reside elsewhere; finally it migrates by way of western New Britain to a village on the north coast. It is this long soul that is stolen by malevolent ghosts and has to be restored to the body. On the other hand, the "short" soul only departs after death and even then lingers about the corpse before going to the underworld, from where it returns to molest the sorcerer who caused its departure and to see that his deed is avenged by the victim's kin.

CEREMONIALISM

The outstanding Bukaua ceremonial is that connected
with the admission of boys to an adult's privileges. There
is indeed a parallel puberty rite for girls: common to both
performances are the segregation of the novices, their instruction by elders, the observance of food taboos and other
restrictions, and the formal promotion to a new status.
But the social import of the girls' ceremony is relatively
slight; or, rather, its significance is essentially of a private
character. While among various African peoples initiation
means entrance into an *organization* of women comparable
to the men's society, no such goal is attained in New
Guinea: the young maiden is merely recognized as of mar-
riageable age. The youths' initiation, on the other hand, leads
to what may be called full-fledged citizenship, from which
women are by the unwritten tribal law forever barred.

This basic distinction in favor of the male sex is prominent throughout the great festival. Women are mystified
and terrorized so long as it lasts. A hoax is propounded
for their exclusive consumption. The Balum, they are told,
is a voracious demon hungering for their sons, but willing
to disgorge them at the price of a fat pig a head. It is also
well to flatten his gullet with taro and other vegetable food.
Thus it becomes the mothers' duty to fatten pigs and amass
provisions for a solemnity they are never allowed to witness. Circumcision forms an indispensable part of initiation, and to account for the wound the women are informed
that the monster has bitten or scratched his victims in spew-
ing them forth again. Under the primitive conditions of
performing the operation it naturally proves fatal at times,
and in that event the unfortunate mother is told that her
ransom was rejected by the ogre as inadequate, or that

the boy failed to conform to the regulations. No wonder the terrified women display great zeal in raising pigs and part from their sons in a state of tremendous excitement. In order to keep the secret from the female sex the newly initiated are warned on pain of horrible penalties never to divulge the real nature of the festivities, while the women must leave the village when the ceremonial structure has been built, for they, too, would fall prey to the insatiable monster if he caught sight of them. To lend verisimilitude to the strange tale, the men simulate the spirit's voice by musical instruments, especially by the swinging of the leaf-shaped wooden slabs known as bull-roarers. Only two or three aged women, in some unexplained manner, are cognizant of what really takes place, and these are bribed into silence by surreptitious gifts of pork.

While the festival is thus a severe test of the women's nerves, it is naturally an at least equally grave ordeal for the tyros themselves. After the heart-rending separation from their mothers they are led blindfolded to the ceremonial building that is to form their abode for from three to five months. There two hidden sentries guard them, terrifying the boys with strange noises and menacing the over-bold with a sharp adze. Novices and guardians alike must practice continence and abstain from pork, lizards, mice, and fresh water. Otherwise the pigs and the novices might both die. Except for the plaiting of mats and the manufacture of flutes, the young men do absolutely no work during the period of seclusion, nor are they permitted to bathe until the morning of the operation. Just before the circumcision itself the elders frighten the boys by every manner of noise,—the swinging of dozens of booming bull-roarers, the clamor of hundreds of human voices, the weird rattling of shells and stones suspended from the tops of trees. The novices' anxiety is not lessened when their hands are tied behind their backs and they are carried or led blindfolded to the site of the operation, where sham attacks are made on them and their guides; nor is circumcision with a splint of obsidian an unalloyed pleasure. Cries of pain, however, are muffled by boars' tusks tied in front of the victims' mouths, and drowned by the elders' thunderous music. After a bath the boys return to the ceremonial house and may join in a vast feast. Any surplus food must be buried lest the women grow skeptical as to the Balum's voracity. This day's proceedings form the climax of the festival and alien visitors depart forthwith. There follows a two or three months' period of convalescence, at the close of which the novices, now conversant with the true state of affairs, are once more pledged to secrecy and receive sage advice as to ethical conduct. Gayly bedecked with ornaments, their faces daubed with paint, finely carved combs stuck in their hair, the boys return to the society of their mothers and the village at large, greeted by a merry and vociferous throng; and with a final banquet the ceremony as a whole comes to a close.

So far, then, the Balum festival appears as a means of exploiting the women and of admitting youths to the grade of adult manhood after a severe test. But this by no means exhausts the content of this composite cultural phenomenon. The occasion has political and economic significance. It unites, at intervals of from ten to eighteen years, not only the Bukaua and the kindred Jabim, but also the Tami Islanders and the wholly unrelated Kai of Papuan speech. Since all feuds are suspended during the course of the ritual, intertribal amity is promoted, and its basis, as so often happens, lies in the trade relations involved, for the foreign guests are invited on the assumption that

they are eager to buy pigs. In other words, the performance by which boys become full-fledged members of their
own community is linked with the quite unrelated idea of
a pig market. Logically enough, the taboos imposed on
the novices are interpreted to safeguard not only their interests, but the health of the pigs destined for sale.

The Balum proceedings evidently loom as awe-inspiring
mysteries in the minds of the women and uninitiated males.
What, however, is their religious significance for the in-
siders, the adult men who conduct the performances? This
inevitable query is not easily answered. It is tempting to
deny the religious feature altogether and to cite in support
the conscious deception of the women for the benefit of
the men. Now of course so much is clear, that the performers cannot have any faith in the cock-and-bull story
told for feminine consumption. But from this it does
not follow that they have no faith in *some* mysterious being associated with the ritual, still less that the ritual itself
is wanting in sacredness from their point of view. As a
matter of fact, occasional utterances by the natives leave
little doubt on the subject. One informant conceives the
Balum as the incarnation of spirits of long-deceased men,
who on reappearing demand a pig; another describes him
as the ancestor of a group of villagers or pictures a weird,
vague personality responsible for landslides and other catas-
trophic events. Moreover, the bull-roarers are far more
than a mere means for the intimidation of women. Each
bears the name of a departed villager, to which is added
the honorific epithet "the old" in the case of those representing distinguished men of the past. In these latter cases
individual peculiarities are indicated; for example, two lateral humps are a reminder of Gumba's protruding hip-
bones, and an obliquely hung instrument perpetuates the

memory of Wabo's disfigured nose. These major or "rul-
ing" bull-roarers enjoy special veneration, are carefully
guarded by the master of the initiation ceremonies, and supply the villagers with a rallying-cry and shibboleth. Some
of the decorative engravings are definitely symbolic of the
spirit presiding over the festival. A design interpreted as
a scorpion or millipede is intended to suggest that the Balum,
like them, can cause sudden poison by his bite, and will do
so if his injunctions are set at naught. On another bull-
roarer a ghost is shown carrying aloft a firebrand and thus
exposing the culprit who has dared divulge the secret of
the Balum. While these decorations may be charged in
part to the gratification of esthetic impulses and the desire
to impress the newly initiated, their elaborateness betokens
that they had some deeper significance for the elders themselves, a conclusion in harmony with the appellations and
uses of the articles as explained above.

But from our broader point of view the religious character of the Balum festival is not dependent on the elders'
belief in *any* spiritual patron, as may be demonstrated by
an extreme case. The bull-roarer initiation ritual has spread
from the mainland about Huon Gulf to Tami and other
neighboring islands and has naturally lost some of its holy
associations in transmission. Indeed, if we can trust our
missionary authority, the Tami elders fail to associate any
conceptions of supernatural beings with either the ceremony or the anthropomorphic representations connected
with it. Nevertheless we are told that the bull-roarers are
treated with reverence, and that the initiation proceedings
are marked by a series of meticulously observed solemnities.
Whether these have for their primary object the magical
preservation of the fattened pigs, as Herr Bamler suggests,
is of subordinate interest. The main point is that even in

the borrowed and apparently weakened form characteristic of these islands, the festival preserves that quality of holiness or supernaturalism which lifts it from the plane of everyday thought to what may properly be called the level of the religious attitude.

It must not be supposed that prior to contact with the Bukaua there was a total absence of pretentious ritual in Tami. First of all, the natives practiced the Tago cult; secondly, there was an elaborate memorial festival that closed the two or three years' mourning period in honor of a dead kinsman. The Tago or mummers' cult, as we may call it, is like the bull-roarer festival an alien feature, though one of greater antiquity in these parts. It is in fact identical with the Dukduk of New Britain, so that Tami ritualism represents the confluence of two cultural waves resulting to a certain extent in duplication, since both cults are associated with ghosts and with the terrorization of women and the uninitiated boys. The Tago is only celebrated once every ten or twelve years, but then its ceremonial period extends over approximately a twelvemonth and throughout its duration the use of coconuts is strictly tabooed. The spirits impersonated by the masqueraders are said to come out of pits in the ground or from across the sea. They receive a formal welcome with a sennet of shell-horn music and are warmly thanked for having braved the long journey. Every morning and evening one or more of the performers, wearing a mask and heavy ceremonial garb, proceed through the village, frightening the uninitiated, while at night distinctive dances are executed to the accompaniment of drums. Each family owns a mask peculiar to its members, and the owner satisfies the hunger of the man performing for him. At the close of the Tago there is a final feast and dance, the performers bid farewell to their patrons and receive provender for the journey, as well as minor valuables; then they disappear amidst general lamentation.

The memorial festival constitutes another grand occasion in the natives' life. All the villagers, and probably the people of a neighboring community as well, are invited and lavishly entertained with pork and taro porridge in quantities that might have been ample for a ten days' normal diet. Every one adorns himself in special fashion,— the mourners by daubing their necks, heads and chests with black earth. With nightfall the dance commences and is continued until daylight, when the food is distributed and the feast begins. The spirits, both those in whose honor the ceremony is primarily held and an indefinite number of others, partake of the food by somehow absorbing its spiritual essence. Finally, the dancers once more appear in a set of pantomimes that make the spectators shake with laughter. Two men pretend carrying a pig, the animal being represented by a piece of wood tied to a pole. Suddenly they are confronted by a thicket,—in reality two dancers,—and the man in front makes gestures to his partner, explaining the nature of the obstacle which is cleared away with a mock-ax. One of the carriers suddenly runs a spine into his foot, which his comrade attempts to extract with a stick an inch in thickness. In another farce of this type one player takes the part of a pig, while two companions are the old women supposed to feed it. The pig grows savage and charges the women, who approach the trough full of fear but are driven to take to their heels. In still other cases actors carry sand in perforated bags. If the deceased was a person of prominence, an offering of food and valuables normally terminates the performance, though some add a further act of devotion, dis-

interring the bones after decomposition in order to daub
them with red paint, and after keeping them in the house
for two or three years rebury the remains for good.

Summary

Bukaua and Tami supernaturalism stands closer to that
of the Ekoi than to that of the Crow: sorcery and ghost-
cults are prominently associated with New Guinea notions
of extraordinary power; and while direct personal communion with the supernatural undoubtedly occurs, it is not
the recognized and generally practiced right of the individual native to seek it. Ceremonially, too, the mystery of the
initiation festival, with the sacrificing of animals and the
subordination of women, savors far more of West African
ritualism than of any Plains Indian performances even
when these are executed by a restricted membership. That
a consistent scheme of the Extraordinary moiety of the
universe is lacking in all three tribes, is manifest; but it is
equally clear that all three somehow respond to the Extraordinary in the routine of existence. What differs is the
technique employed: in one of the typical crises of life a
Crow throws himself upon the Supernatural by going out
for a vision; an Ekoi consults a diviner and prays to ghost
or *njomm;* a Bukaua resorts to the magician, who in turn
falls back upon the traditional recipe.

Let us note again that catchwords utterly fail to penetrate
to the ultimate psychology of our phenomena. In a sense,
both the Ekoi and the New Guinea natives are "ancestor-
worshipers." But in the West African tribe the spirits of the
dead are definitely subordinated to the two major gods and
coördinated with a legion of *njomm;* in New Guinea there
are several categories of supernatural beings, but probably

the ghosts alone are of much religious significance. More important still, these personal beings cannot only be sporadically overcome by the use of impersonal magic, as happens among the Ekoi likewise, but they are regularly ignored in important situations of life in favor of the imitative practices, charms, and taboos described. "Ghosts" in the Kamerun are not what they are in Huon Gulf.

Finally, we may ask, in what sense some of the spiritual beings described in the preceding chapter belong to the realm of religion at all. The *ding,* for example, have the power of shape-shifting. But does that bring them within the range of the Extraordinary, let alone Holy, when they are regularly outwitted by human opponents? The caterpillar, too, undergoes a metamorphosis foreign to man, yet this does not raise it to superhuman status. Let us prepare for the conclusion that non-human personalities, including spirits, may be conceived in such a way as to be eliminated from the domain of the Extraordinary. It is the psychological response to them that is alone decisive in the matter.

References

[1] This sketch is based on Lehner and Bamler, both in Neuhauss.

CHAPTER IV

POLYNESIAN RELIGION [1]

In spite of many local peculiarities the culture of Polynesia presents an essentially uniform character. Certain of its aspects, however, have either been more accurately reported in some of the islands than in others, or were developed with unequal degrees of clarity in distinct sections of the area. Hence, instead of selecting a single group for intensive treatment, I will essay a synthetic sketch of the whole region, though most of the illustrations will be drawn from Tonga, Hawaii, and New Zealand.

A comparison of the Polynesian religion with that of the tribes hitherto considered will once more illustrate the point that cultures are not so much set off from one another by distinctive traits as by the weighting and the organization of these traits into a distinctive whole. So we find that there are features common to the Bukaua and the Polynesians,— noticeably the combination of spells and sympathetic magic for purposes of sorcery. Again, these South Sea Islanders, like the Ekoi, rendered homage to the souls of departed ancestors. Finally, though much has been written concerning the supposedly peculiar *mana* concept of the Oceanians, when we ignore irrelevant philological niceties and minor variations in local usage it unmasks as nothing but a very old friend. "Mana was shown when a man undertook to do an unusual and almost impossible thing and yet succeeded." On the other hand, when a Maori chief was captured by the enemy he had evidently lost his *mana*. It was by no means limited to personal agents, however. Conceived as somewhat in the nature of a transferable fluid, it could be conducted into weapons by placing them in temples, where they might absorb the potency vested in the gods. Wondrous tales are told of clubs mysteriously invisible to all but their rightful owner or so highly charged that they constantly kept moving, and of a quarterstaff that could foretell the issue of a battle. Whether *mana* was always ultimately a gift of the gods, as Mr. Collocott suggests, is not quite clear. It is certain that the term was applied both to persons and things, that it denotes "miracle" in the Tongan rendering of the Bible, that it might designate an unusually protracted spell of rain no less than a mysterious apparition. In short, there is nothing unique in the concept; it corresponds, as exactly as concepts of widely separated peoples can ever be expected to do, to the Crow *maxpé* and the Ekoi *njomm*. The peculiarity of Polynesian religion must be sought in another direction: it will be found, among other things, in the interrelations of social and religious motives.

Religion and Society

In the whole range of human history no people probably ever attached greater significance to distinctions of rank than the Polynesians. There was first of all a division of all society into the nobility and the common herd; and the former were subdivided with an extraordinary degree of subtlety. The basic dichotomy rested in theory on the divine lineage of the aristocrats, and the finer gradations of status depended either on the relative loftiness of the divine ancestors or on the directness of descent from a common ancestor. In practice, many knotty heraldic problems were bound to arise when the dignity of one parental line had to be bal-

anced against the possibly inferior status of the other in
settling the claims of rivals for precedence. Primogeniture,
such as prevailed in some regions, likewise introduced com-
plications. Since all but the eldest-born suffered a degradation of one step in the ladder, it inevitably happened that the
younger children of the lowest title-bearer sank to the level
of plebeians. Now, in Tonga, for instance, the theory obtained that only the souls of nobles survived death; thus, by
a rigorous application of this notion, the soul of one son in
the family would live on, while the souls of his brothers
would perish with the body. Some of them might well balk
at this interpretation and indulge what Mariner quaintly calls
"the vanity to think they have immortal souls as well as the
matabooles (lesser nobles) and chiefs." But whatever in-
tricacies might be presented by everyday experience, the ideal
principle underlying the whole scheme was transparent:
status was correlated with purity of lineage.

This conception appears perhaps most clearly in Tonga,
precisely because there rank and power were in a measure
divorced: while the spiritual supremacy was vested in the
Tuitonga, political sovereignty had been arrogated before the
beginning of the nineteenth century by a presumably distant
kinsman, hence comparatively lesser nobleman. But though
this king might flout the pontiff's counsel in temporal affairs, there was no question concerning the Tuitonga's social
preëminence. Chafing under the humiliation, King Finau
would indeed take pains to avoid a meeting, but whenever it
occurred he yielded precedence and homage in the traditional
fashion.

Within the body of the upper caste there was an interesting sub-group that played a significant part in the culture of
these tribes. They were perhaps the lowest of their class,
yet in some islands, such as Samoa, they rather than the titu-

lar sovereign held the reins of power. They embraced the
courtiers and landed gentry, corresponding at once to the
lesser nobility and the upper middle class of European countries. It was often from this class that the priests were re-
cruited, but though their status appears in such cases inter-
mediate between the pinnacles and the dregs of Polynesian
society, they were essentially to be considered a part of the
regnant caste and as pillars of the established order. However, in Mangaia the noble of highest hereditary rank was
at the same time the priest of the chief deity, and a corresponding union of priestly and heraldic preëminence characterized the Maori. Certain phenomena in the religion of
these tribes become more readily intelligible when one recalls
that it was molded in part by a group of men specially devoted to the management of sacred things and serving as
professional systematizers and standardizers of current
thought.

One of the most remarkable creations of these guardians
of things divine was the taboo concept. Our own word
"taboo" is derived from the Polynesian *tapu* (dialectically,
tabu, kapu), but it is far from designating all the ramifications and shades of meaning that clustered about its proto-
type. The aboriginal term was, like *mana*, the expression
for a highly abstract concept, but while *mana* invariably de-
noted a startling deviation from the norm, *tapu* was distinctly ambivalent: it represented the holiness of the divine,
setting it off from the profaneness of plebeian (*noa*) things
and persons; but that very attitude which lent mystic power
to the deities and their earthly vicegerents invested them with
a "mysterious perilousness and unapproachableness" for the
uninitiated, or indeed, for any one of lesser quality. In
some unaccountable way the sacredness flowed out from the
divine chief and communicated itself to what he ate or drank

or wore. No Tongan durst appropriate the remains of a superior's meal on pain of a sore throat; the cloak discarded by a Maori chief could not with safety be donned by an attendant. A Mangaia pontiff's body could not be tattooed; his equivalent in Tonga could not be either tattooed or circumcised like other men, since no one was competent to touch him with immunity, and when he was buried by his inferiors, as he inevitably had to be, these were reckoned infected for ten months. A number of prohibitions were widely distributed. Thus, no one was allowed to touch a superior's head or pass close behind him or eat in his presence. A Hawaiian whose shadow fell upon the king's house or back or who climbed over the royal stockade was doomed: to defy these taboos was tantamount to asserting oneself an equal or superior.)

Such rigor could not of course be consistently extended to all the numerous ritual prohibitions without extraordinary inconvenience to all concerned. How, for example, could the menial tasks connected with temple-building be undertaken by common workingmen who were bound to pollute the holy site? Polynesian casuistry was equal to the problem by devising a ritual mechanism that transformed the *tapu* spot into a temporarily *noa* one. Again, in Tonga the rule held that any one who, however accidentally, had touched a grandee was infected and might not feed himself with his hands without danger of disease; but that menace was averted if he touched the soles of any superior chief's feet with the palms and backs of both hands. Since the supreme chief was not always present to absolve—as he alone was competent to do—from infractions of the taboo against himself, touching one of his consecrated bowls was considered an equivalent rite of purification. In Samoa, where the gentry rather than the titular chiefs held the reins

of power, the grimly humorous fiction evolved that an un-
popular ruler could be stripped of his sacred character by
being sprinkled with coconut water, whereupon he might be
summarily dispatched.   Practical considerations also dictated whimsical exceptions.   In Tonga, where the kava was
drunk on every possible occasion, both plant and beverage
were held immune to infection by *tapu,* and the meanest cook
might chew the root touched by the Tuitonga.

These concessions to the exigencies of daily life were
doubtless merely unconscious rationalizations and must not
be taken to throw doubt on the sincerity and intensity of native belief in the taboo system.   Of that there is indisputable
and ample evidence.   The strong hold the scheme had on the
Polynesian mind is indicated by its preservation among the
Tikopians, who live in isolation from their congeners, in the
midst of Melanesian populations.   It is shown by the extent
to which even so skeptical a scoffer as King Finau was willing to bow to its decrees.   Above all, it is demonstrated by
the survival of its spirit among the thoroughly Christianized
Tongans of to-day, who have unconsciously applied their
old notions of the inviolability of the sacred to the Sunday
and the churches of the new creed.   As fanatical Sabbatar-
ians they will not even pluck a flower or break a branch on
the *tapu* day, nor will they countenance any dances or social
gatherings in the *tapu* house of worship.   Nay, even water
from the roof of a church is never stored or used, and only
recently the death of a child was traced to the transgression
of this rule.

Under the old régime one practical application of the
principle played a conspicuous part and did much to
strengthen the dominance of the upper caste.   In some of
the islands private ownership was virtually abrogated by
the law that anything touched by a superior became taboo,

hence no longer proper for common use. Thus, the canoe or house entered by the chief became his property. Contrariwise, it was not only inconceivable that a commoner should trespass on a nobleman's traditional domain, but the noble might arbitrarily impose a taboo his inferiors were bound to respect. A piece of white barkcloth in the shape of a lizard or shark would serve notice that the fruits or flowers in its vicinity were not to be disturbed; a similar token by a stream would forbid its use by the common herd.

Thus, social privilege and religious belief were closely intertwined in the Polynesian community. A query that obtrudes itself in this connection can unfortunately no longer be answered satisfactorily. That the beneficiaries of the established order should accept it without reflection is intelligible. But what of the down-trodden masses? Were they uniformly cowed into an acceptance of their lot, content to believe that their masters were the sons and darlings of the gods? Or were there adventurous spirits among them who insisted that there were gods, as well as death-defying souls, for *themselves* in the universe? We shall never know, but we can guess.

PANTHEON

The social organization of Polynesia affected religious culture in a way already suggested: whatever beliefs and rites may have been current among the people at large were coordinated and systematized by a guild of professional theologians. As Gill puts it:

Correct knowledge of these "mysteries" was possessed only by the priests and "wise men" of the different tribes. By them the teachings of the past were embodied in songs, to be chanted at their national festivals.

Even apart from these esoteric elaborations, the bluebloods standardized that part of the tribal theology which linked their line with that of its divine founders. For the patent of nobility sometimes consisted precisely in the knowledge of the poetic chants eulogizing the heroic ancestor of the family. Even lesser men might contribute to the development of religious thought where, as in Hawaii, a retinue of minstrels, irrespective of rank, jointly concocted laudatory songs in honor of their noble patrons. The total effect of these tendencies was a complexity far transcending what would be deemed possible in an illiterate community, nay, rivaling that of ancient classical mythology. A few samples must suffice.

On Tonga six classes of supernatural beings were recognized, one of them being constituted by Móui, who Atlas-like supported the earth and occasionally, like the god Anuto of the Tami, caused earthquakes by turning about in his usual prostrate position. All the other gods were conceived as inhabiting the island of Pulotu, northwest of Tonga, where all good things abounded, but where no mortal could eat the food or breathe the air without subsequently sickening and dying. One of the five groups properly belonging to Pulotu comprised the mischievous sprites or hobgoblins, who play tricks on the natives, trip them up or pinch them in the dark, or otherwise molest them in a minor way, hence spend most of their time in Tonga. Of the remainder, two classes excelled in power and effect on native life,—the primeval gods, numbering about three hundred, and the spirits of the higher nobility. The original attendants of the former were without influence, while the souls of the lesser nobility or gentry played the part of intermediators between their living kin and the major deities, or by sufferance were protectors of the meaner orders of society. In short, only two of the six groups of gods, the original deities and the spirits of the patricians, had independent power and were the objects of a cult; and they alone could make direct revelations to the priesthood. The spirits of the nobles were invoked at their graves, while a limited number of the major deities had special temples dedicated to their worship; indeed, some of them had as many as five or six. Of the major gods, that of war, Taliai Tubo, took precedence, as the patron of the king, with whom he sometimes communicated without a priestly go-between in the manner to be described below. Other deities protected special families or professions or presided over certain departments of nature. Thus, Tubo Totai combined the functions of a tutelary of King Finau's family and of mariners; Alo Alo controlled the weather and vegetation; and Tangaloa was the protector of skilled artisans. One attribute peculiar to this class of gods among the Tongans is the faculty of entering the bodies of lizards, porpoises, and other animals.

Hawaii presents an at least equally impressive array of supernatural powers, but no more than in Tonga were they all uniformly adored by all groups of the population; indeed, Malo cites only four as great national gods, the greatest, Ku, being the special guardian of royalty but worshiped in various forms by lesser men: Ku-ka-oo was the god of peasants, Ku-ula that of fishermen, while carpenters prayed to Ku-pulupulu, and bird-snarers to Ku-huluhulu-manu. Thus, each recognized vocation had a particular patron saint,—the bark-eaters or barkcloth decorators among women prayed to a special divinity, and even thieves had their distinctive god. Apart from these functional deities, there were gods localized in different parts of the globe, such as the four quarters, or residing in inanimate objects ready to execute the wishes of their owners.

But the metaphysicians of the South Sea Islands not only constructed an elaborate pantheon, in connection with it they also created a remarkable cosmology and cosmogony, of which the Mangaian scheme is a fair representative. The universe was conceived as the hollow of a vast coconut shell terminating in a thick stem tapering to a point, with Mangaia above the central aperture at the top of the shell, and at least ten celestial tiers of azure stone arching one beyond the other above Mangaia. The terminal point of the structure was regarded as a spirit but not in human shape: "The entire fabric of the universe is constantly sustained by this primary being." Immediately above it is a stouter demon, and at the thickest part of the stem a third being completes the trio of "the primary, ever-stationary, sentient spirits, who themselves constitute the foundation and insure the permanence and well-being of all the rest of the universe." In the lowest, narrowest portion of Avaiki, the interior of the shell, there sits a woman, Varima-te-takere, so cramped in position that her knees and chin meet. Eager for progeny, she at one time plucked off a bit of her right side, which became a male being, Vatea, half man, half porpoise; and successively produced five other children in like manner. Vatea married a female spirit, Papa, and begot the first beings of purely human shape, viz., the twin gods Rongo and Tangaroa, of whom the former gained the ascendancy; and it was one of his grandsons that pulled Mangaia up from the interior of the great shell to become the center of the universe. Avaiki is peopled by a throng of deities, who marry, multiply, and live like human beings. Thence come all the arts of life, whether peacefully copied from their original possessors or wrested from them like that of fire-making, which the demigod Maui gained from Mauike in mortal combat. There, too, lives the terrible female ogre Miru, who cooks and devours the souls of all who die a natural death. But the warriors slain in battle elude her fires and leap into the blue expanse above to be transformed into the clouds of the dry season. The celestial vault, at first a pitiable six feet above the earth, was raised to its present height by Maui's puissance.

These brief indications must suffice. In contemplating with amazement this wonderful edifice of philosophical fancy, we must discriminate, at least in principle, between myth and religion. Clearly it was not obligatory on a Mangaian to accept each and every element of the theory laid down by his theologians in the sense in which one of our fundamentalists is committed to the acceptance of the Scriptures; for Mr. Gill reports not a few discordant variants. Thus, according to one version the souls that fall into Miru's clutches are annihilated, while another has it that they revive after passing through her intestines. Again, some held that even the braves who have perished on the battlefield are eaten by Rongo and only ascend to the sky after ultimate liberation from his body. In other words, the rigor in the observance of ceremonial to be noted later was not incompatible with a certain latitudinarianism in point of doctrine. Or, rather, cosmology and cosmogony were only in part a matter of dogma or religion at all, whence the observed freedom of belief.

The mutual independence of poetical or philosophical fancy on the one hand and devotional fervor on the other is demonstrated by another reflection. No more than Chronos held the first place in the religious consciousness of

Greece did Vari and Vatea,—let alone the three non-human demons below Avaiki,—gain a hegemony among the gods by their priority in time. As a matter of fact, they had no cult whatsoever, while Rongo, Vatea's son, was the foremost of Mangaian gods. The explanation is not hard to find: these cosmogonic and cosmological subtleties were priestly or poetical glosses on the popular creed and had as little *religious* significance for their inventors as for the populace at large. The delights of untrammeled specula· tion with sacred beings as a starting-point were one thing; illumination through direct intercourse with the divine was something radically different.

Communion with the Supernatural

The deliberate quest of a vision was not practiced, or at all events was not a characteristic usage in Polynesia. But great importance was attached to dreams. The spirit of a deceased parent might appear to a sleeper and map out his course of action, aiding him in the achievement of great enterprises. Again, dreams were interpreted as ominous of impending calamities, as when a Tongan woman dreamt of the Tuitonga leading a force of spirits against the people at the time of the harvest festival; or when another visited the island of Pulotu in her sleep and heard the decree of the god Hikuleo that the inhabitants of Vavau were to suffer some great misfortune. Similarly, a profound impression was created when Funaki, the wife of a great chief, reported that the late king of Tonga had appeared to her in her dreams on several nights in succession and complained of the conspiracies hatched by his son's enemies. Incidentally, the last-mentioned case seems to supply a good example of a transition from an ordinary dream to a sought vision. For Funaki, who was deeply attached to her deceased royal master, who had indeed been suspected of an intrigue with her, slept and mourned regularly on the king's grave for six months; and it is not at all unlikely that this was done at least partly with the expectation of an apparition.

Experiences in swoon or trance also produced an effect at least on the beliefs of individuals. Thus, according to the accepted Maori notion, the soul of the deceased traveled to the northernmost point of New Zealand, where it lacerated itself with obsidian after the manner of mourners; then it slid or leapt into the underworld, undergoing successive deaths, passing to lower and lower regions, and was ultimately doomed to extinction. But this general picture would sometimes receive a personal tinge. For example, there was a woman who died, was pursued by a gigantic bird in the realm of spirits, but escaped to her father, who sent her back to tend her child; he also gave her two sweet-potatoes, and by throwing them to pursuing ghosts on the return trip she succeeded in making her escape. Naturally the priests were conspicuous for their weird experiences and for making them socially significant. Thus, a Hawaiian priest who had seen the wraith of a man and interpreted this as a token of his tribesman's approaching death could readily prevail upon the victim to pledge a propitiatory rite and pay the requisite fees.

The characteristic mode of entering into communion with divine beings, however, was not through a mere theophany but by a veritable inspiration: the visitant was believed to enter the body of the person favored and to speak through him, whence the appropriate Mangaian designation of a priest as a "god-box" and the Tongan term "god-anchor." This custom is as characteristic of remote Tikopia as of Tonga and Hawaii.

A man who is possessed shakes and quivers all over, his eyes get red and he begins to shout and, when the shouting is heard by the people, all run to hear what the *atua* (ancestor) has to say.

The Tikopians, Dr. Rivers informs us, regularly invoke the spirits to determine the future course of events, especially in case of sickness. Apparently, it is not known beforehand which of the summoners is to be possessed; also if an adverse divination is offered, additional ghosts are called in order, if possible, to reverse the prediction. Here commoners, as well as chiefs, may be inspired; but, characteristically enough, the former are possessed only by the spirit of a dead commoner, nor may the spirit of a chief be questioned by any one of lesser dignity.

In Tonga only the major gods and the souls of nobles possessed the priests, who for the time being spoke in the god's name and took precedence of the king himself, though immediately after the performance they resumed their normal station. The session was ushered in by a feast with kava-drinking, the inevitable accompaniment of Polynesian ceremonial. For a long time the priest sat in silence, hands clasped and eyes cast down. In answer to the questions

he generally begins in a low and very altered tone of voice, which gradually rises to nearly its natural pitch, though sometimes a little above it. . . . All this is done generally without any apparent inward emotion or outward agitation; but on some occasions his countenance becomes fierce, and, as it were, inflamed, and his whole frame agitated with inward feeling; he is seized with a universal trembling; the perspiration breaks out on his forehead, and his lips, turning black, are convulsed; at length, tears start in floods from his eyes, his breast heaves with great emotion, and his utterance is choked. These symptoms gradually subside. Before this paroxysm comes on, and after it is over, he often eats as much as four hungry men, under other circumstances, could devour. The fit being now gone off, he remains for some time calm, and then takes up a club that is placed by him for the purpose, turns it over and regards it attentively; he then looks up earnestly, now to the right, now to the left, and now again at the club; afterwards he looks up again, and about him in like manner, and then again fixes his eyes upon his club, and so on for several times; at length he suddenly raises the club, and, after a moment's pause, strikes the ground, or the adjacent part of the house, with considerable force: immediately the god leaves him, and he rises up and retires to the back of the ring among the people.

In interpreting this phenomenon the early observer quoted above was already on the right track. Denying a mere attempt at deception, he writes:

There can be little doubt . . . but that the priest . . . often summons into actions the deepest feelings of devotion of which he is susceptible, and by a voluntary act disposes his mind . . . to be powerfully affected: till at length what began by volition proceeds by involuntary effort, and the whole mind and body become subjected to the overruling emotion.

Similar manifestations were not restricted to the priesthood, and hysteria in some of its forms is still interpreted by Tongans as the result of possession. In Mariner's day the king was occasionally inspired by the spirit of a one-time ruler, and a prince by that of his father's immediate predecessor. The latter found it difficult to describe his subjective impressions in retrospect: he felt himself all over in a glow of heat and quite restless and uncomfortable, and did not feel his own personal identity as it were, but seemed to have a mind different from his own natural mind, his thoughts wandering upon strange and unusual subjects, although perfectly sensible of surrounding objects. When asked how he knew it was the spirit of Tukuaho, his answer was, "There's a fool! how can I tell you *how* I knew it; I felt and knew it was so by a kind of consciousness; my *mind* told me it was Toogoo Ahoo (Tukuaho)." This is an excellent example of the intuitive insight of mystic experience and at the same time of its ineffableness.

Women as well as men were capable of possession. The laity generally reacted differently from the priests and their experiences were ascribed to a deity accusing them of religious negligence "not by an apparent audible warning, but by an inward compunction of conscience." Accordingly, the visitation was marked by low spirits and a profusion of tears, possibly supplemented by a brief fainting-spell. Laymen, like priests, could bring on a paroxysm by an act of will, but Mariner witnessed the interesting case of a native who called for kava in anticipation of a god's visit, yet was obliged to acknowledge amidst general surprise that he was disappointed.

The interpretation offered by this early observer is in accord with recent medical opinion: there is no simulation of the trance, though there is doubtless auto-suggestion in the incipient stage. A number of modern European cases reported by Dr. Stoll are obviously of the same category, and one of the most instructive may be cited here. Dr. Stoll was taking a walk in the vicinity of Zurich one day. Some distance ahead of him an Italian workingman was marching along with a bundle on his shoulder. At a turn in the road this man suddenly tottered backward, dropping his bundle and the stick to which it was tied, and beat the air with his arms as though trying to find a hold. Next he fell on his back, soon rising to the height of a foot but only to fall again head foremost on the hard pavement. His body, supported only by head and feet, curved like an arch, then was jerked up, and altogether he presented the picture of a fish floundering out of the water. When Dr. Stoll came up, the Italian had become quiet and had apparently lost consciousness. After a while he awoke as though from a deep sleep, looked about in surprise, patted his head, which was doubtless suffering considerable pain from its repeated contact with the road, and finally inquired for the road to Lucerne, at the same time presenting a certificate attesting his treatment for epilepsy in a Swiss hospital. He had obviously trained himself to the voluntary performance of epileptiform fits in order to arouse the charitable instincts of passers-by. But as soon as he had decided on an attack, the further course of events was purely automatic; no one could have willed the total series of single events crowded into so narrow a space of time, nor would any sane person have deliberately wished his skull to undergo the maltreatment described above.[2]

Ritualism

As in a sense an outpost of Old World civilization, Polynesia reveals more kinship in the concrete elements of ceremonial procedure with Africa and New Guinea than with America. Among these features of Polynesian ritualism, bloody sacrifices play a prominent part. The Crow limited themselves to self-torture in attempting to placate the powers of the universe, and this practice was by no means unknown in the South Seas. In Tonga, indeed, there was a specific analogy in that people regularly sacrificed a little finger in order to bring about the recovery of a superior relative; hardly an adult had his hands intact, and Mariner witnessed a violent contest between two children five years of age, each claiming the favor of having the ceremony performed on him, "so little do they fear the pain of the operation." Fasting was likewise a Polynesian usage, for example, at a certain stage in the Hawaiian Luakini ceremony. But far more conspicuous were the offerings of domesticated animals, especially pigs, which at the great festivals were sacrificed in droves: thus at the festival just mentioned as many as eight hundred hogs were baked, and even in the normal consultation of an oracle, as described above, a pig was killed. Equally important was the rendering of human sacrifices. Malo would have it that at the Luakini rite only criminals were slain in propitiation of the deity, but his editor's contention that a nobler offering was required is borne out by the data from other groups. When a Maori chief erected a public edifice, he might even offer a favorite child to be buried as a foundation stone for the building. Infanticide, like the finger-sacrifice, was also practiced at Tonga to remove a relative's illness, and when a sanctuary had been defiled by bloodshed a chief was content to have one of his children strangled to avert a calamity.

In the stress laid on omens and the elaboration of a system of divination, though probably not so complex as in some parts of Africa, the Polynesians again reveal their kinship with Old World culture. Weather signs were noted, especially the appearance of the clouds, and as late as the time of Queen Liliuokalani's accession in Hawaii the sight of a rainbow was hailed as a symbol of her dignity. Some soothsayers even paralleled the classical technique of augury by the flight of birds or from the entrails of animals. In Tonga a coconut with the husk on was spun like a top, and the direction of the upper part was taken to indicate whether a patient might be expected to recover or die. Apparently, in contrast with African practice the inquirer might arbitrarily fix the meaning of a given event before consulting such an oracle. The importance often attached to trivial occurrences is well illustrated by Mariner's inopportune sneeze on a solemn occasion, for which he narrowly escaped the death penalty.

Still another trait allying Polynesian with West African ritualism is its iconic character. In Mangaia thirteen pieces of iron-wood roughly carved into the semblance of the human shape and wrapped up in fine cloth represented as many gods and were stored in the pontiff's sanctuary. A procession round an island of the Hawaiian group with one of the idols formed an integral part of the Makahiki ceremony.

The Hawaiians usually worshiped their gods by means of idols, believing that by the performance of certain rites, power, *mana*, was imparted to the idols, so that they became a means of communication with unseen divinities. They imagined that a spirit resided in or conveyed influence through the image representing it.

As these images were physically more impressive than the *njomm* effigies of the Ekoi, so they seem to have been altogether of a more public character,—objects rather to be venerated from afar and only on great occasions, than patrons with or through whom to commune intimately in everyday life.

Next may be mentioned a similarity to Bukaua culture,

to wit, the extravagant reliance on magical incantations with the implied belief in the power inherent in a set formula of words. In New Zealand, especially, every undertaking of any consequence, whether relating to ostensibly sacred affairs or such apparently secular undertakings as the cultivation of the soil, the launching of a canoe, or a hunting trip, was accompanied by the recital of an appropriate spell. Incantations could compel the return of an errant lover, prod the memory of a youthful novice in the arts, or wreak vengeance on a personal enemy, the last-mentioned object being usually attained by a combination with sympathetic magic. Small wonder, then, that in the Maori college the young nobleman, to whom alone its doors were open, had to learn above everything the mystic spells that would bend the universe to his will, possibly by making the gods favor his desires, possibly by their intrinsic efficacy.

The more impressive performances consisted largely in the combination of the aforementioned features, to which some additional elements, often of a dramatic nature or in furtherance of sociability might be added; practices clustering about the taboo concept would almost inevitably be injected into the procedure. Thus, the Luakini of Hawaii may be largely defined in terms of the phenomena already familiar to the reader. Its celebration was in honor of Ku and involved the erection of a special temple to ensure a successful campaign or to promote the crops. The performance involved the imposition and removal of taboos, the carving of images, the destruction of vast numbers of pigs and some human beings, the recital of litanies by the priests and of responses by the congregation. In the Makahiki some of the same elements recur, supplemented by a procession with a sacred idol, a sham attack on the King, the complete cessation of all ordinary labor, and a succession of athletic contests and other games. A taboo on work, coupled with indulgence in such secular pastimes as dancing, wrestling, and boxing, was also linked with devotional exercises in the harvest feast of Tonga, where pugilistic combats, as well as promiscuous fighting, likewise marked the offering of fruits to the weather god, Alo Alo. In the same group kava drinking was the invariable concomitant of sacred ritual, from the invocation of a deity in a private attempt to be inspired to the most elaborate national solemnities.

When we turn from the specific features of religious behavior to the spirit animating it, we can best characterize Polynesia as representing the acme of formalism, as embodying to the greatest degree a tendency displayed by many other primitive groups. Just as some peoples in the course of human history have acquired certain literary devices, say, of versification, and in the joy of discovery have played with their new toy till sense was sacrificed to jingle, so the Polynesians after achieving an intricate series of socio-religious technicalities seem to have reveled in their creature and made themselves its slaves. As among the Crow, sin was independent of intent and consisted in the usually involuntary infraction of an arbitrary rule of conduct, but the Polynesian taboos were incomparably more numerous than those of the Plains Indian and were generally of such a nature as to involve an indefinite number of persons. The punctilio typical of the whole scheme was undoubtedly a powerful instrumentality in the hands of the dominant caste and served to perpetuate its ascendancy. But in its efflorescence it came to subject the original beneficiaries themselves to considerable inconvenience. It was all very well to impose the death penalty on the plebeian idol-bearer who committed an error in running on his ceremonial circuit or who broke the stillness of the air while the priests were chanting some sacrosanct litany. But Hawaiian royalty itself suffered when the accidental barking of a dog or the hoot of an owl nullified the whole ceremony. Similarly in the case of the Maori spells.

The incantations had to be most faithfully and religiously learnt, the least slip was disastrous to the user. If a line or even a word was missed the spell was broken.

Even Maui, demigod and hero, was doomed to destruction from his birth because his father had omitted part of the baptismal service. Practical necessity would require a technique to ward off the perils that constantly beset the taboo-ridden native, yet even these devices were rather palliatives than panaceas or prophylactics. When a Tongan warrior had inadvertently clubbed a foeman on hallowed ground, a chief might save the community from disaster by strangling his own child, but even this sacrifice could not ward off destruction from the culprit, whose death in the next skirmish was anticipated by himself and interpreted by public opinion as due to the unappeased wrath of the gods. For the gods themselves were largely the embodiments or servitors of Polynesian formalism.

REFERENCES

[1] The material used in the preparation of the preceding chapter includes mainly the following: Tregear; Martin; Collocott; Malo; Beckwith; Gill; Rivers.

[2] Stoll: 25 f.

Part II: Critique of Theories

CHAPTER V

ANIMISM

The Primitive Concept of Spirit

Tylor, who gave currency to the term "animism," defined it as the belief in spiritual beings, and only in that sense shall it henceforth be used in this book. But what is meant by "spiritual"? A spirit, according to the dictionaries, may be identified with any supernatural being, good or bad, and the term has doubtless occasionally been so used in the preceding pages. But the time has come for a more rigorous definition.

By common agreement spiritual represents the opposite of material existence. The difficulty is that if we insist on the notion of completely incorporeal being there are probably no examples to be found on primitive levels. Certainly none appears in the beliefs of the tribes hitherto described. The Sun of the Crow Indians lures a maiden to the sky and begets a son; the ghosts of the Ekoi can be thrown and killed in a wrestling-match; Anuto, the Atlas of the Tami, turns about in quite fleshly fashion; and the Polynesian gods procreated by others that evolved from portions of Vari's body are surely not without a taint of materiality. Nevertheless, some of these belong to a different order of existence from that of men, beasts, and rocks. They are not, indeed, immaterial, but they are certainly less grossly material than the bodies of ordinary physical objects; and it is this subtler mode of corporeal existence that may be called "spiritual" in an ethnological

sense. It will be well to illustrate by a few additional examples this double aspect of primitive animism,—the un-
questionable assumption of a relatively tenuous kind of
being distinguished from the cruder reality of tangible matter, and the equally indubitable inability of the ruder peoples
to divest this notion of all marks of materiality.

The Jagga, an East African Bantu people inhabiting the
slopes of Mt. Kilimanjaro, recognize a form of existence certainly differing from that of living man, for their practices
largely center in a cult of the dead, to whom both good luck
and misfortune are ascribed and who are propitiated by their
descendants through prayer and offerings before every important enterprise. But the disembodied soul is not freed
from the exigencies of earthly life: it must be fed and thus
is dependent on the attentions of the living. As in the case
of the Ekoi, these ghosts, then, do not survive because of
intrinsic indestructibility; on the contrary, they grow old,
are deprived of offerings by more youthful and vigorous
spirits, and ultimately die.[1]

The Negrito of the Andaman Islands in the Bay of Bengal have the highly typical belief that man has a soul in the
form of a breath, double, reflection or shadow, which can
leave its owner during his sleep and travel far away. When
a person dies, it is this double that departs, becoming a
spirit either of the jungle or of the sea. These beings sometimes communicate with favored mortals and confer supernatural powers upon them, but are generally dangerous,—
the cause of sickness and death. As a rule they are invisible,
but some people have caught sight of them and give discordant descriptions of their appearance, though mostly im-
puting to them a grotesque or fearful aspect, such as abnor-
mally long legs and arms joined to a small body. Spirits
are attracted by whistling but kept away by singing,—also

by a firebrand or a human bone. As to the habitat of the
ghosts, accounts vary yet bring out clearly their relatively
—but only relatively—immaterial character. The spirits
can travel on rainbows when they visit their sleeping friends
on earth, but their activities have a terrestrial flavor,—they
hunt and fish, eat pork and turtle, dance and sing.[2]

One more illustration will suffice. The Lemhi Shoshoni
of Idaho recognize a life principle, *mū'gua,* which resides
in the head and at death rises cloud-fashion till it reaches
the house of the mythical god or hero called Wolf. The
souls of the Indians are darker than those of the white men
and very small. Half-way up they are met by a spirit of
longer standing, who escorts them to their proper places.
Wolf washes and revives each soul, which then becomes a
ghost, *dzōap.* Ghosts often appear in the form of skeletons
and terrify mortals. They cause disease by entering the victim's body and must be extracted therefrom by the practitioner; but sometimes they fly away with the patient's soul
and make him mad. As a result of an individual experience, Red-shirt Jim had somewhat unusual ideas about the
soul and the hereafter. In about 1890 he fell sick from
breaking a food taboo. He dreamt about a great war and
was suddenly struck by a hailstone. His condition became
serious, and a separate lodge was built for him to die in.

I was still breathing. I thought of seeing my dead father and
mother, brother and relatives. I wished to die immediately.
For three days and four nights I lay in my tent. At last on
the fourth day my soul (mū'gua) came out of my thigh, made a
step forward and glanced back at my body. The mū'gua was
about as large as this (ten inches). My body was not yet lifeless. When the mū'gua had made three steps forward, my body
dropped, cold and dead. I looked at it for some time; it made
no movement at all.

Suddenly something came down and went through my soul. My soul began to go downward. It did not ascend. I reached another world and followed a trail there. I beheld a helper of the Father who was making some dead men over again. I thought I might see the Father, but could only hear him. He was saying to me, "You don't look ill." A kind of thin wire was making a noise at the time. The Father had a buckskin bag; out of its contents he makes everything. He tapped the wire three times. Then I was able to see his hand, which was as small and clean as a baby's. Then the whole world opened up and I could see the earth plainly. I saw everything there. I saw my own body lying there. I saw my own body lying there dead.

The Sun told me I would be restored to life. I did not walk back and I don't know how I returned. Suddenly I was back alive. For a few minutes, I had seen the Father. He was a handsome Indian.[3]

A soul that is washed, a soul that is ten inches tall, does not correspond to our notion of spirituality; yet it is obvious that the Shoshoni conceive it as distinct from and of finer essence than the human body. Without multiplying examples we can accept Tylor's statement that the soul of primitive man is "a thin unsubstantial image, in its nature a sort of vapor, film or shadow."[4] Abundant linguistic evidence could be adduced to prove that it is usually designated by terms somehow denoting this finer type of materiality. This alone would not prove the absence of a purely immaterial soul-concept, for our own abstract terms are reduced to a very concrete basis when etymologically analyzed. But in this instance philosophical thought has not outrun its vestments, as is demonstrated both by the preceding examples and others that will presently be cited.

In many regions of the globe there is a belief in two or

more souls. These are generally localized in the different
parts of the body during life and have separate careers after
death. Thus, the Menomini of Wisconsin, assign one soul
to the head, another to the heart. The former wanders
about aimlessly after the burial of its owner, lingers about
the graveyard, whistles in the dark, and receives offerings
of food; the latter travels to the realm of the spirits, which
it reaches only after conquering various temptations to eat
and drink on the way.[5]

Dualism was found to characterize the psychological notions of the Tami, off the coast of New Guinea, and it is
equally typical of the Bagobo of southeastern Mindanao in
the Philippine Islands, who distinguish not a long and a
short but a right-hand soul and a left-hand soul. The
former, which is good, never leaves the body except to lie,
still intimately associated with it, as the shadow on the
right side; its permanent separation constitutes death. Except for its lesser coarseness, it resembles the living Bagobo,
even to the color of the skin. After death, this soul goes
straight down from the grave to the lower world, which is
called the Great (or One) Country. By purification it becomes a naturalized spirit, who now joins his predecessors
in a mode of life closely patterned on that of the living
Bagobo. While in life the dextral soul is associated with
health, activity and joy, its sinistral counterpart spells sickness, pain, and death. It is this left-hand soul that appears
as the shadow on the left side and also as the reflection in
the water; and it alone leaves the body at night to go flying
about the world. These dream adventures are fraught with
peril for the owner of the soul, for were a demon to catch
it the bodily container would also fall prey to its devourer.
At the moment of death the left-hand soul leaves the body
for the last time and after the funeral becomes merged in

the company of demons who cause disease and dig up corpses in order to eat the flesh. A Bagobo, when expounding these views, is quite capable of theoretically maintaining the tripartite nature of man,—the existence of a body that is buried and dug up by cannibalistic ogres; of a left-hand soul that is ultimately transformed into one of these demons; of a right-hand soul "that goes to the One Country to continue its existence in a less substantial and more highly idealized manner than on earth." The interesting thing, as Miss Benedict informs us, is that in contemplating his own future existence a native will shift his point of view, now merging his individuality in that of the demon, then in that of the denizen of the Great City, according to the emotional reactions of the time being.[6]

Some peoples attribute four souls to every human body. This for instance, is the belief of the Yuchi, who once resided about the banks of the Savannah. One was said to remain rooted to the place of death, two others—not sharply discriminated—hovered near the kin of the deceased, while the fourth departed for the point where earth and sky meet and attempted to leap into the spirit land on a constantly moving cloud. The notion of four mutually independent souls is also attributed to some of the Hidatsa of North Dakota, who account for the gradual sinking of the body by the consecutive departure of the four souls.[7]

A quadruple soul has also been recorded among the Dakota, but Dr. Walker, writing of the Oglala subdivision of that tribe, reports only three souls, all bestowed on the infant at birth and all distinct in the hereafter. The *ni* represents the vital force, being identified with the breath or shadow and causing death by its departure. It accompanies the second soul or *nagi* to the god Skan, testifies on its behalf, and then disappears like smoke among the stars, for it is one of these that Skan had implanted in the new-born babe. The *nagi* controls its owner's disposition and after his decease lingers near his haunts until it appears before Skan for judgment. Finally, there is the *sicun,* which is likened to a shadow; this likewise abides with its owner from birth until death, serving as his guardian angel, and after his demise conducts him to the land of spirits, but without itself entering it. The last term is also used in a radically different sense by the Western Dakota. If the *nagi* does not pass muster, it thereby becomes a *sicun* and must wander over the world until adjudged worthy of admission to the spirit trail, and these roamers are classed with the malevolent beings. But the term is applied with still another meaning, viz., to the tutelary spirits a man of his free volition chooses in the course of his life.[8]

These conceptions, while by no means free from obscurity, are instructive in exemplifying the attempts of the Indian metaphysicians to grapple with the problems of psychology and of existence as a whole.

One remark concerning multiple souls may be offered. As has already been suggested by the French philosopher, Lévy-Bruhl, their precise number may probably be correlated in more than one case with the mystic number of the tribe. Since the Plains Indians constantly associate four with peculiar potency, it is not surprising to find some of them bringing the souls into line with their preconceived idea. All that seems prerequisite is that they should first consider the matter from a numerical angle at all. As soon as that happens the favored number will assert itself with the obtrusiveness of a fixed idea. Thus the Peninsular Malays, who value seven as sacred, are not content with less than seven distinct souls. Considering the arguments advanced in Galileo's day against the possibility of more than seven planets, we need not marvel at the force of such preconceptions.

To the subject of non-human souls the briefest of references will suffice. It is not astonishing that animals should be credited with souls, for primitive man rarely, if ever, draws a sharp line of demarcation between mankind and other animals as a group, though there may be a capricious favoritism in ascribing a soul to some species and not to others. What at first sight arrests our attention is that even the lifeless phenomena of nature are sometimes conceived as endowed with a spirit. We have already seen that when a Bukaua makes sacrifice it is not the food itself that is supposed to be appropriated by the spirits but the spiritual essence of the offering, and this is a far from uncommon practice. To cite another case, the Bagobo ascribe a soul—a single one, incidentally—to such manufactured things as tools, weapons, and clothing.[9]

Tylor's Theory: The Origin of the Spirit Concept

Having briefly surveyed some of the facts of animism we are now ready to examine Tylor's theory of them. His scheme naturally divides itself into two parts. First, he determines how the concept of comparatively spiritual as opposed to grossly material existence could ever have arisen; secondly, he attempts to show how when that concept had once evolved *all* types of supernatural beings evolved from it. Each inquiry is best considered separately.

According to Tylor, the belief in a more refined form of existence than the bodily one of normal experience is based both on an inference from observed facts and on the direct evidence of the senses. Primitive man observes that there is a difference between the living body and the corpse, and he concludes that there must be something in the former, however elusive in essence, that is absent from the latter; hence, the notion of a vital principle. But, secondly, the savage *sees*, either in dreams or in visionary revelations, human shapes different from those of waking experience. "When the sleeper awakens from a dream, he believes he has really somehow been away, or that other people have come to him." But since his body lies where he lay down to rest, since the people he sees are known to be far away, it is necessarily not his normal self or the selves of his dream interlocutors that are concerned, but phantom selves presenting a new category of reality, though bearing the semblance of the fleshly body. Says Tylor:

> My own view is that nothing but dreams or visions could have ever put into men's minds such an idea as that of souls being ethereal images of bodies.

But the vital force and the phantom are intimately connected with the body, the former enabling it to feel, think, and act, while the latter is its image or double. Further, both are separable from the body,—the life principle during insensibility or death, the double when it appears to people at a distance. Tylor argues that primitive man combines the two into the notion of a ghost-soul.

Given the human soul, the extension of the soul concept to other animals was natural considering the primitive view of animals as not basically distinct from man. As for the souls attributed to inanimate objects, Tylor points out that even they may be regarded as endowed with life, while in any event they will appear as phantoms in dreams and visions alongside of persons wearing, carrying, or otherwise using them.[10]

Let us understand clearly the relations of Tylor's theory to the phenomena to which it pertains. That even extremely rude tribes believe in the existence of a spiritual, that is, relatively immaterial, reality, is the starting-point of the inquiry. Whence, asks Tylor, do they derive this belief, which is apparently not suggested by experience? His answer is that the lack of an empirical basis is only apparent; and he cites two sets of phenomena that conjointly may have led to the notion of spirit as here defined. He does not pretend to have historical records for the origin of a conception that belongs to dim antiquity. His theory is avowedly a psychological interpretation pure and simple, but inasmuch as it not only explains the empirical observations, but operates exclusively with facts like death, dreams and visions, all of which demonstrably exercise a strong influence on the minds of primitive men, it must be conceded to have a high degree of probability. I, for one, certainly have never encountered any rival hypothesis that could be considered a serious competitor. However, the eminent French sociologist Durkheim has raised objections to Tylor's theory, and it will accordingly be necessary to examine his arguments.[11]

One criticism offered by Durkheim seems to coincide with what I have myself said in the Introduction concerning Tylor's intellectualistic bias. Why, asks the French scholar, should primitive man crave a theoretical interpretation of dream life? He is not a philosopher who deliberately concocts theories of the phenomena observed.

Now it is undoubtedly true that Tylor's phraseology is often tinctured with rationalistic psychologizing. But Durkheim does not put his finger on the right spot. Tylor is at fault in so far as he limits the consideration of religion almost wholly to the belief in spiritual beings, that is to the conceptual aspect of religion without due regard to its emotional concomitants. But in the present context the charge of intellectualism is pointless because Tylor is concerned with tracing the origin of a concept, that is, of a cognitive element of consciousness. Further, he derives it very largely not from ratiocination about observed phenomena but from the immediate sensory testimony of dream life.

As a matter of fact, Tylor's errors in the way of intellectualism are the veriest peccadilloes beside his critic's. For Durkheim's remarks in part involve an intellectualistic notion of the savage that is well-nigh incredible. How, he asks, could a dreamer fail to discover that he has been the dupe of an illusion? Say, he has been disporting himself in his sleep with some fellow-tribesman; all he has to do on awakening is to compare notes with his friend. Has *he* undergone similar experiences? In most instances there will be discrepancies, hence no reality will be attached to the adventures of dream life.

This is almost beneath criticism. In the first place, the persons seen in sleep are not always so close at hand as to be readily interviewed about the precise simultaneity of their dream experiences. Secondly, what evidence is there that primitive men would naturally resort to such a checking process? From what we know it would appear that in proportion as they attached emotional value to their dreams they would be reticent concerning them. But, waiving that point, let us suppose that our inquirer categorically confronts a camp-mate with a tale of joint nocturnal wanderings. Which one of us is able to recall with complete sharpness all the varied details of a night's dreams? How, then, could the person consulted be sufficiently certain of the facts to make a categorical denial? His reactions, when he is so confronted, would certainly depend solely on his inborn suggestibility and his psychological relations to the questioner. They would correspond, in some cases at least, to the response given under comparable conditions, already mentioned, when a Hawaiian priest would announce to some native that he had seen the latter's wraith misbehaving himself, that such conduct had aroused the anger of his familiar, and would result in dire consequences unless a rite of atonement were undergone.

At this speech of the *kahuna kilokilo* [priest], the man whose soul was concerned became greatly alarmed and cast down in spirit, and he consented to have the *kahuna* perform the ceremony of *kala,* atonement, for him.[12]

Other arguments advanced by Durkheim suffer from the same combination of arbitrary assertions and rationalistic psychologizing and, above all, from a misunderstanding of the question at issue. We are told that Tylor simplifies the problem by representing the soul merely as a separable double; to be sure, it may be so conceived, but it also figures as something not radically separable, as something fusing with the organism it animates, so as to be affected by bodily wounds. Tylor, then, fails to explain why the dualism of soul and body does not exclude a profound unity and an intimate interpenetration of the two.

The obvious answer is that that is beside the problem; the problem is not why primitive man does not attain a logical consistency rarely encountered among learned metaphysicians, but how the empirically observed notion of relatively spiritual being came into existence. Whether that notion solely dominates the view of mental operations, or is coupled with contradictory notions, is irrelevant. Specifically, the transmission of a wound from the body to the soul is wholly

intelligible from Tylor's scheme whenever the soul is represented as an image reflected by the body.

Again Durkheim contends that dream phenomena are not
most simply explained by the assumption of a double; for
example, it would have been simpler for a dreamer to imagine himself endowed with telescopic vision when he sees
remote regions in his sleep. *That* would make lesser demands on the imagination than "cette notion si complexe
d'un double, fait d'une substance étherée, à demi invisible, et
dont l'expérience directe n'offrait aucun exemple."

Let us remark again that the question is not to show
how the savage might in simple fashion explain his dream
life but how the empirically noted idea of a double could
arise. Durkheim misses the point of departure for Tylor's
investigation by thus inverting the problem. Further, the
assertion that telescopic vision is simpler than the double-
concept is at best an idle conjecture. As a matter of fact,
there is nothing complex about this notion, which is according to Tylor directly yielded by the sensory experience
of dreams and abnormal mental states. Finally, how would
telescopic vision explain those cases in which the dreamer
does not observe remote happenings but is visited in his
own habitat by persons known to be far away?

Durkheim is not more fortunate when he argues that
our dreams very often relate to past experiences, that we
survey once more what we have already seen, do again what
we have done. All this, he insists, cannot be explained by
the double; even if that were capable of traveling in space,
no human being, however devoid of intelligence, could invest it with the power of traveling in time. It is much
simpler for early man to regard such dreams as what they
are, namely, as particularly vivid recollections of the past.

But again we must insist that a theory which purports

to derive the soul-concept—partly, it should be noted—
from dream life is under no obligations to outline a savage
theory that shall consistently explain *all* dream experiences.
When the theory has explained how some of the ordinary
dream phenomena yield the notion of a double, it has
achieved all that can reasonably be expected. The very assumption that primitive man must be credited with a consistent scheme of things reveals a strange lack of insight
into his mental operations. Apart from this, it would be
interesting to know whence Durkheim derives the information about the relative frequency of dreams that must necessarily be referred to the past.

Finally, a chronological stricture cannot be ignored.
Durkheim is willing to grant that nowadays the savage uses
the concept of the double to account for dream apparitions;
but he maintains that this represents a later stage of development. Primitive man, he argues, does not explain all
dreams alike, but disregards the majority of them; he pays
attention only in so far as they are sanctified by a pre-
existing religious system. The Australians, in particular,
neglected dreams unless they exhibited souls of the deceased:
the soul-concept thus precedes and underlies the conception
of dream experiences and cannot be derived therefrom.

In answer to this, we may note once more, in passing, the
inversion of the real problem and the one-sided emphasis
on dream life, which Tylor considers only one, though a
very important, source of the spirit-concept. For reasons
to be explained below, we cannot accept Durkheim's bland
assumption that Australian usage, even if correctly reported,
is decisive as to primitive, let alone primeval, belief. But
even if it were, what is meant by "ignoring" dream experiences? It would be entirely possible not to weight them
emotionally yet to apprehend them intellectually. As a

matter of fact, it is improbable that repeated nocturnal apparitions in sleep should fail in the long run to yield evidence of a relatively immaterial form of reality, and that is all that is required by the theory. The point that there is discrimination exercised as to the value of different dreams is valid enough but irrelevant. Incidentally, I suspect that in a good many instances the appraisal of a dream has a purely subjective basis, that it is due to a simple thrill which carries with it immediate conviction.

To sum up, Durkheim's objections leave Tylor's explanation entirely unshaken. Certainly the alternative proposed by the critic cannot be regarded as an adequate substitute. Durkheim assumes that the most archaic religious conceptions are those found in Australia. Typical of the island continent is the belief that each sib (clan) in the tribe has peculiarly intimate relations with a species of animals or plants,—its "totem." Diffused throughout the sacred species there is an anonymous force. But the individual Australian is himself a part and parcel of the group that comprehends alike his sib and his totem species: the totemic principle is incarnate in him as his soul, which is really only part of the collective totemic soul. Since, nevertheless, each individual is distinct from animals or plants, the notion of a dual form of existence naturally arises.

Since this is not a treatise on dialectics, it is unnecessary to examine the numerous allegations bound up with Durkheim's scheme, together with their logical ramifications. We shall content ourselves with putting the ax to the root of the theory. It is ethnographically unwarranted to deduce primeval conceptions from Australian conditions. The Australians are not so primitive as, certainly not more primitive in their culture than, the Andaman Islanders, the Semang of the Malay Peninsula, the Paviotso of Nevada. In these sociologically simplest tribes totemism does not occur. Totemism is a widespread but far from universal phenomenon, while the belief in spiritual beings is universal; precisely these rudest tribes which have a decisive bearing on the question are non-totemic animists. Hence, the notion of spirit cannot be derived from totemism. Moreover, the totemic ideas of the Australians represent a highly localized product and cannot even be accepted as the earliest form of *totemism*.

Durkheim's argumentation may therefore be dismissed as in no way invalidating the core of Tylor's hypothesis in the absence of historical evidence.

Quite recently an objection to Tylor's theory has come from another quarter. An eminent anatomist, Professor G. Elliot Smith, has broached the view and impressed it on the minds of several students of cultural anthropology, that animism is not a product of the primitive mind at all but was transmitted to the ruder peoples of the world from Egypt since, say, 2600 B.C. Thus Mr. Perry, a disciple of this school, does not hesitate to pronounce it as probable that

prior to the coming of this (Egyptian) civilization, the native peoples were devoid of any magical or religious practices or ideas.[13]

The historical evidence adduced to support this inference seems to me to be precisely nil. The conclusion is based partly on an irrational pan-Egyptological bias that impels members of the school to trace practically all arts and beliefs to the banks of the Nile, partly on the dogma that it is a psychological impossibility for any belief, custom, or art to be re-invented independently. Even were this

psychological principle fully demonstrated, the Egyptian
origin of animism, or of anything else, would not follow as
a logical corollary; for it is entirely conceivable that the
beliefs shared by the ancient Egyptians with the modern
Australians or Andamanese are in all three instances sur-
vivals of an extremely ancient and deep-rooted human set
of ideas.   That is, of course, the implication of Tylor's
theory.   Tylor, disavowing historical knowledge, has shown
to my mind a satisfactory correspondence between the primitive concept of spirit and certain psychological phenomena,
known to occur among primitive folk, that would produce
that concept.   I, for one, shall not be bulldozed into the conviction that it was psychologically impossible for primitive
man to arrive at animistic ideas before the ancient Egyptians
are proved to have had a unique innate mentality that would
enable them alone, of all hominids, to evolve the spirit-
concept.

Tylor's Theory: Nature and Sequence of Supernatural Beings

Tylor represented in admirable fashion the characteristics
of the English intellect.   Fine-spun dialectics and their elaborate speculative products were little to his taste.   He
reveled in facts, burying his arguments and his readers under
their solid array, and approached his problems with a punc-
tiliously judicial frame of mind.   But even the most cauti-
ous and open-minded are not immune to the subtler influences of their intellectual atmosphere, and so Tylor, the
compeer and comrade-at-arms of Darwin and Huxley,
could not but insensibly transfer to his field of inquiry the
basic principles of biological evolution that were then being
rapidly extended to every branch of learning.   The biolo-

gists were asserting that an essential unity underlay the apparent diversity of organic life; and for the student of comparative religion it was a tempting conclusion that the varied forms of religious belief were likewise linked by a fundamental likeness. Zoölogists were passing from the general proposition that species hitherto regarded as distinct were related by blood to the elaboration of family trees; and the anthropological investigator of religion spontaneously followed suit and, naturally enough, regarded it as a foregone conclusion that as man had been derived from a unicellular ancestor so the beliefs of the most highly civilized peoples had evolved by a corresponding series of progressive changes from the faith of the tribes lowest in cultural rank. In other words, when Tylor had answered the question how humanity ever came to conceive such a thing as spirit at all, and next confronted the varied manifestations of belief in supernatural beings, he automatically attempted to bring order into the welter of facts by a theory monistic in its psychology and unilinear in its historical implications. As to the psychological interpretation, indeed, nothing could be more explicit:

It seems as though the conception of a human soul when once attained to by man, served as a type or model on which he framed not only his ideas of other souls of lower grade, but also his ideas of spiritual beings in general, from the tiniest elf that sports in the long grass up to the heavenly Creator and Ruler of the world, the Great Spirit.

And again we read:

The idea of souls, demons, deities, and any other classes of spiritual beings, are conceptions of similar nature throughout, the conceptions of souls being the original ones of the series.[14]

In part the argument on behalf of this basic unity is quite convincing. It is easy to understand how the souls of the living, postulated for reasons set forth in the first part of Tylor's scheme, should assume the character of malignant demons or of benign patrons after the death of the body.[15] There is also a good deal to be said for the interpretation of what Tylor calls "fetichism": as the human soul can exist in the human body or leave it in dream life and abnormal states, so spirits modeled on the soul may either flit about freely or become temporarily housed in material bodies, which through this incorporation become sacred objects or "fetiches."[16] But here a difficulty arises that is indeed explicitly expounded by Tylor. Plausible as this interpretation may be, have we the right to assume that sacred objects *always* derive their mystic character from spirits embodied in them? We have not, Tylor candidly explains; but his monistic bias is too strong to be seriously shaken by the caution felt and expressed *in abstracto*. That is to say, what he is really interested in demonstrating is the omnipotence of the animistic principle not only as an explanation of all spiritual beings but of all objects whatsoever that possess religious value. Hence these are brought so far as possible into the animistic category. Yet there is now considerable evidence that precisely in some of the regions where fetichism flourishes most, viz., in West Africa, the power of the fetich is derived not from an embodied spirit but from, say, some magical substance that is smeared over it and is inherently endowed with supernatural potency.

Doubts likewise arise as to the alleged identity of nature-spirits with human souls. "As the human body was held to live and act by virtue of its own inhabiting spirit-soul," the argument runs, "so the operations of the world seem to be carried on by the influence of other spirits." There is an infinite multitude of spiritual beings in primitive belief to serve as causes of natural phenomena: "these spirits are looked upon as souls working nature much as human souls work human bodies." Thus, the firmament is explained "by an indwelling deity, modeled on the human soul. We may best understand what was meant by the Heaven-god, if we think of him as the soul of the sky." At first the spirits are merged in their element, later as anthropomorphic gods they are independent controllers of the phenomenon. Thus, the barbarian's fire-worship is at first directed to the spirit supposed to be animating "the actual flame which he watches writhing, roaring, devouring like a live animal," but at a subsequent stage any particular fire is a manifestation of a general elemental being, the fire-god. Similarly, the sea divinity of the older period evolves into Poseidon "so little bound to the element he governs, that he can come from the brine to sit in the midst of the gods in the assembly on Olympus, and ask the will of Zeus." [17]

Undoubtedly the facts can be consistently explained along these lines. But if we ask whether Tylor has demonstrated his interpretative principle to the exclusion of all others, it must be said that no such rigid proof is to be found. As a matter of fact, the data will be seen below to admit in part of a simpler explanation.

Turning from the psychological to the chronological aspects of Tylor's scheme, I must confess that it is not in all details perfectly clear to me, for the overwhelming mass of concrete illustrations is leavened by a minimum of logical correlation. Thus I am not sure whether fetichism is conceived as a definite stage succeeding ancestral cults and antedating nature-worship; or whether it is merely considered an outgrowth of the basic soul-concept, such as

might appear in any and every period after the initial establishment of the spirit idea.   Two facts, however, are quite
beyond the possibility of doubt: according to the theory, the
soul concept is the earliest because it is "based on evidence
most direct and accessible to ancient man"; and a belief in
a Supreme Being is the last in the series, arising from a
preceding polytheism through the ascendancy of one deity,
—presumably on the pattern of the earthly supremacy of
the chief or king.[18] Moreover, when such a belief is
reported for primitive peoples, Tylor is strongly inclined to
scent the influence of contact with higher cultures, those of
Christianity and Islam.

In the interests of the reader I have seen fit to punctuate
my exposition with an occasional anticipatory query.   However, for a long time after its appearance Tylor's theory
remained unquestioned in anthropological circles.   Its consonance with the thought of the period, the wealth of its
documentation, Tylor's well-earned reputation as a leader
of the new science, all served to silence dissent.   When, indeed, doubts were at last voiced, they did not issue from the
ranks of the academic guild.

Andrew Lang, who in 1898 ventured to challenge one of
the most impressive parts of Tylor's scheme, was indeed
very much more than a mere amateur.   Though a professional man of letters with primarily literary interests, he
was widely read in folklore and related fields of anthropology.   He serves as an illustration of the fact that at a
certain stage in its development a branch of knowledge may
well profit from the labors of a nimble-witted outsider.
Precisely because Lang stood aside from the intellectual
currents that could not but affect a man like Tylor, he was
able to preserve a greater freshness of outlook.   He was
not interested in natural science and the catchword "evolu-

tion" that held many of his contemporaries spellbound did not accordingly stir his imagination at all. However, it would not be just to ascribe his attitude wholly, or even predominantly, to mere aloofness from the contemporaneous philosophy of natural science. Lang belonged to that rare company of men who do not readily bow to the mere authority of learning. He displayed a certain mental affinity with writers like George Bernard Shaw or, to take academic men, like William James and Gustav Theodor Fechner. So far from being cowed by the pronunciamento of an acknowledged master, the very idea exerted upon him a contrasuggestive influence. With specific reference to Tylor, Lang felt and expressed the admiration common to everyone who could appreciate vast knowledge coupled with sound judgment; but he was not hypnotized into blind acceptance of Tylor's theory and preferred to draw conclusions on the basis of a personal scrutiny of the data.

I have pointed out that what were foregone conclusions for Tylor would necessarily appear to Lang as highly dubious propositions. [Why must all notions of supernatural beings be ranged in a unilinear series? Why must loftier conceptions of the deity grow out of less worthy ones? History, as a matter of fact, seemed to demonstrate that gods do not always improve ethically with advancing culture.) Why, then, could not the conception of a "high-god" be held by the very simplest tribes,—a god, that is to say, who could be described as a "primeval eternal Being, author of all things, the father and friend of man, the invisible, omniscient guardian of morality"? Lang contended that such a notion of divinity actually existed among a number of rude peoples and that it was not introduced by white missionaries, or that at least such alien influences were highly improbable. He was by no means disposed to challenge

Tylor's scheme *in toto*. He had no particular quarrel with
Tylor's derivation of the spirit-concept and freely admitted
that the cult of demons and ancestral spirits naturally
flowed from the idea of the soul. What he denied was
that it ever culminated in the conception of a high-god.
Referring to Tylor's suggestion that it had arisen out of
ancestor-worship and on the pattern of earthly royalty, he
pointedly asked how such a process was possible among
those peoples who did not worship their ancestors and who
were not governed by kings. He thus arrived at the theory
that the high-god faith represented a line of development
radically independent of that which held for the soul-ghost
idea. But, though radically distinct, that faith did not remain so. The high-god was conceived as sublime in such
measure as to be removed from direct relations with human
needs and received neither prayer nor offerings; these would
be rendered instead to the ghosts of the deceased, who thus
came to occupy in increasing degree the center of the religious stage and arrogated to themselves all cult activities.
In addition, the myth-making tendency would come to over-
lay the originally sublime character of the high-god with
human and even contemptible traits. Thus, the Creator of
primeval days would secondarily fuse with the idea of an ancestor and might assume the mutually contradictory characteristics of a hero and a trickster. This, for example, is
supposed to have happened among the Zulu: in the beginning the Unkulunkulu of their mythology was, according to
Lang, a typical high-god, but the intense development of
ancestor-worship led to his identification with the first man,
while the myth-making fancy of the natives made him the
hero of adventures hardly consistent with a monotheistic
divinity in our sense.

But the chronological aspect of Lang's theory is at least

equaled in interest by its psychological complement. Lang denies flatly that the high-god of primitive tribes need be a spiritual, i. e., soul-like being.

To us, such a being is necessarily a spirit, but he was by no means necessarily so to an early thinker, who may not yet have reached the conception of a ghost.

The savages conceived their high-gods as "undefined eternal beings," to them the deity was "a magnified non-natural man,"—one, in other words, vastly superior to natural human beings but not envisaged as resembling the shadowy double inhabiting the human body,—a conception that may have been of later origin. In answer to the question, how primeval man could evolve such a high-god, Lang appeals to the human desire for an explanation of origins, which would naturally stimulate the conception of a Maker or Creator.[19]

In the course of my exposition of Tylor, I have already hinted at a criticism of the same nature as this psychological one advanced by Lang but of even broader application. If it is possible to doubt that the high-god is necessarily conceived by primitive man as spiritual, the same skepticism is surely permissible with regard to other supernatural beings. We cannot blame Tylor for striving to bring the greatest possible number of phenomena under a single formula, for that is the aim of all science. But it is the duty of subsequent scholarship to test the evidence on which the bold generalizers of an earlier age based their conclusions and to disclose whatever gaps appear. Approaching the subject in this temper, I find no proof in Tylor of the assumption underlying his theory, that *all* supernatural beings are "spiritual," that is, modeled on the idea of the human soul. It is

of course, possible that, say, the sun-god is conceived as the
soul manipulating the solar body to which it is somehow attached. But it is at least equally probable that the savage,
without splitting up the phenomenon by a dualistic point of
view, directly apperceives it as a person of vast power,—in
other words as "a magnified non-natural man." To take an
actual case, among the beings who bless the Crow Indians
the benevolent Dwarf plays a part, but there is not the
slightest hint that he is soul-like: he has all the earmarks of
robust non-natural anthropomorphism, he belongs as it were
to a distinct and powerful, though stunted, branch of the
family Hominidæ, localized near Pryor Creek. For North
America generally, Dr. Ruth Fulton Benedict has proved
that the so-called guardian spirits are only in a few
tribes the spirits of dead people, and even there these never
constitute a majority of the tutelaries acquired.[20] In this
area, in short, the "spirits" of descriptive monographs are
not comparable to the ghosts of the Ekoi or Bukaua.

I do not wish to deny that it is possible for the soul-concept to color the deities of primitive man without their being
expressly identified with the deceased, but I think more definite indication of that fact is required in each instance. Certainly, great caution is obligatory in the use of the term
"spirit" and its equivalents. Many writers freely employ it
to designate any supernatural being. This may be convenient, but in the interest of clarity such usage should be
tabooed. For example, Dr. Radin, after defining Indian religion as animism "in the old Tylorian sense of the term,"
speaks of certain monsters as spirits generally distributed
over North America, and particularly of the Horned
Snake.[21] Now Tylor would undoubtedly have tried to bring
these, together with all other supernatural beings, under the
head of "spirits," but always with the explicit or implicit

understanding that they are derived from the concept of soul. Dr. Radin, however, in no way indicates any features of the serpent that suggest such an origin, and altogether reveals a quite un-Tylorian indifference concerning this point.

Some additional comments on Tylor's animistic interpretation will be offered below under the heading of "Animatism."

We shall thus not merely recognize as valid Lang's objection to the alleged psychological unity of high-gods and souls but are willing to extend his skepticism to other supernatural beings. Let us now revert to Lang's critique of the historical aspects of Tylor's scheme. On this subject Lang has found a vigorous adherent in the person of Father Wilhelm Schmidt, the combative editor of *Anthropos,* one of the keenest and most erudite writers in the domain of anthropology to-day. Schmidt has independently developed and systematized Lang's views while fitting them into the total scheme of culture-history first propounded by Dr. F. Graebner. In the modified form of that system elaborated by Father Schmidt himself, the most archaic form of culture accessible to inquiry is that common to the rudest peoples of the globe, including the Tasmanians, Bushmen, Andaman Islanders, Semang of the Malay Peninsula, Congo Pygmies, and a few others of comparable grade, including some native tribes of the New World. All these share the belief in a high-god, the argument runs, hence Lang's contention of the great antiquity of the high-god concept and its contemporaneousness with the crudest culture stands confirmed.

Though the basic assumption here made is one that I am myself willing to accept, it obviously requires justification, for as has been pointed out in the Introduction, "primitive" and "primeval" are two distinct concepts. To review what was explained there, even the Tasmanians, however isolated and culturally stagnant compared with more progressive peoples, were not absolutely stable in their ways of life. They have indeed been compared with Palæolithic man, but the very fact that they had evolved some sort of adjustment to local conditions proves that they had added something to whatever cultural techniques they may have brought with them to their new island home. In other words, Tasmanian culture, too, had a history, and we cannot simply equate it with the culture of the ancestral immigrants of five—or ten—or twenty—thousand years ago. Now it would be strange indeed if what obtained for material culture were wholly inapplicable to the field of religion. In other words, the beliefs of the Tasmanians recorded by their observers cannot be set down as of Palæolithic antiquity without further inquiry. And the same skepticism will be in place with the corresponding ideas of the Andamanese, Semang, and their compeers.

But fatal as the criticism may appear at first blush, it can be fairly answered. In the first place, the tenacity with which all religious beliefs are maintained in spite of the superficial adoption of later creeds is notorious. The Mohammedanized Malay will still in the hour of need pray to the older gods of Hinduism and, if the worst comes to the worst, fall back upon the pre-Hindu deities of the pagan pantheon. So the modern Greek peasant along with his Christian faith preserves fragments of belief that can be traced back for well over two millennia into ancient Hellas.

Accordingly, since the force of conservatism is certainly not less in the rudest communities than among the representatives of a more sophisticated civilization, we can fairly assume that each of the very simple peoples cited will preserve *some* archaic elements. If, moreover, all, or most of them, should turn out to share certain conceptions of the religious order, the probability that these common features are very old will be considerable. For their likeness cannot be explained either by mutual borrowing or by borrowing from a common source since the isolation of these groups has been precisely one of the most important determinants of their backwardness. An alternative presents itself: each tribe in isolation may have evolved the same idea through the obscure workings of the "psychic unity" of mankind. But on that principle it would not be clear why such unity should have brought about the high-god idea precisely among all the simplest tribes and not in the whole of the human species. Finally, it might be argued that though the several "simplest" peoples had brought their common religious notions into their present habitat this implies only a moderate antiquity for these beliefs in so far as the tribes in question are racially akin to one another. This contention might indeed be properly advanced against ascribing great age to features common to the Andamanese and the Semang, both of whom are of Negrito stock and have presumably separated in relatively recent times. But even the Bushmen, though sometimes classified with the Negrito, represent so specialized a physical type as to demand a considerable period of time for their development; and the Tasmanians, while Negroid, are definitely not in the Negrito family. Hence, any religious traits held by these Negroid groups prior to their specialization must be of hoary age; and if these features are common to them and the rudest American aborigines, we are indeed carried back to as early a period of human belief as we can reasonably expect to attain by means of an historical reconstruction.

In short, on the score of logic I have no objections to Father Schmidt's premises: if, nevertheless, I demur to his conclusions it is on the score of facts. In other words, *if* all the rudest peoples share a distinctive high-god religion, then it represents an element of archaic culture; but do they?

At this point it will be useful to outline somewhat more fully Father Schmidt's conception of that cult as sketched by one of his associates and disciples.[22] The high-god is supposed to live in the sky and is not clearly soul-like. He is, however, eternal, omniscient, omnipotent without ever abusing his power. He acts as the founder of moral law, rewards the good and punishes the wicked by disease and death, nay, even in a hereafter. He is asexual, and such anthropomorphic traits as are ascribed to him result from the later influence of mythology. A being of this type, representing a union of ethics and religion, naturally inspires the believers with awe, so that they are reluctant to name him. They do not worship him in temples or through images, but address him in spontaneous unstereotyped prayer and offer him first-fruits as a tribute of adoration, *not* in the frame of mind of ghost-worshipers offering food to the souls of the departed.

The points of agreement with Lang's position are obvious; the main difference lies in the stressing of the occurrence of a definite, though as yet little standardized, cult in the form of supplication and sacrifice.

We must, then, inquire to what extent the beliefs and practices cited are really characteristic of the tribes that in recent times correspond most closely to the archaic substratum. And here we are at the very outset confronted by not inconsiderable technical difficulties. To determine accurately the religion of an alien people is at best a difficult task, as shown by the contradictory nature of the views found among such relatively high and well-known tribes as the Crow and the Polynesians. But concerning many of the simplest tribes we know nothing. Mr. Ling Roth has faithfully collected everything written about *The Aborigines of Tasmania,* but the evidence is so vague, fragmentary, nay, contradictory that beyond the conviction that they had some form of belief nothing positive can be gleaned from the compilation. About the Pygmies of the Congo forest we have no trustworthy data because their shyness has hitherto defied attempts at intensive study. Similar timidity has been noted as characteristic of the Semang, and though it can not be said that we are wholly ignorant regarding their creed, it remains true that our knowledge is of the scantest kind and that we are tantalized once more by conflicting testimony.[23] Concerning the rudest North American tribes, such as the Shoshoneans of the Great Basin, our information is far from satisfactory, though a fair body of mythology has been collected.

Certainly for the determination of those singularly elusive points involved in Schmidt's theory, the evidence for any of the tribes cited is inadequate. For example, an earlier observer among the Semang records a belief in Kari, to whom his informants ascribed various attributes of a monotheistic deity; but a somewhat later investigator, Mr. Skeat, failed to find the slightest corroboratory testimony. Instead he was told about a very powerful and benevolent being named Ta'Pönn, who was pictured as the creator of the world and as inhabiting the eastern heavens. Now the *name* of the high-god would hardly affect the argument; what does matter is that Ta'Pönn is anthropomorphically described as the husband of the moon, the father of four children, and the son of Earth-mother and her obscure spouse. Furthermore, in the western heavens the high-god has a powerful adversary, with whom is associated a giant monkey; this ogre pelts into space any would-be intruders into his abode and the belief is held "that when the end of the world came, everything on earth would fall to his share."

In these conceptions the idea of moral retribution is lacking; further the benevolent deity is clearly not all-powerful, nor eternal, nor asexual. In other words, he is not a high-god in Schmidt's sense. Perhaps the earlier reporter's account is authentic, but until that fact is established by new field-work the Semang data will not help support the theory of an archaic high-god cult.

The difficulty urged above has been on the score of inadequate descriptive material. Let us now turn for a final test of Schmidt's theory to tribes better known,—to the Andaman Islanders and the Bushmen. The former seem especially favorable since we have two independent accounts by good observers, Mr. E. H. Man and Professor A. R. Brown. What, then, can we learn from these concerning the religion of the natives? First of all, it is clear that, whatever may be the high-god conceptions held by them, these are coupled with animistic beliefs. This fact of course does not militate against Lang's or Schmidt's theory but is worth remembering. The spirits, who are definitely associated with the souls of the dead, are generally conceived as bizarre and fearful beings who cause sickness and death. Nevertheless, they sometimes befriend mortals and impart to them some of their own supernatural powers either on chance encounters or during serious illness or in dreams, and cures are sometimes effected through their aid. The only persons who in any way correspond to the priests and shamans of other peoples derive their authority from these spirits alone.

But in addition to these animistic figures there is a character, variously named according to locality, Biliku, Bilik or Puluga, who suggests a monotheistic deity. It is true that he has a counterpart in a being known as Tarai, Teriya or Daria, but since Biliku (to use a single term regardless of dialectic variants) is clearly more powerful the dualism is more apparent than real. The question then narrows itself down to a determination of Biliku's personality, and here we find our two witnesses in direct disagreement. Mr. Man pictures him as an eternal, omniscient creator who punishes iniquity both in this world and the hereafter; according to Professor Brown, he is the Northeast monsoon (Tarai representing the Southeast), is not omniscient since the natives try to deceive him when committing ritual offenses, and is not in the least interested in inflicting penalties for anything but the breach of purely ritualistic, i. e., non-ethical, taboos. Before discussing the data furnished by this more recent investigator, it is worth noting that in spite of his predecessor's enumeration of Biliku's divine characteristics this deity is far from wholly conforming to the high-god standards set by Father Schmidt even on Mr. Man's own *concrete* testimony. For one thing, he eats, drinks, sleeps, mates, and reproduces like a human being; for another, the natives of South Andaman do not scruple to threaten him with the bite of a mythical snake to prevent him from causing rain. It is of course very easy to say that anthropomorphic traits are a later blot on the loftier archaic picture, but where is the proof for this assertion? It is not contained in the empirical data but represents a superadded and arbitrary interpretation.

Turning now to Professor Brown's material, one of the most striking facts we encounter is the lack of agreement among his Andamanese informants, both individually and locally. Even on so fundamental a point as Biliku's sex, there is division. Such variability need not unduly surprise us in view of our experiences with the Crow and the Polynesians. But its bearing on the present argument is a peculiarly significant one. We are trying to establish as an

archaic substratum of human religion those elements shared
by the Andamanese with the Semang, Bushmen, and so
forth.   But what if the Andamanese themselves failed to
share in a common belief?   That would be reducing the basic
argument to an absurdity.   As a matter of fact, the case is
not so desperate.   There is absolute unanimity concerning
the identification of Biliku with the Northeast wind, and
also as regards the taboos he insists upon.   Other features,
such as the association of this character with the discovery
of fire, are at least sufficiently common to be reckoned possibly ancient beliefs that have merely dropped out here and
there.   But the striking fact is that precisely the data that
would vindicate the monotheistic character of Biliku are
rare and of localized occurrence.   It is only sporadically or
in the south that he (she) figures as a beneficent creator;
the common view, supported with much legendary evidence,
makes him (her) hostile to mankind, or at best reluctantly
benevolent.   Thus, we find the ancestors of the natives steal-
ing fire from this deity, exiling him, nay, even killing him in
revenge for his attacks.   In other words, the lofty conception of a high-god dissolves into nothing on closer scrutiny:
even if we admit Mr. Man's evidence on a par with Professor Brown's, the new data demonstrate the absence of a
general Andamanese belief in a high-god and its rarity precludes great antiquity.[24]

Finally, a few words may be devoted to the case of the
Bushmen of South Africa.   According to an early observer,
they differed from their neighbors in not praying to their
ancestors and in so far were less animistic; but this
does not by compensation imply monotheistic ideas of the
type under discussion.   If we turn to the incontrovertible
evidence of the natives' own literature,[25] we find no being of
monotheistic dignity.   Prayers are addressed to the moon

and stars. But the moon is now represented as the Mantis's shoe, now as a man gradually sliced down to almost complete extinction by the Sun; while the stars are made from roots hurled into the sky by a girl of the mythic race of First Bushmen. The Mantis is a typical trickster. The Sun was a man different from the mythic people; he illuminated only the space about his own habitation by raising one of his armpits, the sources of light; but an old woman induced some children to throw him into the sky. In all this there is not a suggestion of an eternal, primal, benevolent creative lawgiver. It is of course conceivable that myths developing at a subsequent stage would obscure the character of such a divinity; but here as in other instances of this type, actual evidence for the sequence postulated by Lang and Schmidt is not forthcoming.

To sum up, Schmidt's logical premises are acceptable, but it is impossible to reconstruct an archaic monotheistic layer of religion from the data on the simplest peoples. On some of these tribes, such as the Tasmanians and the Congolese Pygmies, information is practically non-existent, hence they must be completely disregarded. In the case of the Andamanese, for whom our accounts are most satisfactory, individual and local variability is so great that only certain features can be assumed to represent the proto-Andamanese creed, and these are precisely not in harmony with the monotheistic theory.

It may appear that this is a discouragingly negative result after our appreciative introduction of Lang's and Schmidt's views. But as a matter of fact, their labors have not been in vain. First of all, there is the important anti-monistic conception of supernatural beings. Whether the high-god is later or earlier than the conception of a soul, the two notions are distinct in origin, and this emboldens us to inquire

whether other forms of supernatural beings, say, nature-
gods, are necessarily derived from animistic ideas.   Secondly, though in the absence of adequate data for at least
half of the simplest tribes no archaic layer can be recon-
structed from this comparison, the occurrence of a creative
personality in the thought of peoples so lowly as the Andamanese and the Semang is a phenomenon of the greatest
psychological interest, even though we must divest that personality of the monotheistic halo with which Lang and
Schmidt surround it.   Biliku, for example, may not be
omniscient or omnipotent, but she is the inventor of basketry,
the maker of celestial bodies, the discoverer of edible roots.
It is true that such a figure is perhaps primarily no more than
the product of intellectual and esthetic fancy, but it is equally
true that it may easily acquire religious character.   The
germ of a non-spiritual type of deity is thus actually demonstrable here.   These results are admittedly not so sensational
as would be the discovery of Christian theology on the Negrito level; but they do not for that reason lose all value.
In this moderate appraisal of the high-god phenomena I am
glad to be able to coincide in the conclusions of the learned
Archbishop of Sweden.[26]

ANIMATISM

Tylor's bias in favor of the soul-concept led him, as we
have seen, to conceive fetiches, that is, inanimate objects of
sacred character, as hallowed by the presence of a spirit.   As
a matter of fact he was inclined to apply the same view to
all instances in which inanimate reality is personified by
primitive man.   But as Dr. Marett has convincingly shown,
this involves an unnecessary hypothesis, and he has introduced a useful conceptual and terminological distinction by

segregating as "animatism" those cases in which there is mere evidence that the savage regards as living what we class as lifeless. When, to use one of his own illustrations, a South African yells at a hurricane, he is personifying the natural phenomenon, but we have no right to assume that he is thinking of a being of relatively refined bodily essence residing in and directing the storm. Similarly, we may add, when a Crow picks up a curiously shaped rock and hits upon the quaint conceit that it can reproduce its kind, he is putting it into the organic kingdoms, but it no more follows that he attributes spirit to it than that we ascribe a soul to a cat when we describe it as animate.

Dr. Marett makes a further point that I unhesitatingly endorse: both animism and animatism are essentially non-religious, or only potentially religious, becoming religious only in so far as the emotional attitude characteristic of religion clusters about their objects. When a Melanesian distinguishes between a yam and a pig by ascribing to the latter a vital principle, he is, so to speak, on the level of comparative biology; he still adheres to that level when he distinguishes between a pig and a man by attributing to the latter exclusive transformation into a ghost after death. But when he proceeds to differentiate among the ghosts of the deceased and to ascribe mysterious potency to the ghosts of distinguished men only, he passes the threshold that separates the everyday world from the universe of religion.[27]

REFERENCES

[1] Gutmann: 127, 142-145.
[2] Brown: 136-147, 163-179.
[3] Lowie, 1909 (a): 226-229, 301.
[4] Tylor, 1913: I, 429.

[5] Skinner, 1913: 85.

[6] L. W. Benedict: 49-65.

[7] Speck: 97. Matthews, 1877: 50.

[8] Walker: 86-88, 155-159.

[9] L. W. Benedict: 54, 64.

[10] Tylor, 1913: I, 428-479; esp., 428 f., 442, 445, 450, 477-479; id., 1881 : 343.

[11] Durkheim: 66 sq., 78-84, 347, 355, 370, 378.

[12] Malo: 150.

[13] Perry: 480.

[14] Tylor, 1913: II, 109 f.

[15] Tylor, 1913: II, III sq.

[16] Tylor, 1913: II, 123, 144.

[17] Tylor, 1913: II, 185, 247, 255, 277; id., 1881 : 357 sq.

[18] Tylor, 1913: II, 110, 331 sq.

[19] Lang, 1909: 160-190; id., 1901 : 15-45, 224 sq.

[20] R. F. Benedict: 43-49.

[21] Radin, 1914 (b) : 351, 356.

[22] Koppers: 145 sq. Schmidt, 1908-1909: III, 590-611; IV, 244-250.

[23] Skeat and Blagden: II, 173 sq.

[24] Brown: 136-288, 354 sq.

[25] Bleek and Lloyd.

[26] Söderblom: 151, 162.

[27] Marett: 14, 18, 118.

CHAPTER VI

MAGIC

FRAZER'S THEORY

In Murray's Dictionary magic is defined as

the pretended art of influencing the course of events, and of producing marvelous physical phenomena, by processes supposed to owe their efficacy to their power of compelling the intervention of spiritual beings, or of bringing into operation some occult controlling principle of nature.

If we rapidly pass in review some of the data presented in the synthetic sketches, we find many phenomena that fall under the definition. To resuscitate a dead being, man or ghost, by a particular substance, after the Ekoi fashion, is surely to apply an occult natural law; the binding of a victim's soul by a Bukaua shaman, and the Polynesian priest's muttering of a magical incantation fall within the same category. The presence or absence of spiritual assistants is considered immaterial: what counts is how such spiritual helpers are regarded. If they are used as mere tools, as a specific type of device for attaining certain ends, then we are dealing with magic, even though the feeling accompanying such procedure may lift it into the religious sphere as defined in this book. The difference between the Crow and the Winnebago attitude towards supernatural beings is instructive. The Crow supplicates the powers of the universe, who may yield to his entreaties or withhold favors at will;

the Winnebago spirits are constrained: if a man "make the requisite offerings to the Thunderbirds they must accept them and bestow on the suppliant the powers they possess." For at the time when the earth was created Earthmaker ordained that in return for tobacco the spirits were to bestow blessings on man.[1]

So cavalier a treatment of personal beings, however, seems devoid of the peculiar flavor of religion; and the whole apparatus employed by the magical practitioner, with or without spiritual agencies, suggests other things than religion as popularly understood. Accordingly, it is not surprising that in his great work Tylor separates Magic from Religion by a chasm of several hundred pages. Magic is to him a pseudo-*science* based on the erroneous association of ideas; and divination, in particular, which he considers under the same general head, is characterized as "a sincere but fallacious system of philosophy."[2]

This general point of view has been elaborated by Sir James George Frazer, whose latest exposition shall be followed here.[3] In this connection we are concerned mainly with two points in his treatment,—the relation of magic to science, and its relation to religion. In essential agreement with Tylor, Frazer sees a basic unity in magic and science. Both assume immutable laws: so long as the magician adheres to the rules of his art he is infallible, resembling the scientist who repeats the same experimental conditions and thus produces the same reaction. It is true that magic is false and science valid, but the mental operations of the two are alike. Both employ the association of ideas; the sum-total of empirically tested and established associations constitutes science, the sum-total of illegitimate associations is magic. Taboo is merely negative magic involving the belief that harmful consequences are averted when certain acts are *not* performed. In contrast to both science and magic, religion does not assume the immutability of nature. On the contrary, since it is "a propitiation or conciliation of powers superior to man which are believed to direct and control the course of nature and of human life," its central assumption is the variability of natural phenomena as determined by the will of supernatural personalities. While the scientist or magician assumes an arrogant attitude towards the conditions he controls, the religious devotee grovels before the beings who are masters of the universe and sway its manifestations according to their caprice.

Frazer himself cites instances to show that this clear-cut distinction does not obtain everywhere. In ancient Egypt and India, nay, among the peasantry of Europe, we find that gods are prayed to, while the supplicants simultaneously resort to magical processes; or that gods themselves reveal the magical knowledge that gives miraculous powers to its possessor. But such fusion, we are told, is a relatively late development; and this brings us to a cardinal part in Frazer's scheme,—its chronology.

According to our author, the Age of Religion in the sense defined above has been everywhere preceded by an Age of Magic, the regularity of this sequence rivaling the established succession of the Stone and Metal Ages. Two arguments are advanced on behalf of this conclusion,—one of them resting on a priori grounds, the other on the empirical facts of distribution. First of all, it is contended that the association of ideas constituting magic is psychologically simpler than the conception of personal beings, is indeed so simple that it occurs even among animals. Hence it is probable

that man essayed to bend nature to his wishes by the sheer force of spells and enchantments before he strove to coax and

mollify a coy, capricious or irascible deity by the soft insinuation
of prayer and sacrifice.

The second argument again divides in two. On the one
hand, the Australians, "the rudest savages as to whom we
possess accurate information," universally practice magic
and eschew religion; they are all magicians, none of them
priests. On the other hand, magic is essentially uniform
wherever found, while religion is notoriously diverse. But
generally the range of a cultural element is proportionate to
its antiquity. Hence magic, the invariable, is older than religion. Only gradually the leaders of thought came to realize the futility of magical procedure, which they supplanted
with religious rites, while the weaker intellects continued to
cling at least partially to their faith in magic.

Frazer's theory has the merit of throwing into relief two
divergent primitive attitudes,—the one implying an appeal
to personal helpers in the form of prayer, the other resting
on the application of a formula that may or may not involve
the constraint of such helpers but excludes supplication.
The differentiation is a useful one, most useful, however,
when considered as defining two limiting cases, two types of
reaction conceivably antithetical, yet often coexisting among
the same people.

For example, on Frazer's theory the Winnebago who ad-
dresses a "spirit" with a tobacco offering forces him to
grant the favor desired, hence we are dealing with magic.
But from our observer's concrete illustrations—and, indeed,
from some of his explicit statements—it appears that the
matter is not quite so simple. There are certainly individual differences in the attitudes of Winnebago visionaries, by
no means all of whom adhere to the mechanical theory of
cause and effect broached by some of Dr. Radin's witnesses.

Nay, we can go farther and declare categorically that, whatever these Indians may say or think they think, their attitude practically *never* corresponds to that of Frazer's magician. For, we are told:

> The personal religious experiences were very sacred and rarely told even to near relatives. As far as I know, they were only told before death or when a person was very ill. . . .

If it is merely a case of compulsion of spirits by recourse to a set recipe, whence the sanctity of the encounter? The case is really typical. As Dr. Marett has shown, the error of Frazer's interpretation lies in false intellectualistic psychologizing. There is no evidence that the magician among the Winnebago or elsewhere normally postulates the uniformity of natural phenomena. On the contrary, there is everything to suggest that he performs his acts "solemnly, earnestly, in short, in a spirit of reverent humility which is surely akin to homage," and what applies to "positive magic" in Frazer's sense holds equally for his "negative magic" or taboo.[4]

To revert to the Winnebago, if they are not uniformly religious according to Frazer's definition, neither are they by any means pure magicians in his sense. There is certainly a vacillation in the attitude of different Indians, perhaps even of the same Indian at different times.

This lack of a sharp distinction can be illustrated by material from other areas. As Dr. Marett points out in one of the essays of the book quoted, thin partitions often divide the spell from prayer: a slight change in the formulation of words, a possibly transitory personification may convert the magical formula into a religious petition. This is well brought out by an intensive comparison of the sev-

eral magical performances of the Bukaua. As demonstrated
in the sketch presented above, these conform generally to a
single style of procedure. But while in many cases the incantation is a mere recital of incidents without the suggestion of prayer, there are equally stereotyped formulas in
which an ancestor is supplicated to grant a request. Are,
then, the Bukaua to be classed as magicians or as religious
devotees? The instance illustrates the arbitrariness of which
we should be guilty if we assigned them wholesale to either
category.

With these qualifications Frazer's definition of the two
types of attitude may be accepted; that is, they do not correspond to uniformly identifiable modes of tribal behavior
but roughly describe the more or less prevalent character of
individual reactions. Apart from this, I cannot concede to
Frazer's scheme the slightest basis: it seems to me to mis-
represent grossly the psychological situation, while its historical contentions are equally devoid of validity.

The psychological error has already been exposed above
in the treatment of the Winnebago case and the exposition
of Dr. Marett's views. For good measure I will throw in
a discussion of divination, for though not dealt with as
magic by Sir James it offers an a fortiori case inasmuch as
it represents a phase of primitive thought strictly comparable and is saturated with intellectual motives to a degree that
preëminently seems to warrant its definition as a pseudo-
science.

Divination is probably nowhere more highly elaborated
than among the Thonga of Southeastern Africa, who shall
therefore serve for purposes of illustration. M. Junod,
our authority, is full of admiration for the intricate system
of these natives, for the skill with which they have inter-
woven with the practice every aspect of their social life. In

a sense it is a national pastime to interpret the meaning of a throw of the astragalus bones and other objects constituting a complete divination set; nevertheless, only the initiated pass as fully equipped diviners. Now what, we ask, is the attitude of one of these adepts toward his apparatus (*bula*)? Is it the attitude of a surveyor toward his theodolite, of a chemist toward his reagents, of an architect towards his scaffolding? Not at all. One of M. Junod's informants once ejaculated: "You Christians believe in your Bible. Our Bible is much better than yours! It is the divinatory bones!" Mankhelu, we are told, "was attached to his divinatory bones by all the fibers of his heart." He had two sets, one called the "Father" and used at home, while the "Son" was taken along on travels. M. Junod tried to buy one of them for his ethnographical collection, but the wizard could not be prevailed upon to sell either. All this hardly betokens the attitude of a nascent Helmholtz or Galileo.

It might be suggested that the reverential attitude here displayed has its psychological basis in that association with supernatural beings which, according to Frazer, may set in as a secondary development. But the argument remains unshaken by this consideration. To be sure, *some* connection with religion in Frazer's sense exists. The ancestral gods were themselves bone-throwers and are invoked to give or to revive the spirit of divination. Mankhelu, for example, derived one of his prophecies from his father's spirit. But such association is definitely incidental and unessential:

The Bula, the Word, is not generally considered as being the utterance of the ancestor-gods. The bones are, in a certain sense, superior to the gods, whose intentions they disclose. The

Bula is the revelation of a somewhat impersonal power, independent of the gods." [5]

In other words, the Bula is sacred and supernatural, and is so not in a derivative fashion but in its own right. Its emotional concomitants are not those of mere intellectual curiosity but are closely similar to those evoked by the objects of religious devotion. Both the parallelism of magic and science and antithesis of magic and religion thus rest on inadequate psychological analysis.

To turn next to the chronological sequence advanced by Frazer, the a priori argument adduced is absurd. It is for comparative psychologists to decide whether and how far down the scale of the organic kingdom animals can be credited with the power of associating ideas. But even if we make the most liberal concessions in this respect, it remains true that while all magic may consist in the association of ideas (though we have just seen reason to repudiate such a purely rationalistic interpretation) it does not follow that all association of ideas leads to magical beliefs and rites. After asserting that without associating ideas beasts could not survive, Frazer triumphantly asks:

But who attributes to the animals a belief that the phenomena of nature are worked by a multitude of invisible animals or by one enormous and prodigiously strong animal behind the scenes?

The fact is that the things compared here are not on the same plane. We ask in reply, "Who attributes to animals a faith in the uniformity of nature, a belief that the same ceremony accompanied by the same spell will produce identical results? What animal has ever made an effigy of its hunter to cause his destruction? What beast ever secured an enemy's hair to croon a spell over it?" The logical error involved here is really of an incredibly elementary character. As soon as we pass from the mere association of ideas underlying magic to magical processes themselves the extreme simplicity alleged by Frazer vanishes in thin air.

The inductive proof for the priority of magic does not indeed rest on a patent logical absurdity but is unacceptable on empirical grounds. It is not true that the Australians are the "rudest" savages concerning whom accurate information is available; it is not true that they practice magic to the virtual exclusion of religion; it is not true that magic is essentially uniform in the world as contrasted with religion.

In a previous chapter we have already listed those peoples who may fairly be regarded as the "rudest" known, and certainly they do not represent a higher level than the Australians. Let us take the three best-known, the Andaman Islanders, the Bushmen, and the Semang of the Malay Peninsula, and examine Frazer's thesis in the light of our information about their beliefs.

Among the Andamanese there are certainly magical practices of some sort: thus human bones are believed to drive away evil spirits, and the same property is attributed to fire, which is accordingly always kept burning by the side of a patient. A practitioner may avail himself of such methods if he chooses; but he has other means of dispelling the disease-causing spirits, viz., "addressing them and conjuring them to go away," for "in his dreams he can communicate with the spirits and can persuade them to help him to cure the sick person." This is manifestly a case of the conciliation of superior beings. It is worth adding that whatever extraordinary knowledge of the magical properties of objects a shaman has is supposed to be derived from his spirits.[6]

The Bushman data are of the same general tenor. Magic was performed, as when a man unable to reach home threw earth into the air so that his wife at home might see the dust. But there is also positive evidence for prayer to the moon and stars.[7]

Finally, the Semang perform various acts typical of magic, such as the sending of a bamboo sliver against the enemy's heart. But though this tribe displays a very weak development of religious ritual, invocation and sacrifice are not absent. The more important of their deities are addressed in spontaneous prayer; and blood drawn from the region of the shinbone is thrown to the skies as a sacrifice to Kari or the ghosts.[8]

But the Australians themselves, surely rude even though not "rudest," fail to support Frazer's arguments. It is indeed a fact that the Central Australians described by Spencer and Gillen constantly utilize magic and are reported never to appeal for assistance to supernatural beings. But congeners of theirs not one whit more advanced in general culture by no means uniformly refrain from such propitiatory rites. Thus, the Dieri perform a ceremony directed towards the alien race of sky-dwellers called Mura-mura, who in times of drought are asked to supply rain, while, on the other hand, in case of excessive showers they are invoked to restrain the precipitation. To this must be added the unimpeachable testimony of Mrs. Parker, a life-long observer of the Euahlayi. The "high-god" of this people, Byamee, is invoked on a number of occasions. People pray to him at funerals on behalf of the souls of the dead; orphans successfully address him to secure rain; at the close of initiation rites the oldest attending medicine-man prays to him for long life; and even a female shaman, debarred by her sex from communing with him under his proper name, has been known to supplicate him for rain through the intercession of a tutelary spirit.[9]

The only inference that can fairly be drawn from the facts is that among very rude peoples magic and religion (in Frazer's sense) coexist.

What shall, however, be said of the argument from distribution? Admitting with qualifications that the range of a cultural element is proportionate to its age, we must reject the conclusion drawn, because once more Sir James is not comparing comparable phenomena. If religions are compared in their specific characteristics and magical faiths only as regards their most abstract common traits, the former will of course appear diverse and the latter uniform. A fair survey, on the other hand, will bring out frequent recurrences of religious no less than of magical practice.

On the other hand, magic is very far from presenting that uniform character one might infer from Frazer's statement. Even one of the two main branches into which he divides magic, to wit, contagious magic, is not represented among the Arunta and their Central Australian neighbors. For, if we can rely on the definite statement of Spencer and Gillen, Frazer's favorite authorities, the custom of bewitching a person by first securing and then charming a lock of his hair or some detachable part of his body does not occur in this area.[10] To take another aspect of magic, in our sense, divination as a definite art is far from universal and is certainly less pronounced in America than in the Old World; and within the Old World we find a definite regional distribution for such divinatory techniques as scapulimantia, the art of foretelling events from the cracks in an animal's shoulder blade. Again, the practice of chanting spells, universally recognized as magical, which was found so highly elaborated in Polynesia and New Guinea, is far less conspicuous in North America, where the extensive use of magical formulæ is restricted to special districts, such as northern California.

In short, Frazer's argument breaks down at every point, and even if we adopt his definitions there is no reason to ascribe greater antiquity to magic than to religion. *Ipso facto,* our broader definition of religion will not support such a chronological hypothesis. In the state of our knowledge, both magic and religion are best regarded as extremely ancient components of the human world-view. But since the magical has been found to partake of the psychological character of the religious, no good ground for a sharp division of the two remains, and it is permissible to regard the magical beliefs and practices as religious in *our* sense of the term. If this seems unacceptable, it will be necessary at least to follow Drs. Marett and Goldenweiser, who conceive of Magic and Religion as two distinct compartments or branches of one larger whole, Supernaturalism.

In the interest of clearness, however, a few supplementary statements seem called for. Magic—not only as generally defined, but as specifically dealt with by Frazer under the headings of "imitative magic" and "contagious magic"—is assuredly akin to religion if the psychological factors are taken into account. On the other hand, primitive man undoubtedly does form a vast number of associations in a matter-of-fact way, and the generalizations based on these constitute his lore, the *psychological* equivalent of our science irrespective of its objective value. Some of this—indeed an appreciable portion of it—is genuine knowledge resting on sound observation and inference, as Drs. Golden-

weiser and Marett contend.[11]   But the residue, which *we*
are obliged to reject when testing it in the light of *our*
knowledge, does not, for that reason, belong to a different
category from a psychological point of view.

It is the native's frame of mind that invariably decides
the matter.   In so far as he observes and reasons without
enveloping his mental operations with the atmosphere of
supernaturalism he is none the less a scientist or at least a
precursor of science because of his errors, for mistakes
from sheer ignorance are committed by our greatest thinkers.   When a Bukaua hears the call of the *moqua* bird,
he infers that the enemy is planning an attack; when he
hears the *soqueng,* this is accepted as the harbinger of a
visit from a neighboring village.   These are associations
of ideas, devoid so far as one can see of any trace of
religious sentiment, mere summaries of experience: *they*
are pseudo-science.   Again, when a Crow in Montana or
a Jagga on the slopes of Mt. Kilimanjaro assures a sneezer
that some one is calling him by name, we are once more
dealing with false science, though this is magic neither in
Frazer's sense nor in any one else's.   On the other hand,
the attitude of the Bukaua sorcerer, the Thonga diviner,
the Maori spell-chanter, is different not because they are
objectively farther from the truth, but because one and all
they err not as cool observers who happen to be only partly
familiar with a range of facts but as inveterate devotees
of supernaturalism.

This conception of a domain of supernaturalism embracing both magic and religion and opposed to the sphere of
the everyday world that includes as a late product scientific
thought runs counter to Durkheim's theory.   For while the
French sociologist likewise dichotomizes the universe into
two antithetical principles, the Sacred and the Profane, *his*

Sacred does not coincide with ours, which is merely synonymous with the Extraordinary or Supernatural, often modified, by an additional affective tinge, into the Holy. Natural and Supernatural, Durkheim argues, are correlative concepts; the Supernatural is merely the negation of Nature. Then, how can the Supernatural have been conceived by early man, who had no notion of a natural order in the universe? For that is demonstrably a late development; and before it evolved, human beings had no reason to reject the most marvelous occurrences as impossible.[12]

To recognize the false intellectualistic psychologizing behind this specious reasoning is to knock it into a cocked hat. Dr. Marett anticipated and clearly refuted the objection when he wrote:

The savage has no word for "nature." He does not abstractly distinguish between an order of uniform happenings and a higher order of miraculous happenings. He is merely concerned to mark and exploit the difference when presented in the concrete.[13]

A man does not need to have studied comparative anatomy to see that a bird is not a fish, nor to have analyzed his sensations to know that one woman inflames him with ardor while another leaves him cold. So an Ekoi does not keep a double catalogue to which he refers as occasion arises to decide whether an audition is normal or abnormal: he hears his Oji tree calling and in the middle of the night, regardless of consequences, he dashes towards it. He knows intuitively, immediately, spontaneously, that the summons is generically different from that of a tribesman, even of a chief, and he reacts accordingly with the precision of a lower organism exhibiting its tropisms. Our conception of the Supernatural involves nothing but such differential response to external or internal stimulation.

DURKHEIM'S THEORY

Durkheim, like Frazer, separates magic and religion; but, as might be expected, his reasons are quite different.[14] While he regards religion as founded in a sense of the Sacred, as contradistinguished from the Profane, he adds a vital differentia: religion in its historical forms is invariably linked with a church. That is to say, there is always a body of votaries united by the same ideas of the Sacred and by the same practices revolving about it. Now such a bond, the argument runs, is lacking in magic. The relations of a sorcerer to his clients are like a doctor's to his patients; they form no basis for any kind of church. This situation is not altered when the magician works for the public good rather than for private individuals: there is still no permanent or durable tie established between the practitioner and his beneficiaries.

It is true enough, Durkheim admits, that sometimes magicians assemble in fraternities. But, first, such association is not essential to the practice of magic; secondly, even at best it does not supply a parallel to a church organization. For a brotherhood of wizards would correspond merely to an association of priests without the congregation of laymen; and where is there a *church* made up exclusively of priests?

Anticipating a protest from another angle, the French sociologist takes cognizance of such individual subjective experiences as have been described in our first synthetic sketch. He does not deny their existence but explains them away as constituting not so many individual, that is, churchless forms of religion but so many minor variants of one social religion corresponding to a single church.

In this last contention there is indeed a germ of truth. We have seen that even the extreme subjectivism of the Crow is quite consistent with a spontaneous conformity to tribal standards. That, however, is a subordination not to a clear-cut church doctrine but to that far vaguer thing, a common cultural background. The same objects are *not* held sacred by all the Crow, nor do they display an identical behavior toward their respective sacred objects. When a Crow shaman allows a young warrior to go out with his own medicine, his attitude does not differ fundamentally from that of a magician towards *his* client. And when a number of braves singly resort to him, there is still no necessity for a congregational development; there is certainly a possibility for it, but so there is in the case of a magician's clients. In so far, however, as such a group is united, the members are segregated from, not merged in, a tribal Church. Precisely as the Crow shaman's notions and practices are circumscribed by the traditional Crow culture, the Bukaua magician's technique, taboos, and spells are determined by Bukaua culture. There is as much or as little of a church in one case as in the other. In both there is automatic acceptance of the received beliefs, while in neither is there a rigid conformity to a set of tribally established dogmas and observances. The sociological distinction between magic and religion is untenable.

REFERENCES

[1] Radin, 1923: 279, 289.
[2] Tylor, 1913: I, 117-136.

[3] Frazer: 11-60.

[4] Marett: 29, 38, 73, 190.

[5] Junod: 11, 488 sq., 493 sq.

[6] Brown: 178 f., 184.

[7] Bleek and Lloyd: 57, 81, 339, 385.

[8] Skeat and Blagden: 11, 174, 198 f., 205 f., 233.

[9] Spencer and Gillen, 1904: 490 sq. Howitt: 395 sq. Parker: 8.

[10] Spencer and Gillen, 1899: 553; ei., 1904: 478. 605.

[11] Goldenweiser, 1922: 154.

[12] Durkheim: 33-40.

[13] Marett : 109.

[14] Durkheim : 60–65.

CHAPTER VII

COLLECTIVISM

In the preceding chapters I have several times referred to Durkheim's theories, and uniformly in a critical spirit. This attitude will not be abandoned in reviewing the core of his system, hence a prefatory word of explanation seems desirable in order to guard against misunderstanding. I am convinced that the cardinal tenets of Durkheim's scheme are unacceptable, but I should not like to be understood as denying that it represents an estimable intellectual achievement. Indeed, so far as I can see, it is the only comprehensive effort since Tylor's day to unify religious data from a wholly novel angle. Moreover, Durkheim's incidental interpretations of religious phenomena in the concrete sometimes reveal considerable acumen, and we shall have occasion to adopt his views on at least one important subject.

Let us recall that Durkheim's minimum definition of religion implies an antithesis of the Sacred and the Profane, and the union of fellow-worshipers of the Sacred in a sort of church. In casting about for the key to the mystery of religion, that is, of its origins, our author goes to the Australians because they are said to represent the primeval condition of human communal life. Their concepts of sacredness are all wrapped up in totemic ritualism, hence the essence of their totemism will be the essence of archaic religion. What, then, is the essence of Australian totemism? On the surface it seems that certain species of the animal kingdom are the sacred objects of adoration. But that is only a superficial view, says Durkheim. For many of these sacred totems are such insignificant specimens of organic life as the ant, the lizard, or the rat. Surely these are too insignificant to thrill primitive man with a sense of holiness; and more impressive phenomena of nature, such as the stars, rarely function as totems in Australia. Moreover, it is not the animals and plants themselves to which the natives attach the maximum of holiness, but to their representations, the totemic symbols. The problem thus narrows down still further and becomes equivalent to that of the significance of the symbols.

Durkheim has a ready solution: the symbols are emblematic at the same time of the totemic principle or "god" and of the clan. "Si donc il est, à la fois, le symbole du dieu et de la société, n'est-ce-pas que le dieu et la société ne font qu'un?" In other words, the social group or clan *is* the god of the clan, *is* the totemic principle, but disguised and "représenté aux imaginations sous les espèces sensibles du végétal ou de l'animal qui sert de totem."

It remains to show how society could have the power of calling forth the sense of the divine. According to our author, this results from the fact that the relationship of society to the individual parallels that of the typical deity to the typical worshiper. On the one hand, society dominates every member by its superior authority, overriding the individual will regardless of personal considerations; on the other hand, it is a source of strength, for to be in harmony with one's fellows is to be inspired with confidence and courage such as the devout believer enjoys when he is conscious of the benevolent gaze of his god. Furthermore, all of a man's cultural possessions are the gift of

society. In short, the individual consciousness finds an
environment peopled with forces at once transcendently
potent and helpful, august yet benevolent; it objectifies its
relevant impressions as we objectify our sensations, but
with a significant difference: these sensations do not evoke
the sentiment of awe, they correspond to the profane as
contrasted with the sacred part of the universe. In the
case of primitive man, Durkheim further contends, the
religious sentiment would be inspired primarily not by
society as a whole but by the immediate group with which
he is related, viz., the totemic clan.

For the origin of the fundamental difference between the
sacred and the profane which he regards as essential to
religion, Durkheim has recourse to the antithesis he notes
in Australian society between the workaday and the ceremonial season. The former is characterized by the peaceful monotony of isolated economic activity, the latter by
the all but frenzied excitement incident to the big festive
assemblies, a contrast which prefigures that of the profane
and the sacred.

The question is naturally asked, why it was necessary
for the native to conceive the social forces in the guise of
plant and animal symbols. Durkheim answers the latter
query by pointing out that the primitive Australian is above
all a hunter and that animals most naturally suggest themselves to his imagination; such phenomena as the several
stars are not sufficiently distinguishable to serve as badges
for a considerable number of distinct clans. On the other
hand, the choice of *some* symbol is imperative: the clan
is too complex a concept to be grasped in its concrete unity,
while the totemic symbol is the flag of its group, the visible
body of its god. Moreover, that period of excitement
which gives rise to the sense of the sacred passes away;

if there were no outward sign to survive as a rallying-point, the religious sentiment itself would vanish.

In this interpretation of totemism there is something like an anticipation of the Freudian interpretation of dreams. Things are not what they seem on the surface but have a hidden meaning. Totems are not the real objects of worship but acquire sacred character in so far as they symbolize the clan, which is the real god. Nevertheless, once sanctified by this symbolization, they become the center of ritual performances and themselves appear as the source of awe-inspiring and benevolent activities. By contact with them, in turn, other objects, intrinsically of a religiously indifferent character, also acquire sanctity, and thus whole systems of sacred things evolve. The relationship of the totemite to the totem which looms so large as the manifest content of the faith is a secondary attempt by the natives to explain why they believe and act as they do.

. Durkheim especially piques himself on having escaped what he considers the vital error of the two most significant rival theories, animism and naturalism. Both of these derive religion from illusions. But a phenomenon of such vital importance in the life of humanity as religion cannot be founded in unreality. Durkheim's view avoids such error, he thinks, by basing religion on an indubitable verity, —the social group. Specifically with reference to naturalism, Durkheim contends that it is incomprehensible how such erroneous notions of nature as are implied in naturalism could have persisted among mankind. If, however, the clan is god and if the latent goal of religion is not the adjustment of man to the outer world but the integration of society, then the most absurd notions of nature might be entertained and would be irrelevant, hence would not affect the believers' attitude. Further, nature is incapable of arousing the religious sentiment. It is too uniform to produce deep emotions; and even if it could evoke surprise and admiration it nowhere suggests a duality of the sacred and profane, such as is indispensable for the concept of religion.

While by no means inclined to join in the pæans of praise that have been intoned in Durkheim's honor, I repeat that his essay is a noteworthy mental exercise and would rank as a landmark if dialectic ingenuity sufficed to achieve greatness in the empirical sciences. Even as it is, the freshness of his approach is at times stimulating and reconciles us somewhat to a narrowness that balks at no measure of absurdity.[1]

The present book is not a treatise on logic, and it would profit us little to follow Durkheim's thoughts into all their ramifications. Without slavishly summarizing Dr. Goldenweiser's exposition and critique, let us rather follow the broad sweep of this writer, who, more appreciative of the French sociologist's mental operations than we profess to be, has nevertheless repeatedly made his system the butt of his critical acumen.[2] His strictures fall into three categories,—the ethnological, the sociological, and the psychological.

From the ethnological point of view Dr. Goldenweiser pertinently asks whence the non-totemic peoples have derived their religion. Durkheim proceeds on the assumption, now thoroughly discredited, that the sib (clan) in the typical form of the totemic sib is a universal trait of very rude cultures. As a matter of fact, it has already been shown that the simplest tribes in both the Old World and the New World lack sibs and totems. No such institution occurs among the Andamanese of the Bay of Bengal or the Chukchi of Siberia, nor has it been reported from the Tasmanians, the Congolese Pygmies, or the Bushmen. If it be objected with some plausibility that our knowledge of the three tribes just mentioned is too inadequate to permit negative data to weigh heavily, there is the wholly unobjectionable evidence from the Western Hemisphere, where the sib organization is uniformly absent from all the rudest hunting tribes and in North America is an almost regular accompaniment of horticulture. The Mackenzie River Athabaskans, the Shoshoneans of the Great Basin, the tribes of Washington and Oregon are sibless, while the sedentary Iroquois and Pueblo tribes are organized into sibs with at least totemic names, if not with a full-fledged totemism; for, as we cannot resist mentioning incidentally, the sib organization is by no means uniformly linked with totemism. These simple facts had been pointed out by Dr. Swanton some years before the publication of Durkheim's book, but the French sociologist prefers to ignore them and to take for his point of departure a demonstrably false theory of primitive society.

In short, then, there are many non-totemic peoples and among them precisely are those of simplest culture. But they all have some sort of religion! Shall we assume that they only obtained their beliefs and practices by contact with and borrowing from the higher totemic cultures? The assumption is not a priori probable, and empirically there is not the slightest proof for it except as respects specific features of religious culture, such as may be borrowed back and forth under favorable conditions. Dr. Ruth Fulton Benedict has recently examined Durkheim's thesis with reference to the North American data, selecting for discussion the relations of totemism to the most persistent of North American religious traits, the guardian-spirit complex.[3] This feature is not only by virtue of its range

far older than totemism but also turns out to be highly
developed where no traces of totemism have ever been recorded. It is therefore impossible to derive the guardian-
spirit belief from totemic conceptions. On the contrary,
there is good evidence that in certain regions totemism,
which otherwise has a very meager religious content, "tends
to take its coloring from the guardian-spirit concept, and
the high-water marks of a religious attitude towards the
totem, which beyond doubt are found on this continent,
are intelligible from this fact."

To summarize the essentials of the ethnological argument, Durkheim—like Frazer—has been deceived by the
rash assumption that the primeval culture of humanity is
represented in Australia. In reality, the Australians have
only a moderate, certainly not an exclusive, claim to being
reckoned among the rudest peoples, and what holds for
them in the way of religion does not correspond to a universal archaic faith of mankind.

From the sociological angle, Goldenweiser objects that
while ostensibly Durkheim deifies society his conception
of it in the rôle of god is a singularly narrow one since
he practically identifies society with the *crowd*. While this
may not be a wholly accurate statement of the case, our
critic is undoubtedly right as regards the origin of the religious sentiment, for *that* Durkheim surely traces to the
crowd-psychological situation typified by the atmosphere
of the Australian ceremonial season. Now, as Goldenweiser
remarks, man does not objectify his crowd as something
distinct from and superior to himself, but identifies himself with it: "the crowd or group self *is* the self *par excellence*." Again, a crowd setting never creates a specific
psychic state: crowd ecstasy is merely a feeling of joy
carried to an extreme degree, and so with all other emo-

tional states; they are not originated but merely intensified by the crowd. As Goldenweiser trenchantly asks, Why is it that the gatherings of Indians for secular dances are not transformed into religious occasions if the assembly itself gives rise to the sentiments of religion?

To these comments I should like to add another. In so far as Durkheim does not identify divine society with the crowd, he rather lightly fixes upon the sib as the social group that would at the same time loom as the god-like protector and curber. No doubt the individual derives sustenance and protection from his own sib, but that is equally true of his local or tribal group as a whole. Why, then, should the sib alone function as the nascent god? On the other hand, restraint is precisely what one's own sib does not usually exercise,—that is left to the other sibs. If by special act of grace we follow Durkheim to his favorite Australian field, special difficulties arise. He insists that the individual acquires his culture from society. But the society from which he acquires it is only in small measure his sib. For example, in a matrilineal Australian tribe a boy belongs indeed to his mother's sib, but his training in woodcraft is derived from his father, regardless of rules of descent, and later his education is completed in the camp that unites all the bachelors, irrespective of kinship. The leap from society as a whole to the individual's own sib seems to be in no way justified by Durkheim's reasoning. We are obliged to conclude that his theory neither explains how the assemblages of the ceremonial season create religious emotion nor why the sib should be singled out for masked adoration from among all the social units when it is only one of a series all of which jointly confer on him the blessings of culture and of protection.

To turn to the psychological aspect of the case, under this head we must consider first of all the idea that nature cannot inspire primitive man with religious emotion and that he does not feel the superiority of natural forces over human beings. Durkheim's error here is all the more regrettable because with his initially skeptical attitude on the subject he might have made a perfectly valid and interesting ethnographic point in correction of a widespread fallacy. There is really no *necessity* for attaching religious value to cosmic phenomena, plausible as that may seem to the closet philosopher. For example, the Thonga of Southeast Africa never personify or worship the sun or moon, while the stars also play an insignificant part in their thought. In fact, altogether the forces of nature are quite subordinate to the ghosts of ancestors in the religious life of these people.[4] What we require here, as in so many other phases of culture-history, is an investigation of regional distributions. The best prophylactic against baseless speculation that man must believe this or do that is the actual knowledge that throughout a definite part of the globe he believes and does nothing of the kind.

But any such ethnographic point of view is quite foreign to Durkheim, who merely combats one psychological dogma with another. So far from the truth is the alleged impossibility of nature to impress mankind with religious sentiments that perhaps a majority of North American Indians have the most specific myths and rites in connection with natural phenomena. The sun and the thunder, for example, are widely reverenced, and the Pawnee of Nebraska developed a veritable astral cult. To return to Africa, the great deities of the Ekoi were found to be associated with sky and earth, while among the Andamanese the two main gods direct the principal winds of the area. Without going further, we can safely reject Durkheim's anti-naturalism as absurd.

But, as Goldenweiser has forcibly explained, Durkheim is guilty of false psychologizing in another direction also, for he underestimates to an incredible degree the capacity of *individuals* for religious experience, quite independently of the crowd, which prophets and seers often notoriously shun. The typical North American vision-quest, as among the Crow, involves a *lonely* vigil, and the thrill that comes to the successful seeker may possibly remain his life-long secret.

Finally, there is something almost pathetically inept about Durkheim's plea that unlike animism and naturalism, his collectivist theory rests on the solid rock of reality. In this context the objective reality of the religious construct is irrelevant: the sense of sacredness remains a fact whatever may have produced it and its subjective value remains unaffected by metaphysical considerations of illusion and reality arising in another consciousness. Incidentally we may well ask in what sense natural phenomena are less real than society. It is true that as religious objects they may be fantastically personified, but then society in the form in which it is pictured by Durkheim as capable of becoming a "god" bears very little resemblance to the society of actual experience. As for animism, Durkheim ignores once more the fact that the concept of spirit is not exclusively derived from the illusions of dream life but in part from the contrast between the living body and the corpse, which is real enough.

Before parting from the French sociologist's original but unsound speculations, I should like to direct attention to one phase of his work that rests on a surer foundation. His treatment of symbolism seems to me excellent. There is little doubt that symbols may concentrate the worshiper's religious fervor upon themselves and that their holiness may in turn flow into still other channels. We have seen how devoutly a Crow will regard the feather that is basically merely a badge of his vision yet becomes glorified out of proportion to its intrinsic value through that association; and the communicability of holiness is one of the striking features in the Polynesian taboo system.

In this connection Durkheim's view that the specific nature of the object worshiped is immaterial may likewise be cited as coinciding. altogether with the position here assumed. It is hardly susceptible of doubt that the person of a sovereign may call forth a sentiment hardly distinguishable from religious emotion; and the abstractions labeled "Country" and under certain conditions "Liberty" and "Reason" have an equal potency. If we adhere to the psychological point of view, we shall find no reason to exclude such ideas from the rank of "gods." Of this, more anon.

We leave Durkheim with the consolatory reflection with which Mach once commented on Herbart, that after all this eminent thinker has not been exclusively a perpetrator of. errors.

References

[1] Durkheim: 97-121, 293-334.
[2] Goldenweiser, 1917: 121 sq.; id., 1922: 360 sq.
[3] R. F. Benedict: 61 sq.
[4] Junod: ii, 281-285.

Part III: Historical and Psychological Aspects

CHAPTER VIII

HISTORICAL SCHEMES AND REGIONAL CHARACTERIZATION

To apply a historical point of view is to the minds of not a few scholars equivalent to elaborating a scheme of sequences. Tylor's theory of animism is historical in that sense, though he assumed a unilinear development which modern representatives of the historical schools reject. With some writers the tendency to predicate relative chronology is so strong that they cannot help ascribing a like disposition to others who do not share their obsession. Thus, because Dr. Marett insisted on the antiquity of the sense of the supernatural and its independence of the ghost-soul concept, he has been credited with the assumption of a pre-animistic era, which he expressly disavows.[1] Those who have been most active in repudiating unilinear evolutionism have not abstained from outlining a generalized scheme of religious history,—generalized not in the sense of ascribing one course of development for all peoples but as purporting to sketch along its several distinct paths the religious history of all humanity.

Father Schmidt's scheme, while not accessible in this country except in summary form, serves as an ideal illustration of a multilinear system.[2] First of all he assumes an archaic culture now only represented by the very rudest peoples, whose faith is characterized positively by a belief in a high-god, by the union of religion and ethics, and the beginnings of prayer and ritual, while negatively the lack of ancestor-worship and magic are noteworthy criteria. Upon this common substratum three diverse structures were reared in mutual independence,—the horticultural, the totemic, and the pastoral. Horticulture was a feminine invention and produced a corresponding social preponderance of the female sex, which found expression in matrilineal descent and in the worship of a female deity, the Moon. Animism and an ancestral cult also arose, largely in connection with a revolt of the masculine underdog, which led to the organization of men's associations, that is, secret societies designed to curb woman's power. In the second, totemic culture, which evolved elsewhere, masculine precedence was mirrored in the adoration of a solar deity of male sex; totemic beliefs and the excessive reliance on magic as contrasted with archaic dependence on a high-god were significant features. Finally, pastoral nomadism adhered more tenaciously to primeval monotheism: neither sun nor moon but a sublime heaven-god, the Jahve of the Semites and the Dyaus pitar of Indo-Germanic peoples, occupied the first place among divine beings. As for subsequent events in the history of religion, they were the result of interaction among these three primary differentiations of the archaic culture.

Much might be said concerning the sociological assumptions underlying this theory and especially with reference to its naïve economic determinism, but detailed criticism is hardly in place so long as the full evidence adduced by the author of the scheme cannot be examined. Our present concern is with quite a different phase of the matter. I must repeat what I said in my discussion of animism, that Father Schmidt and his school quite underestimate the technical difficulties to be overcome in a historical reconstruction where religion is the subject-matter. Every such reconstruction obviously rests ultimately on the descriptive data, and it is precisely these which, even when abundant, are usually far too intricate to admit of a convenient summary by one or two catchwords such as "solar cult" or "animism" and "magic." Even in so rude a tribe as the Andamanese we have to reckon with a supernaturalism of at least triple form,—Biliku and his counterpart Tarai; the spirits of the deceased; and a variety of magical conceptions. We have already seen that in spite of the simplicity of such conditions the relative weighting of factors is far from easy. No wonder that in circumstances of greater complexity the problem may become practically insoluble. On how many peoples is the evidence even approximately so complete and so trustworthy as for the Ewe of Togo, West Africa? Herr Spieth, as the result of his years of missionary experience, has given us in *Die Ewe-Stämme* an admirable account replete with documentation in the vernacular. Yet when Spieth in another treatise essays to give a general summary of Ewe religion, a fellow-missionary cannot assent to some of his most important propositions, those relating to the high-god and to the hereafter. The critic concludes: "Die Arbeit ist mit viel Fleiss geschrieben; und doch legt sie der Leser unbefriedigt beiseite, da sie so viele Fragen nicht oder nur unklar beantwortet." [8]

To cite another example, the Crow seem unable to decide as to the character and identity of the Sun. No doubt by making an indefinite number of arbitrary auxiliary hypotheses a skillful dialectician could explain away the obscurities, but that would be the lawyer's rather than the scientist's procedure; and in the present instance even the special pleader's task would be an arduous one. If he set out from the plausible proposition that the Sun is the archaic high-god obscured by mythological fancy and what not, he would be confronted forthwith with the query why the Crow, who are matrilineal, have given to their supreme being the solar and masculine character that might be expected from a patrilineal group, while the moon, which is really conceived in feminine guise here, is of quite subordinate importance. But to leave dialectics for scientific argumentation, the whole discussion on this basis is from our point of view a meaningless irrelevancy because we have found that the specific nature of the "god" is immaterial to the Crow and that it is the subjective experience that is really significant to him. In characterizing the religion of this tribe I have actually shown how at all events the greater part of their beliefs and practices can be connected with the vision. Nevertheless, the catchword "vision" is no more successful than other catchwords in doing justice to the marvelous wealth of concrete situations that are invariably bound up with religion; and still less is it capable of even remotely indicating the historical relations of Crow religion, which are manifold and point in diverse directions.

I should not like to be misunderstood as opposing historical reconstructions on principle; quite the contrary is the case. But in this field of inquiry there is still so much doubt as to the raw materials themselves that historical schemes, except if confined to narrow limits, are likely to come to grief. How can we reconstruct history if even the facts of regional distribution are far from clear? About ten years ago Dr. Paul Radin surveyed the data of North American religion and concluded that a belief in the localization of spirits, in *genii loci,* is prevalent in this continent and underlies the guardian-spirit concept. But Mrs. Benedict has recently shown that what Dr. Radin considered a universal correlation is a strictly localized one and that generally the guardian spirit is in no way associated with the local genius.[4]

The immediate task of the comparative student is therefore a sifting of the material, an accurate determination of specific tribal religions and upon this basis a series of intensive distribution studies covering successively culture areas, continents, and the whole globe. In the absence of adequate preliminary regional surveys, the following remarks on some, not all, major areas are to be taken as purely tentative.

North America is characterized by the conspicuousness of the subjective experience conveniently labeled "vision" and by the frequency with which tutelaries are derived from such abnormal psychic states, a correlation which Mrs. Benedict has shown to be by no means an organic, logical correlation but a fortuitous historical conjunction.[5] This author has demonstrated the basic importance of the vision in this continent by producing evidence that even among the Pueblo Indians, where the hypertrophy of group ritualism dwarfs the significance of individual revelations, such experiences are far from wholly lacking. But though the vision itself is ubiquitous, its correlates vary considerably: in one area, for instance, all men strive for a revelation, as among the Crow, while elsewhere, as in California, vision and tutelary are the shaman's prerogative. Compared with other divisions of the globe, North America is likewise distinguished by the extreme development of more or less spectacular ceremonialism, often bound up with definite organizations. This trait is weakly developed only in the extremely rude cultures of the Mackenzie River region, the Great Basin, and adjoining territories.

The South American phenomena are not sufficiently

known to admit of a comprehensive statement, for such meaningless catchwords as "animism," which in no way differentiate one area of the world from another, must be rigidly barred in the interests of an ultimate comprehension of the facts. On the other hand, it is worth noting that direct intercourse with the supernatural—in short, the equivalent of the vision—is distinctive of native doctors in the tropical forest region, nay, as far south as Tierra del Fuego. In the latter region the investigations of Fathers Koppers and Gusinde have brought to light a number of interesting parallels between the southernmost Yahgan and North American tribes. The Fuegians represent the Californian and Siberian rather than the Crow or Winnebago type, for there is no universal seeking of a revelation but a sudden imperative call to special individuals in the form of some soul-stirring psychic experience. To be sure, there is a deliberate attempt to induce hallucinations by rigorous fasting in a wizards' school, but only persons with a specific vision or a definite predisposition enter the fold of pupils, and to become a full-fledged shaman the vision is prerequisite. Again, as in California and Siberia, resistance to the supernatural summons is fraught with danger. Another definite resemblance consists in the acquisition of a song taught to the visionary by his supernatural protector. In order properly to appreciate the significance of such analogies it would be necessary to possess fuller data on other South American tribes than are at present available. However, the possibility should be kept in mind that the Fuegians may have preserved very ancient elements of New World religion. From the point of view of ceremonialism, the simpler South Americans do not rival the Northern peoples of corresponding status; however, even the

Fuegians have secret cult organizations and performances with simple masks.

The higher American cultures from Mexico to Peru are naturally associated with a great elaboration of ritual, which reveals certain marked features. Most noteworthy is the excessive development of bloody sacrifices, human sacrifices being especially common among the Aztecs. In North America bloody sacrifices, even of animals, are definitely rare, the Pawnee (Nebraska) offering of a maiden and that of a white dog by the Iroquois being notable exceptions. The apparently systematic practice of divination in the more complex cultures likewise merits consideration.

Asia, the home of many higher centers of civilization, largely falls outside the scope of our present survey, but regarding one of its larger subdivisions, Siberia, some statements are called for. It is to a remarkable degree a region of shamanistic activity; in other words, the direct intercourse with the supernatural world is in the foreground. However, it seems that here communication with beings of another sphere is restricted in the main to definite individuals instead of being sought by all or the majority of men, as in many North American tribes. Among the Turkic tribes the tutelaries are predominantly ancestral, while the more important Chukchi equivalents belong to other categories of supernatural beings. Turks and Mongols are further characterized by the dualistic conception of a good and an evil being of great power. From the ritual point of view we may note the wide occurrence of bloody animal sacrifices, whether of dogs, reindeer or horses; also, the method of divination known as scapulimantia, that is, by the cracks in a sheep, reindeer, or other animal shoulderblade held above a fire, a usage which

Dr. Andree has traced from the Chukchi to the Mongols and Turks, and indeed into westernmost Europe. The special regard shown to the bear, culminating among the Ainu and Amur River peoples in a great public festival, will engage our attention a little later.

In Africa the ancestor-worship appearing in Siberia and carried to extremes in the higher Chinese civilization is a widespread phenomenon,—certainly far more so than "fetichism" in the sense of a cult centering in carved effigies of divine beings, for this appears in typical form only in the West. Sorcery is of tremendous practical importance, and in association with it the appeal to ordeals and such elaborate systems of divination as have been described for tribes so remote from each other as the Southeastern Thonga and the Ekoi of Kamerun and Nigeria. Ceremonial activity is often linked with two ideas,—the initiation of one or both sexes into the status of an adult, and a definite cult belonging to a secret fraternity or sorority, which not infrequently employs masks. These religious brotherhoods thrive especially in the West but have been found as far east as Ruanda, a country east of Lake Kivu. Bloody sacrifices are probably common throughout the Dark Continent.

The Polynesian religion has been characterized at some length in a previous chapter, and for the simpler Melanesian area, including New Guinea, we content ourselves with referring to the prevalence of ghost-worship and magic. This latter, in the form of sorcery, finds an extraordinary development in Australia. Here, too, is found an elaborate ceremonialism, connected on the one hand with the initiation of boys into the status of full-fledged tribesmen, on the other with totemic conceptions, such as the desire to multiply the totem animal.

This brief and wholly inadequate summary must not, I repeat, be taken too seriously; least of all, should negative conclusions be drawn from it in an absolute sense. For example, sorcery is given as a characteristic of the Australians and Negroes, but not of the North Americans. Nevertheless, tribes like the Menomini of Wisconsin had sorcerers who destroyed their victims by imitative and contagious magic, deriving their power from the mythical horned snake. Guardian spirits bestowing the arts of black magic upon their protégés have been noted widely in the Algonkian family, and also among the Takelma of Oregon. The Pueblo Indians, indeed, possibly dread witchcraft quite as much as the Africans and explain by it such afflictions as droughts and disease; the Cochiti imputed to sorcery so recent an epidemic as that of 1896.[6] Nevertheless, when the totality of religious phenomena in these several cases is considered, there is warrant, I think, for assigning to this phase of supernaturalism a comparatively humble place.

Again, it is safe to say that the lack of ancestor-worship is a significant negative trait of North American religion. As Mrs. Benedict has shown, even ghosts, irrespective of their kinship, rarely become tutelaries and never to the subordination of other beings. Nevertheless, the suggestion of an ancestral cult appears in the Pueblo area. Thus, the Cochiti believe that the dead go to Wenaima in the west to become *shiwanna* and on the order of Uretsete, the mother of the Indians, give rain to the people, who make offerings of pollen to the spirits and impersonate them in ceremonial masquerades. But, as Kroeber explains for the parallel Zuñi case, the Pueblo Indians pray to the dead as a generality and there is accordingly no genuine equivalent of the adoration of a particular ancestor by his surviving kin.[7] In other words, while it would be rash to say that the dead play no part in North American belief, a relative appraisal of the facts lends corroboration to the general statement made above.

Our conclusion, then, comes to this, that in the present state of our knowledge world-embracing schemes purporting to account for the great variety of religious beliefs are premature; that first of all the facts themselves and their distribution must be ascertained with a reasonable degree of certainty if we are not to build a house of cards. Nevertheless, even with the information at hand it is by no means necessary to despair of the possibility of establishing historical connections, and in some instances the inferences that can safely be drawn are sufficiently comprehensive to satisfy all but the most insatiable synthetic palates. A few examples must suffice.

Let us consider for one thing some North American conceptions of disease. Over a wide area we find the theory and the practice recorded by Dr. Walker among the Oglala of South Dakota:

All diseases are things which get into the body and do violence to it in some way. The thing to do is to get these things out of the body.

This is the dominant idea east of the Rockies: it is noted for the Montauk of Long Island as early as 1761, for the Yuchi of Georgia and South Carolina, for the Natchez of the Lower Mississippi, and in the Plains area. As a matter of fact, it is found widely also in the Far West and on the Pacific. In California the Colorado River people form the only exception, and the Takelma of southwestern Oregon also entertain the characteristic Californian view that sickness is a "pain" lodged in the patient's body, from which it may be extracted in the form of a splinter. In the Southwest, the Zuñi and Pima are known to practice medicine on the extraction theory. But when we turn to the region of the Pacific slope somewhat farther north than the examples cited, a rival conception appears, either in addition to the other or possibly even as a complete substitute, viz., the notion that illness is caused by the loss, usually theft, of the patient's soul and that accordingly the doctor must recapture and restore the kidnaped vital principle. Among the Chehalis and Chinook of the lower Columbia River this looms as the major cause of disease. The ghosts carry away the patient's soul, and it is the shaman's task to recover it and put it back into the patient's body. But it is essential that the truant shall not have taken anything belonging to the ghosts or drunk of their water, otherwise the sick man must die: the doctors may seize the soul and bring it back but it has shrunk to so small a size that it can no longer fill its owner's body. Sometimes a sorcerer abstracts the soul and hides it near a corpse or in some other uncanny place, and then some other man with supernatural power is hired to find the soul lest the victim die. However, the doctrine of soul-loss is combined in this region with that of intrusive causes: and the shaman may have to take out the disease in the form of a rope or pieces of bone or a wolf's claw. This double notion of soul-loss *and* intrusion also occurs among the Northern Athabaskans, the Coast Salish of Puget Sound, the northern coastal tribes of British Columbia, and the Eskimo; while both ideas again appear in the Southwest among the Cochiti of New Mexico.[8]

It is the apparently complete lack of the soul-loss theory and the correlated method of curing over a vast and continuous part of the New World that is historically significant. Miss Lublinski has recently summarized the South American data, and it seems that intrusion coupled with extraction by blowing or suction alone occurs according to her records. Mr. M. R. Harrington informs me that Dr. S. A. Barrett found soul-capture in Ecuador, which would thus define the southernmost range of the idea. According to Father Koppers's quite recent data for the Fuegians, however, an apparently spontaneous wandering of souls may figure as the cause of illness, though the extraction of pathogenic agents is probably more common than the conjuring back of errant souls by means of sacred chants. From a survey made by Mr. Forrest Clements under my direction it appears that the Greenland Eskimo are the only North American people of the East who entertain the theory of soul-kidnaping. Indeed, with a few exceptions to be noted below, we must go to the Far West to find evidence of this notion: according to my own inquiries, it is absent among the Ute of Colorado and Utah and does not turn up in the Basin area until we get to the Lemhi of Idaho and the Paviotso of northern Nevada. Yet there is not the slightest *psychological* reason for this limited distribution. One and all, these American aborigines believe in the existence of the soul; some South American tribes go so far as to have the shaman's soul leave his body to consult the spirits in the course of medical practice. Yet the idea that disease results from soul-snatching has not been evolved.[9] Why this geographically restricted occurrence of a conception so plausible on the uniformly distributed animistic basis?

The answer is to be found not in psychology but in the historical connections between America and Siberia. The basic disease-concept of America is clearly that of intrusion, for it occurs virtually throughout; and even in the Northeast, where the rival idea is most intensely developed, it is almost everywhere coupled with intrusion. The only reasonable supposition, then, is that locally soul-theft has supplemented or even ousted the ancient American theory of disease. But this can hardly be regarded as an autochthonous product of Far Western America, for while in the Western Hemisphere the feature is almost wholly marginal it has a considerable range in Siberia, embracing the Chukchi, the Buryat, of Mongolic stock, around Lake Baikal, and the Turkic people of the Altai. Hence we are probably dealing with a relatively late borrowing from Siberia.[10]

The few exceptional instances ostensibly contravening this assumption can be readily explained. Among the Central Algonkians in the Great Lake region the soul-loss principle once more turns up. Thus, certain Menomini wizards not only extract bones, worms, or other pathogenic agents shot into the patient by a sorcerer, but on occasion may cajole back a wandering soul by whistling and cause it to reënter the sick Indian's body. Since some of the Central Algonkians have been in direct contact with the Eskimo, who have demonstrably carried the soul-loss concept as far east as Greenland, this sporadic occurrence of the trait in the East is quite intelligible.[11]

In America, then, intrusion represents an old cultural layer that has been partly overlaid by the soul-loss stratum. But the question can be studied from a broader point of view. Even in Siberia the Yakut practice the cure by extraction, which indeed is not unknown as a subsidiary method among the Chukchi themselves; it is coupled with other theories in Africa and Malaysia, and is dominant in Australia. The chief facts of distribution are already sketched in one of Tylor's earliest books. Tylor, without working out the hypothesis in detail, definitely espouses the view that only some historical connection can account for the resemblances of belief and practice as to sickness in South Africa, Australia, Borneo, America, and Europe.[12] I adopt this assumption in the following specific form. The doctrine that disease is due to a tangible intrusive body is probably of very great antiquity,—is a genuinely Palæolithic feature. Originating somewhere in the Old World, it was carried into the New by early immigrants, while in the Eastern Hemisphere it likewise came to cover an enormous stretch of territory, so that while often superseded by other conceptions it still persists to some extent in every major area.

The definite proof that the American and Siberian conceptions discussed above had a common origin emboldens us to look for further resemblances between these two areas. In passing we may call attention to the quite arbitrary association of shamanistic activity with a tambourine, which links some of our Eastern Indians not only with Siberia but with Lapland. Mythological parallels between Asia and America have been repeatedly pointed out by Bogoras, Jochelson, Boas, and others, and have been generally accepted as proof of historical contact. Here it is merely necessary to mention the remarkable recurrence among the Chukchi, Yukaghir, Mongolic, Turkic, and Finnic tribes of the widespread North American "earth-diver" motive, viz., the diving into water for mud from which the earth is created.[13] At present, I am interested in indicating more elusive instances of dissemination. Thus, Mrs. Benedict has shown that in Eastern North America and the Plains a revelation is normally sought by fasting and even torture, but that in the Ultramontane area a different idea occurs widely, viz., the conception of the vision "as un-sought, involuntary, a thing of predisposition"; and she further indicates that that is precisely the attitude among the Koryak and, she might have added, other Siberians.[14] Another feature that may be mentioned is the "berdache" custom, the notion that a man as a result of a ·psychic experience must change his sex and thereafter fulfill all the duties of a woman. This phenomenon has been amply described for the Chukchi in Bogoras's classical monograph and is attested for a great number of North American tribes, where religious associations may or may not be present. A similar usage has been reported from Borneo, and the question arises whether we are dealing with a phenomenon calling for an historical interpretation or with one rooted in a general tendency of human groups to produce a certain proportion of aberrant individuals. That an abnormality of this type might be regarded with more or less awe and thus be linked with supernaturalism, seems plausible enough. A satisfactory answer to this query, however, will be possible only when the distribution of the trait is more definitely known.

Finally—though I should not like to suggest that additional parallels are not present in abundance—the reverential attitude assumed toward the bear on both sides of Bering Strait merits intensive comparative study. Characteristic of the Asiatic point of view is the Koryak festival in which the slain bear is entreated not to be angry and is equipped with traveling provisions, the object of the ceremony being to secure success in future hunting. Corresponding ideas exist among the Yukaghir and Lamut, while the Chukchi likewise stand in awe of the bear and commonly refer to him by such euphemisms as "grandfather" or "the old man." Now among people so far to the east as the Cree and Saulteaux about Hudson Bay Mr. Skinner has found elaborate practices connected with a slain bear: the bones are cleaned, the skull is painted, kept for months and finally put into a tree, and there are various taboos.   All this is conceived as a prayer and offering to the great chief of the bears who would otherwise prevent the Indians from killing any more members of the species. Even before killing his game, the bear-hunter would address him in a conciliatory speech.   Further west, the Assiniboin made offerings to a bear's head, praying for future success in bear-killing, and conciliatory prayers to the carcass are noted for the Shuswap, who also put the skulls of bears on tall poles.   An apologetic. statement is recorded for the Tlingit, who paint the grizzly's head.[15]

It is thus not at all improbable that central and even eastern North America can be connected as regards a whole series of religious traits with central and even western Siberia.   This does not mean that all the features in question originated in one area and were thence disseminated in a body to the other.   The simplicity of such an assumption has tempted many scholars, but historical phenomena are *not* simple and a *simpliste* view is more likely to be wrong than right.   We know that the American Indians borrowed many things from the Caucasian intruder, but we also know that the Caucasian obtained maize and tobacco from the aborigines.   We know that the Chinese formed a center for the diffusion of culture in Eastern Asia, but we also know,—thanks to Dr. Laufer,—that they borrowed more than one element from the ruder tribes to the north and to the southeast.   Sane historical reconstruction will not assume as a foregone conclusion that historical connection is equivalent to a steady irreversible stream of cultural traits from an active initiator to a passive recipient.

That theory breaks down even when material culture alone is considered and is obviously less tenable in matters of the spirit, where man is less dependent on the knowledge of technical devices.

It would of course be folly to deny the far-reaching influence of higher cultures on the beliefs of simpler peoples when specific evidence is available. A superb illustration has been cited by Kroeber.[16] Hepatoscopy, that is, divination by examining the liver of sacrificial animals, occurs in modern Indonesia, including Borneo and the Philippines; but it was a usage in ancient Babylonia possibly as early as 2,000 B.C. and spread thence both towards the east and the west. We know that Indonesia derived many cultural features from Hindu and Chinese sources; hepatoscopy is too specific a trait to be readily intelligible as due to a repeated invention; and our earliest record of the usage points to Western Asia. Hence we can safely infer that an ancient Babylonian practice survives in modern Malaysia.

It should be clear to the reader that what divides me from the diffusionist school of Father Schmidt is not a denial of diffusion nor even parsimony in the use of the principle of historical connection, whether in point of space or of time. The difference lies merely in my insistence on an incomparably greater difficulty in the determination of what is fact in religion, on an incomparably greater complexity of the historical process itself than Father Schmidt seems willing to admit. Hence, I prefer to practice the historical method by tracing the distribution in time and space of traits with sharply defined individuality and to establish sequences where the distribution is spatially continuous or rendered plausible by documentary evidence or at least by known ethnographic principles; and the establishment of more ambitious schemes strikes me as distinctly premature.

REFERENCES

[1] Marett: IX, XXVI.

[2] Koppers, 1921: 145, 150, 168, 170.

[3] Witte *in* Anthropos, 1913: 1162.

[4] Radin, 1914 (b) : 357. R. F. Benedict: 46 f.

[5] R. F. Benedict: 20 sq.

[6] Skinner, 1915 (a): 182, 188. R. F. Benedict: 44 f., 74. Dumarest: 151-165.

[7] R. F. Benedict: 47. Dumarest: 170-175. Kroeber, 1916: 277.

[8] Walker: 163. Skinner, 1915 (b): 67. Speck: 132. Swanton, 1911: 80, 180. Lowie, 1922: 375, 380. Kroeber, 1922: 299. Sapir, 1907: 40. Stevenson: 393, 396, 414. Russell: 261. Boas, 1894: 205 sq. Morice: 206, 209. Haeberlin *in* Amer. Anth., 1918: 249-257. Boas, 1916: 475, 559, 561. Jenness: 172 f. Dumarest: 151-161. Densmore: 127 sq.

[9] Lublinski. Koppers, 1924: 173, 175.

[10] Bogoras: 463 sq. Czaplicka: 158, 282, 287.

[11] Skinner, 1915 (a) : 194 sq.

[12] Tylor, 1865: 275 sq. Gutmann: 158.

[13] Jochelson, 1905-1908: 351 f.

[14] R. F. Benedict: 27.

[15] Jochelson, 1905-1908: 88. Bogoras: 325. Skinner, 1911: 68 sq., 162 sq. Teit: 602. Lowie, 1909 (b) : 56. Swanton, 1908: 455.

[16] Kroeber, 1923: 209.

CHAPTER IX

HISTORY AND PSYCHOLOGY

SOMETIMES the historical and the psychological point of view are contrasted as if they were necessarily antithetical. Nothing is further from the truth. The psychological facts of religion are the most fundamental that a history of religion can deal with; without them, indeed, such a history would be well-nigh meaningless. On the other hand, it is equally true that an insight into the psychology of religious phenomena is impossible without reference to the conditions that preceded and accompanied them. This is seen forthwith when we consider some of the definitions by poets or philosophers that purport to penetrate the subjective aspects of religion without the drudgery of historical research. Place the Roman poet's saying that fear created the gods alongside of the divine beings described in the synthetic sketches. Did fear create the Crow visionary's equestrian patron who promises his "son" invulnerability in battle? It may indeed have led the American aborigines to worship the Thunder, but how could it have evoked the characteristic association with a bird? Fear is prominent enough among the Ekoi; but it is bound up primarily with their ideas of sorcery, to a lesser extent with their ghosts and Nimm, least of all with the greatest of their deities. It is quite true that their supernaturalism largely revolves about the practice of sorcery; but the specific ways of using it or averting its effects are not at all explained by the simple psychological motive of fear. The Polynesians, too, with their taboos and formalities were prey to religious dread; yet this emotion seems hopelessly inadequate to account for their system of beliefs and practices. We should not fare better if we substituted for the Roman epigram the German philosopher's "Der Wunsch ist das Wesen der Religion." The wish, like fear, can surely be detected in religion, but it quite fails to explain what we should like to understand, viz., the concrete diversity of religious phenomena. Why does a Crow try to secure his wishes by fast and prayer, an Ekoi by bloody sacrifice, a Maori by a sacred incantation? The high-sounding aphorism leaves us in the lurch. It and all its congeners seem to postulate that individual man reacts to the universe religiously in response to certain inborn instincts and in complete independence of time and space, whereas the most obvious illustrations from our own culture suffice to demonstrate the shallowness of such an assumption.

Thus, eliminating all controversial discussion as to the Gospel of St. John, let us examine for a moment its opening sentence: "In the beginning was the Word, and the Word was with God, and the Word was God." If we attach to the term "Word" its everyday English connotation, the meaning is nil, and we cannot picture its author as thus spontaneously voicing his religious sentiments. Certainly the instinct of fear and the craving for wish-fulfillment help us not a jot. It is otherwise when we turn from random psychologizing to history.

Our "Word" then turns out to be the equivalent of the Latin *Verbum,* Greek *Logos;* and this Greek term not merely designated a vocable but stood in Hellenic philosophical literature for the rational order of the universe, the rational principle immanent in the cosmos. Introduced by Heraclitus (ca. 500-450 B.C.) and adopted by the Stoics, the concept was assimilated by Philo, a Jewish thinker born in

Alexandria about 30 or 20 B.C., who absorbed features of Greek metaphysics while still retaining his faith in the God of the Old Testament. He harmonized the two views by characterizing the Logos as indeed a creative principle but as one subordinate to God. On the one hand, it appears as a mere faculty of God, by which He thought out the nature of the universe; on the other hand, as a being derived from God and carrying His influence into the world. Philo's Logos is of course not identical with that of the Gospel, where it is not a secondary but a second Divine Being, not an intermediary but a Mediator uniting divine and human nature in one person. Yet it is in a sense an anticipatory conception, and a conception identical with that of St. John but as yet unlabeled appears among his Christian predecessors, as when Jesus figures as an "image of the invisible God" (Ep. to Col., 1, 15), as his Son, "whom he hath appointed heir of all things, by whom also he made the worlds" (Ep. to Heb., 1, 1-2). As the *Catholic Encyclopedia* puts it, nothing was lacking but the name "Logos." In short, the initial sentence of the Fourth Gospel translates these earlier expressions into the nomenclature of Greek speculation, borrowing a term there used for a comparable concept. Without a knowledge of the historical relations of Hellenic to Western Asiatic thought, St. John's opening sentence remains a psychological enigma, but the puzzle is instantly solved when the historical facts are elucidated.

The same point could be demonstrated for other parts of the Johannine writings. An important purpose of them was to safeguard the Christian faith against the attacks of heretics, and specifically against the teachings of Gnosticism. Thus, St. John's assertion that a claim to sinlessness is erroneous seems to be not an abstract proposition laid down regardless of all temporal circumstances but a rebuke admin-

istered to the hostile faction that associated purity from sin
with the gnosis, or intuitive spiritual insight, characteristic
of their sect.[1]

But enough has been said to suggest the interdependence
of psychological and historical factors on higher levels of
civilization. In consonance with the plan of this work we
turn now to a fuller consideration of two remarkable examples of fairly well-known primitive cults, the Ghost Dance
of our Plains Indians, and the Peyote religion of the Winnebago of Wisconsin and Nebraska. Apart from illustrating
my main point, both are interesting as illustrations of a
proselytizing tendency that is on the whole very rare on the
primitive level.

The Ghost Dance

In 1890 a Martian visitor to the Teton (Western Dakota
or "Sioux") reservations of South Dakota might have summarized his outstanding impressions in some such terms as
the following:

At frequent intervals, usually once a week, these people
undergo solemn preparations for ceremonial activity. They
will fast for twenty-four hours, purify themselves at sunrise by a vapor bath, and are then decorated by some of their
great men, such as Short-bull or Sitting-bull, who paint each
person's forehead, face and cheeks with a circle, cross, or
crescent. Next every one dons a shirt likewise ornamented
with symbolic figures. Finally the whole community to the
number of several hundred adults gather round a tree hung
with streamers, cloth, feathers, and what not. The leaders are
seated at the foot of the tree, and before anything vital happens a young woman within the circle lets fly four bone-
headed arrows towards the cardinal directions and remains

standing by the tree with a redstone pipe extended toward the west. There follows a plaintive chant by the whole assembly, whereupon food is passed and shared by every individual. Then at a signal by the leaders all rise, sing the initial song, standing motionless with hands stretched out toward the west, and join hands. Soon other songs are intoned, the dance begins, and the steps are accelerated till the performers are going round at topspeed, bodies swaying and hands tightly clasping the neighbors'. Now a woman with hair disheveled, staggers from the ring, panting, groaning wildly, and waving her arms, and soon falls unconscious and twitching to the ground. Now a man follows suit, then a second woman, and still another. After a while possibly a hundred are lying on the ground. As each recovers from his swoon, he is brought to the center where he makes some statement to the master of ceremonies, who heralds it to the crowd. At last they all shake their blankets and disperse.

If our hypothetical Martian knows the language of his hosts or commands the services of an interpreter, these proclamations, together with the songs of the dancers and Shortbull's harangues to the crowd will give him some notion of what ideas are associated with the strange performance he is witnessing. The Indians are hoping to be reëstablished as supreme rulers of the country. Their white oppressors are to be overwhelmed,—smothered by a terrific landslide or destroyed by whirlwinds; their firearms will be powerless against the Teton, whose painted shirts render them invulnerable. The spirits of all the dead Indians are returning to reinhabit the earth and are driving immense herds of buffalo before them. The dancers who have fallen into a trance see visions in earnest of this glorious destiny. The maiden over there has seen her dead mother and is now imploring her to return and tend her orphaned infant. That

man has taken part once more in an old-fashioned buffalo
hunt and beheld the scouts dashing back to proclaim the
sighting of a herd. Yonder hag has helped in making pemmi-
can after a successful chase. A dozen men and women have
seen the spirit of a deceased kinsman, who suddenly vanished in the guise of a beast or bird. But in order to see
the spirits and bring them back for good, and to destroy the
enemy, it is necessary to dance the Ghost Dance and to dis-
card the gewgaws and trappings of the white man.

Now, how much of all this is amenable to a simple psychological interpretation? Very, very little. Of course, certain
general motives are involved here as they are in every human activity. Naturally enough, men do long to see their
departed kin and resent the intrusions of foreign invaders.
But such generalities not only leave the greater part of the
story unexplained, but become progressively less illuminating
as our visitor extends his inquiries in time and space. Why
has the desire for union with departed relatives never been
voiced by the Teton prior to 1890, at least, never in comparable fashion? Why are they rising in armed rebellion
against the United States, while the Arapaho and Cheyenne
are content to leave the destruction of the whites to the
supernatural powers of the universe, nay, even deprecate the
use of the painted shirt because it is a symbol of war? Why
are the pipe and the dancers' hands extended toward the
west? Is it perchance because that is the home of the setting
sun and the land of the dead? (Our visitor may have fa-
miliarized himself with the theories of sublunary mytholo-
gists.) These questions and many others are unanswerable
or answerable only in demonstrably incorrect fashion so
long as we conceive of the Ghost Dance as a direct religious
response by such and such an individual or tribe. But they

can be illuminated at once if we resort to the sane method
of historical reconstruction. Let us begin with the last-mentioned query.

The pipe and the dancers' hands are extended towards the
west because it is from that direction, viz., from Nevada,
that the Teton have received the new ceremony and its
doctrine, which was promulgated about the beginning of
1889 by Wovoka ("Jack Wilson") of the little-known Paviotso tribe, otherwise known as the Northern Paiute. It
seems that at the time of a solar eclipse, probably on Jan-
uary 1, 1889, Wovoka fell asleep during the daytime and
was taken up to the other world, where he saw God and all
the dead of long ago, who were happy and young, playing
at their old games and engaged in their old occupations in a
land of joy and plenty. After showing him everything, God
bade him return with a message of peace, good-will and
moral exhortation. If the people obeyed instructions, they
were to be reunited with their dead friends. They were to
practice the dance revealed to Wovoka in his vision. "By
performing this dance at intervals, for five consecutive days
each time, they would secure this happiness to themselves
and hasten the event." Finally he was given control over
the elements by means of five songs, each with a distinctive
effect on the atmosphere.

The first point of contrast with the Teton variant of the
cult that strikes us in Wovoka's revelation is the genial attitude assumed towards the whites. This may indeed have
been modified in occasional audiences as a concession to Indians from hostile tribes, but everything goes to show that
primarily Wovoka brought a gospel of universal brotherhood. This is borne out not only by his statements to Mr.
Mooney, which might be construed as designed to curry

favor with a white man, but by the report of an early Chey-enne delegate, which must be considered free from this source of adulteration:

> He also told us that all our dead were to be resurrected; that they were all to come back to earth. . . . He spoke to us about fighting and said that was bad and we must keep from it; that the earth was to be all good hereafter, and we must all be friends with one another. . . . He told us not to quarrel or fight or strike each other, or shoot one another; that the whites and Indians were to be all one people.

Wovoka's friendliness, or at least freedom from fanatical hatred, for the whites is further indicated by his attitude toward the elements of our material culture. While the Teton made a deliberate attempt to dispense with the enemy's artifacts, even to the point of not using beads for decorative purposes, the Paviotso prophet did not scruple to wear good trade clothes and a white man's hat.

Another point of considerable interest is that, at least occasionally, Wovoka pretended to be Christ returning after hundreds of years to renew the world, which was getting too old, and to instruct mankind once more.

All this is quite intelligible from Wovoka's antecedents. As a young lad he began to work for a white farmer, David Wilson, and because of his close attachment to the family, he was dubbed "Jack Wilson." Through this contact he evidently acquired not only a smattering of English but also some notions of Christianity, possibly enlarged by other white acquaintances; and these associations explain both certain specific features in the original Ghost Dance code and also its freedom from racial antipathy.

Why the Teton so strangely altered the harmless conceptions of Wovoka, will be discussed below. For the present it is important to note that we have not yet ascended to the fountainhead of the Ghost cult. Wovoka had a forerunner in the person of his possible father and probable kinsman Tävibo, whose appearance dates back to about 1870. As to his precise doctrine, especially as regards the prospective destruction of the whites, there is conflicting evidence. But he certainly went into trances and declared that the spirits of the dead were about to return to earth, and that game animals together with the ancient life were to be restored. In one version he is even credited with a definitely ethical doctrine. However this may be, there is manifestly a historical connection between the elder and the younger of the two related prophets, and the Ghost Dance of the Plains tribes is thus ultimately traceable to the preachings of a Paviotso antedating their adoption of the ceremony by nearly twenty years. Here the question naturally obtrudes itself, why the Teton, instead of waiting for Wovoka, did not welcome the earlier Messianic teaching.

Before attempting to solve this problem, it will be worth while noting a point that eluded Mr. Mooney. It was not by sheer whim or accident that Wovoka set the period of the dance at *five* days and acquired *five* songs for controlling the weather. As no reader of that half-educated Paviotso, Sarah Winnemucca, can fail to observe, five is the mystic number of her tribe as definitely as four is that of the Plains area. Hence, in so far as the Prairie tribes adopted the idea, they were acting under the prestige suggestion of an alien leader, who was himself quite spontaneously bowing to the accepted folkways of his own people.

When we set side by side the beliefs and observances that constituted the Ghost cult of the Paviotso with those characteristic of the Teton variant, the differences are more striking than the resemblances. Let us turn first of all to two

closely connected queries: Why did the Teton fail to adopt
the gospel of 1870 when they espoused with such ardor the
gospel of 1889? And why did they alter not merely lesser
details, but the very spirit of Wovoka's teaching? In order
to solve these problems it is necessary to consider the change
in outward circumstances effected among the Western Sioux
during the intervening periods. In 1870 they were still able
to subsist in large measure on the products of the chase; by
1889 the virtual extinction of the buffalo had reduced them
and neighboring tribes to a precarious economic existence.
But the Teton were worse off than other Plains Indians because of a variety of special conditions. Not only had they
lost their favorite game animal, but for two successive years
they had suffered a failure of crops, had seen their livestock depleted by disease, and their Government rations materially reduced, so that they were literally threatened with
starvation. Add to this a series of epidemics that wrought
havoc in their midst, the chafing of a nation of warriors
under the encroachments of whites, the recollection of recent
conflicts with the Government and of various grievances
against their official guardians: and the intense emotional
stress predisposing a people to yearn for deliverance from
their ills is amply accounted for. In 1870 all these conditions were either lacking or much less acute, and the soil was
therefore but indifferently prepared for the reception of a
Messianic faith. But even apart from the inevitable difference in psychological attitude, there were circumstances that
would greatly impede the rapid dissemination of Tävibo's
teachings: the means of transportation that enabled delegates
from a thousand miles away to make their long pilgrimages
to Wovoka were still in their infancy, and the number of
educated Indians who might spread knowledge of a new
revelation in Nevada by writing to remote tribes was ex-

tremely small. It is not at all unlikely that in Tävibo's day not a single Teton had ever heard of the Paviotso. But even if the Paviotso were known, their ability to propagandize the proud Plains Indians in a relatively normal state was more than problematical. Could anything good come out of the country of the seed-gathering kinsmen of the "Bad Lodges," as even the more eastern Shoshoneans were contemptuously designated on the Prairie? It was otherwise with the Teton when decimated by disease, deprived of their livelihood, and incensed against the oppressor to the point of clutching at any hope of salvation.

With this major difference of initial attitude interpreted, various special features are directly explicable from a knowledge of Dakota ethnography. When the Teton introduced decorated shirts to ward off the enemy's bullets, they were merely, as Wissler has demonstrated, reviving the hoary custom of averting darts by the designs on shields, for in either case the protective virtue was believed to lie in the decoration, supposedly revealed in each instance by a supernatural power. Why did the Dakota, unlike the originators of the ceremony, begin with a sweat-bath? Because while among the Paviotso the sudatory was of little significance, the Teton regarded it as a regular preliminary to any rite dedicated to the major gods. Why did the Dakota erect a tree in the middle of the circle when no such feature appeared in Nevada? Probably because in two of their greatest festivals, the Sun Dance and the Round Dance, a tree was erected in the middle of the site. Again, the visions of buffalo, scouting-parties, and pemmican-making were faithful reflections of normal Plains Indian life that were manifestly impossible to natives of the Basin area. The departure of spirit visitants in animal shape is once more a trait highly characteristic of Dakota visions generally but never recorded for the Paviotso. In this connection another difference may be noted: while in Nevada the Prophet himself was the only one to go into a trance, the Teton and some other Plains tribes developed the mass ecstasies described above, another possible influence of the Sun Dance pattern.

As for the Christian elements of Wovoka's revelation, they completely evaporated on Dakota soil. There is no trace there of the ethical doctrines proclaimed by the Prophet. Already familiar through contact with missionaries with the notion of the crucified Christ, the Teton did not indeed spurn it but subordinated it to their own desires, corrupting it into the conception of an avenger of their wrongs. He merely served the function of any one of their own guardian spirits. Indeed, he was very far from supplanting the figures of their pantheon; the protective shirt designs recorded by Wissler demonstrate the old reliance on Sun, Thunderbird, and their mates.

In short, the Teton Ghost Dance involved essentially the assimilation of a single novel idea, that of the returning dead and the restoration of the old-fashioned life, in consonance with the preëxisting Teton system of religion; and the total result was applied to the solution of the critical situation in which they then found themselves.

This last statement may be extended to other tribes. Though not animated by the fanatical hatred for the whites nourished by the Western Dakota, the Arapaho, Cheyenne, and Kiowa—to mention only a few cases—had enough grounds for discontent in the inevitable conflicts with the intruders to welcome a revelation that promised freedom from their yoke. They were ready to accept the leadership of an alien prophet, nay, in their exaltation might raise him to divine dignity and invest with a halo of sanctity even such trivialities as the ochre he used to decorate the faces of dancers, or might attach veritably sacramental value to piñon nuts from Nevada, which in that country were a common enough article of diet. It was indeed possible for the Ghost Dance to supersede all the older ceremonies of the Cheyenne and Arapaho,—but only because they largely retained the ancient ceremonial *pattern,* automatically molding the new cult into harmony with it. Seven was one of the mystic numbers of the Arapaho; and the apostle of that tribe would ordain seven priests, or seven of each sex, to superintend the dance. It had been customary to make ceremonial pipe-offerings to the sun, the earth, the fire, and the four cardinal points, and this usage was followed in Arapaho song rehearsals. In Plains Indian theory every mode of decoration for a ceremony was the result of inspiration, and the Ghost Dancers strictly adhered to this conception. A certain flat pipe was the Arapaho holy of holies, and it held its place despite the new cult, entering into some of the new chants. The Thunderbird was one of the great figures in Plains Indian religion, and so far from abjuring it, the Ghost Dancers frequently wore its effigy on their heads. In short, the Plains Indians gave up next to nothing that was really vital in their old faith; and what they adopted could be easily made to fit into the system of inherited belief. The basic conception of a revelation from a supernatural power was one of the most deep-rooted traditions of their culture. Whether Wovoka was himself divine or merely the recipient of divine blessings, there was nothing shocking to their sense of verisimilitude in his dispensation of miraculous favors. Since the quest of a vision was practically universal, at least among the men of the Plains area, the striking fact that many individuals experienced visions, which in Nevada were restricted to the Prophet himself, is at once intelligible. It was natural for the Pawnee shamans to interpret all the relevant phenomena as merely revivals of the traditional type of revelations with a mere modification of content; and there is little doubt that that was essentially the view held throughout the region. Even the extensive employment of hypnotism in some of the tribes had its parallel in earlier practices. Of the Crow we know that the conductor of the Sun Dance would deliberately put the pledger of the ceremony into a trance if mere dancing before the sacred doll failed to produce the desired result; and similar customs were doubtless found among neighboring tribes as well.

Let us now revert once more to the basic question, in how far the Teton cult as practiced in 1890 is intelligible apart from the historical setting described above. In other words, in how far could any individual separated from those specific conditions be expected to express his relations to the supernatural in like fashion? The answer is, Not at all. Even disregarding all matters of ritual detail, we cannot fail to recognize that the receptiveness toward Wovoka's message and its peculiar elaboration with the stressing of the trance idea, were directly dependent on the Plains Indian worldview. In the Ghost Dance as it developed in the Prairie region possibly three factors stand out above the rest,—the return of the buffalo, the return of the dead, and the destruction of the whites. Of these, the first and last were *in principle* of old standing. Rites for luring the herds of game animals towards the encampments in times of famine were prominent among most of the Plains groups. Similarly, the destruction of the enemy through supernatural sanction was a well-established principle, so that no Crow war party was organized without a corresponding revelation. The economic plight of the Plains people was only a particularly accentuated instance of a situation with which they had often had to contend in the old days; and the whites were only a particular type of especially obnoxious enemy. Even as early as 1881, eight years before Wovoka's name had traveled eastward, a Kiowa shaman had sought to recall the buffalo, prescribing to his people a mode of ceremonial conduct revealed in a dream. In 1887 the Crow prophet Wraps-up-his-tail laid claim to a vision that would enable him to drive the whites from the country. In the same year a second Kiowa shaman not only pronounced himself heir to his forerunner's powers but declared that since the whites had caused the destruction of the buffalo he would destroy them all.

There was a Plains prehistory, as it were, to the Ghost Dance, and that prehistory made the cult different from what it would otherwise have been anywhere else in the universe.

But is not at least the longing for the deceased a phenomenon of universal occurrence and a human motive that requires no historical interpretation? Undoubtedly, but alas! it fails to explain the case at issue. For that supposedly abiding motive had never before produced the conception of a re-peopling of the world by the spirits of the dead. The Plains Indians were for the most part conspicuously little interested in the hereafter, and it required the suggestion of Wovoka, established and fostered through the circumstances already sketched, to implant his eschatology among these tribes. In other words, a Teton unaffected by Wovoka's evangelists might have yearned for a sight of the dead in 1890 as he might have done in 1790 without more than dreaming of a visit to the land of spirits. If in 1890 such dream experiences were linked with the expectation of a definite reunion, not through the dreamer's journey to the dead but through their reëntrance into this world, it was simply because by historical accident the gospel of Wovoka, itself the resultant of Paviotso and Caucasian culture, that is, of another historical accident, had reached Dakota territory.[2]

THE PEYOTE CULT

An excellent illustration of my thesis is provided by the history of the Peyote cult, which in several of our Western tribes has manifested a strong tendency to supersede the ancient ritualism. The peyote, incorrectly called "mescal," is a species of small cactus that grows along the lower Rio Grande and in Mexico. It resembles a radish in size and shape and has a white blossom, which is displaced by a tuft of white down. North of the Mexican boundary only the top is used, being sliced and dried to form the "button," while in Mexico the whole of the plant is sliced, dried and used in decoction. The Peyote worship centers in the eating of the button or drinking of its infusion. Professor Kroeber, who partook of peyote among the Arapaho, thus describes its effects:

It affects the heart, produces muscular lassitude, is a strong stimulant of the nervous system, and has a marked effect on the general feeling of the person, giving the impression of stimulating especially the intellectual faculties. In most cases it produces visions of a kaleidoscopic nature. Its emotional effect varies greatly, being in some cases depressing or intensely disagreeable; in others, which are the more frequent, producing quiet but intense exaltation. There is little subsequent reaction.

Now in perhaps the majority of cases this modern faith clearly combines Christian elements (including such features as Bible-reading, testimony, puritanical ethics) with the adoration of the cactus plant. Yet it is not a concise historical formula any more than a psychological formula that really sheds light on the psychological processes involved, but only a painstaking consideration of each step in the historical development, such as has been furnished by Dr. Paul Radin for the Winnebago.[3]

Since the cactus in question is indigenous only in the South, the Winnebago naturally derived its cult from that direction. John Rave, who introduced the new faith among his people, had learned to eat peyote while visiting an Oklahoma tribe in 1893-94. He was a member of the important Bear sib, but personally had a bad character as a shiftless drunkard. When visiting in the South he was in a very unhappy frame of mind, for he had recently lost his wife and his children. At the invitation of his hosts, he ate peyote and saw some horrible monsters that threatened to devour or spear him. To quote his own words:

There seemed to be no possible escape for me. Then suddenly it occurred to me, "Perhaps it is this peyote that is doing this thing to me?" "Help me, O medicine, help me! It is you who are doing this and you are holy! It is not these frightful visions that are causing this. I should have known that you were doing it. Help me!" Then my suffering stopped. "As long as the earth shall last, that long will I make use of you, O medicine!"

Rave ate more peyote and saw God and the morning-star, also his dead wife and children and other kinsfolk, and all seemed well. Then he ejaculated, "Ah! Peyote, you are holy. All that is connected with you I should like to know; for now I first realize what holiness is."

On his return he cured himself of a disease of old standing and likewise his new wife, who had also suffered from the same affliction. He further treated several other people with the aid of the peyote. Yet in the beginning, despite his propagandist fervor, the cult spread slowly, embracing only Rave's immediate family. But after four or five years there was a marked increase in membership and with it the apparently spontaneous development of an organization with a leader and four deputies. Towards the traditional Winnebago faith Rave's initial attitude was that of passive indifference, but for various reasons—doubtless in part owing to the unreceptiveness of the conservative element—this changed into violent antagonism.

At this point a fundamental innovation was introduced by another personality. Hitherto the faith had been essentially of aboriginal cast with possibly a slight tinge of Christian ethics. Rave, it must be remembered, was an illiterate and hence incapable of reading the Scriptures. But now there appeared on the scene a Carlisle graduate named Albert Hensley, who revolutionized the cult by introducing Bible readings and making Rave baptize the members with an infusion of peyote. Hensley, who was an epileptic, experienced frequent trances with glorious visions of Heaven and Hell, which he subsequently interpreted in terms of the Revelation. At the same time he explained the Bible in terms of the peyote, assuming the position that the Bible was intelligible only through the supernatural cactus. Rave himself preserved an attitude of indifference towards the Scriptures. He was quite willing to accede to the introduction of Christian features if craved by his flock. To him the peyote was the end-all and be-all of the cult, the source of all blessings: if a peyote-worshiper reckoned the Bible among the life-values, then naturally the peyote as the fountainhead of everything precious would open up avenues for its comprehension that otherwise would remain closed.

Subsequently a schism was precipitated by Hensley's puritanism. He objected to the appointment of a deputy leader of notorious character, while Rave insisted that official position in the organization was independent of moral character. Hensley seceded with a number of adherents, but the majority of peyote-eaters remained under Rave's guidance and even some of the dissenters returned to the fold. However, a new competitor arose when in 1912 Jesse Clay returned from the Arapaho and introduced *their* form of the Peyote ritual, thus establishing a distinct sect, in which Christian symbolism is conspicuous while Winnebago conceptions, at the time of Dr. Radin's inquiries, were wholly absent. It is important to note that even in Rave's congregation the increasing number of young educated Indians tended to preserve the Christian elements due to Hensley, despite the latter's withdrawal. Our authority notes, indeed, a virtually complete adoption of Christianity by some of the members balanced by the relapse of others into paganism, while many had lost their ardor for Rave's cult. The subsequent fortunes of the Peyote sects of the Winnebago in the last decade have remained unstudied.

Now when we examine the phenomena outlined above we find that here, too, any attempt to understand their subjective aspect is doomed to failure if divorced from the historical facts. To begin with the most recent innovation, Jesse Clay's separatist movement is psychologically in a quite different category from Hensley's: learning from the Arapaho a form of the cult diverging from Rave's, to whose influence he had apparently remained immmune, he naturally became to all intents and purposes the prophet of a new creed rather than a dissenter from an established one. Again, Hensley's innovations are not spontaneous products of the religious sentiment but represent a quaint attempt to unify two currents of thought that had come powerfully to affect his mystic's soul,—Christianity and the Peyote complex.

Without alien contact of a specific sort the former influence could never have been exerted, and as a matter of fact it was practically non-existent for Rave, the illiterate founder of the Winnebago cult. It is in considering how Rave and his early followers elaborated the "Peyote cult" that the indispensability of a historical point of departure for psychological understanding appears most clearly. For the attitude of these devotees is unintelligible except on the basis of the traditional Winnebago faith. Unlike the later prophet Clay, Rave was not the passive recipient of an alien creed but automatically transformed what he accepted by casting it into the traditional Winnebago form. The peyote plant had cured him, had put him into a state of exaltation, and he forthwith ranged it in the category of sacred substances with supernatural curative powers, assuming towards it the typical attitude of a Winnebago shaman. It was customary to offer tobacco to supernatural entities, and accordingly he offered tobacco to the peyote. There were five leaders in the ancient Medicine Dance, and accordingly the new society had a leader with four deputies. The old cult societies derived their origin from the revelation granted in a fasting experience, and consequently even Hensley, Christianized as he was, could not free himself from the influence of this tribal pattern. Thus we find once more that the path to psychology lies through history. Only when we know the Winnebago heritage of belief and ceremonial, can we appreciate the psychological reactions of the peyote-eaters, whether as a group or as single individuals.

REFERENCES

[1] *Catholic Encyclopedia:* VIII, 437, 442; IX, 329. Scott. Schmiedel, 1906 (a) and (b).

[2] Mooney: 701-704, 706 f., 764-842, 894-926, 958-1075.

[3] Radin, 1914 (a) ; id., 1923: 388 sq. Bartlett: 160 sq.

CHAPTER X

WOMAN AND RELIGION

IF we were asked whether women or men are the more religious, most of us should unhesitatingly answer in favor of women and should presumably · cite their proverbially greater emotionalism as an explanation. On the Continent —say, in Spain—it is a familiar enough thing to have women go to mass while their free-thinking brothers and husbands never enter a church, and in Anglo-Saxon countries pietism or any obtrusively religious or ethical reform movement is more definitely associated with the feminine psyche,—and this irrespective of the fact that in most denominations women are barred from the positions of priest or minister. But when we survey the corresponding phenomena of ruder cultures, the significant fact appears that in various regions women are not only ineligible for office but seem to be shut out from all religious activity. In most Australian tribes it would be death for a woman to witness the initiation procedures; corresponding conditions have been described for New Guinea and Melanesia and have a sporadic distribution elsewhere. Does this mean that women in such areas are really debarred from religious manifestations? And if not, how do they display the relevant sentiments? To what extent are their disabilities founded in some innate peculiarity, how far are they due to a specific cultural environment? And how do woman's subjective reactions differ from man's?

At the present stage of our knowledge some of these

questions are more easily asked than answered. If in spite of our ignorance a special chapter is devoted to the topic, it is in order to direct attention to an interesting but neglected field of inquiry. On the last-mentioned problem in particular I have ransacked the literature in vain for even a shred of enlightening material. One turns naturally to those regions in which women are least hampered by social conventions. Thus, among the Northwestern Californians the part of shaman is most commonly played by the female sex, and Professor Kroeber has secured the confessions of one of these medicine-women. Yet when one analyzes her statements, the personal factor seems wholly submerged in the characteristic tribal (Yurok) trait of greed for money: she is obsessed with the desire of acquiring wealth through her practice, precisely as her fellows, male or female, are in the ordinary business of life: "So whatever I did I spoke of money constantly . . . I said to myself: 'When people are sick, I shall cure them if they pay me enough.'" From such stereotyped longings of avarice it is impossible to distill the faintest flavor of distinctively feminine character.

Among the Crow there are relatively few restrictions because of sex. Women, as well as men, have the right to seek visions and if they avail themselves more rarely of the privilege it is because in so intensely martial a culture the craving for success in war is the most usual impetus to a vision-quest. In the important ceremonial society concerned with the sacred Tobacco there are no offices for which members are ineligible because of sex, and the part played by women in the dances is a conspicuous one. Of the women I knew, Muskrat was probably the most positive personality that figured in religious activities. She was very well informed and intelligent, but inordinately vain, and her attempts at self-aggrandizement were some-

times ridiculed by her fellow-tribesmen—in her absence.
She had been Mixer in the Weasel chapter of the Tobacco
society, and to the resentment of some old people she continued to exercise the duties of the office after having sold
the prerogative. She herself explained that she had only
sold part of it and at all events remained a dominant figure
in the organization. I repeatedly interviewed her and
obtained much interesting information but nothing that
would suggest a positive sex difference. Thus, she had a
revelation of a particular tobacco-mixing recipe such as any
man might have secured; on another occasion a weasel
entered her body, a not uncommon experience of either
sex; precisely like any other member of the Tobacco organization she adopted new members; and again like other
Crow Indians with corresponding revelations she exercised
specific functions, such as charming an unfaithful husband
or doctoring broken bones. Her taboos also wholly re-
semble those of other visionaries in principle.[1]

It is of course conceivable—though hardly a priori probable—that no sex differences exist. On the other hand,
it is possible that our field methods have hitherto been too
gross to sense such elusive differences as may occur; and at
all events a resolute attempt in that direction—if possible,
by a woman anthropologist—would be eminently worth
while.

If very little can be said on the subjective side, I think
we can definitely dispose of a plausible misconception based
on objective observations. It does not follow that women
are excluded from the religious life of the community because their social status is inferior or because certain spectacular features are tabooed to them. In the striking Ekoi
case we found that women were indeed prohibited from
touching a strong *njomm* or seeing a bull-roarer or a stilt-

walking exhibition and from ever intruding into an Egbo meeting; but by way of compensation they ·exclude men from the Nimm sorority and through that cult play no mean part in tribal ritual.   Elsewhere in Africa the legal subordination of women in no wise interferes with very important religious offices.   Among the Zulu, women no less than men detect sorcerers, and the same is reported for the Thonga, where Mholombo, whom M. Junod not unnaturally describes as "an extraordinarily acute woman," would confound evil magicians, work such miracles as walking on the water, and interpret the divining-bones through the agency of a spirit possessing her.   Other women have been known to become diviners, though not so often as men, and to be possessed by ancestral ghosts; and though normally the eldest brother acts as priest in ancestral worship the duty may also devolve on the eldest sister.[2]

The condition characteristic of these African tribes is of very wide distribution: that is to say, women may not participate so frequently or so fully as men, yet their rôle is far from negligible in the religious life.   For instance, the highest reaches of Chukchi shamanism—those connected with the practice of ventriloquism—are inaccessible to the female sex, yet lesser forms of inspiration are more commonly bestowed on women than otherwise.   In the Andaman Islands women do not join in ordinary dances, though they attend to form the chorus; but they have a mourning dance of their own and act as shamans, though less frequently than men.   In Polynesia, again, all kinds of taboos hedged in the life of the women: in Hawaii they were obliged to eat food apart from the men and were not even allowed to enter a man's eating-house prior to the abolition of the old rule by a decree of Kamehameha II in 1819;

they were not admitted to the sacred college of the Maori of New Zealand and might not travel by boat in the Marquesas. But in spite of Malo's statement that in Hawaii the majority of them "had no deity and just worshiped nothing," his own description tells of their worship of female deities; and in Tonga inspirational dreams of consequence were not denied to women.[3]

It is, however, particularly noteworthy that even in regions where some rigid penalty seems wholly to eliminate women from ceremonial participation closer scrutiny reveals a very different state of affairs. Oceania and Australia furnish stock examples of the former, but the less obtrusive assertion of women in religious life has not been adequately recognized. Thus, among the Tami of New Guinea we have seen that while the female sex was excluded from the initiation ceremony and terrorized by its performers, women normally call the spirits of recently deceased tribesmen. An equally striking illustration is provided by Australia. Among the Euahlayi of New South Wales the inner mysteries of the initiation ritual also remain a sealed book to women, nay, even the usual name, Byamee, of its divine inaugurator is concealed from them. But this does not prevent them from praying to him under another designation, as did that remarkable old shaman, Bootha, whose portrait has been so vividly painted by Mrs. Parker. When probably well over sixty, she absented herself from camp in order to grieve over the loss of a favorite granddaughter. After a long seclusion in more or less demented condition she returned a full-fledged medicine-woman. Henceforth she was able to summon and interrogate the guardian spirits acquired; with their aid she performed miraculous cures and produced rain at will, evidently exerting a considerable influence on the aborigines in the vicinity and apparently in no way inferior to her male colleagues.[4]

An American instance may be added for good measure. The Northern Athabaskans generally are hardly conspicuous for their chivalrous attitude toward women, and the Anvik, who inhabit an Alaskan village some hundred and twenty-five miles inland, form no exception. Even from infancy a girl is carefully watched lest she step on anything lying on the floor that might affect the welfare of her family. "The spirit of the boy is stronger than the spirit of the girl, so a boy may step where he pleases." As the child grows older, restrictions multiply, especially from puberty on, nor has the girl a will of her own in the choice of a mate. Again, there is discrimination in the ceremonial use of masks: men may wear female masks, but no woman is allowed to put on a man's mask. Yet, all these taboos to the contrary notwithstanding, the weaker sex is by no means wholly debarred from participation in the religious activities of the community. Some women own sacred songs and chant them at the tribal festivals. There are female shamans who treat sick members of their sex, and the wives of shamans are favored to the extent of being allowed to sing at the more important dances and to inherit something of their deceased husbands' supernatural gifts. Individual cases are known of women who gained great influence.

Cries-for-salmon's mother is a woman with power. She has many strong songs. Her father had been a great hunter, with wolverene and bear songs. She is always consulted in the village, she knows her power, and there is no one to check her or to talk about her.[5]

This notable trio of instances establishes a sort of a fortiori conclusion. Evidently even marked sexual disabilities do not exclude women from exercising religious functions of social significance, and there is not the slightest indication that their limitations are the consequence of innate incapacity or that a lack of emotional interest in religion has been engendered by compulsory disuse. As a matter of fact, as soon as outward pressure is somewhat relaxed the sexes share quite equitably in ceremonial duties. This is clear even from the African cases cited above, and the case for North America could be easily strengthened by additional instances. Among the Plains Indians the custody of sacred objects, such as shields, was regularly entrusted to a favorite wife; membership in secret organizations was often open to women on equal terms with men; nay, they were even at times eligible to the highest ceremonial offices. To turn to another area, nothing could be fairer than the allotment of ritualistic privileges among the Bagobo of Mindanao, and indeed other natives of the Philippines. Old men offer sacred food, recount their exploits while holding the ceremonial bamboo poles they have cut, prepare for human sacrifices, perform magical rites, while old women conduct altar rites at the harvest, make offerings at shrines, and recite the accompanying prayers. If the men direct the ceremonial as a whole, it is virtually a feminine prerogative (as in New Guinea) to summon the spirits at a séance. Indeed, the women "direct many ceremonial details and are often called into consultation with the old men; they exercise a general supervision over the religious behavior of the young people." [6]

Where pronounced religious disabilities occur, I am inclined to impute them predominantly to the savage man's horror of menstruation. Lest this seem a fanciful suggestion, I offer by way of substantiation a part of the abundant evidence.

Among the Ila, a Bantu tribe of Rhodesia, a woman during her periodic illness is dangerous "and must be separated as far as possible from contact with her fellows." A man eating with her would lose his virility, and sick people would be most injuriously affected by her. She may not use the common fire or handle other people's pots or drink from their cups or cook or draw water for others. In Central Australia a menstruating woman is carefully avoided, while in Queensland she is secluded and must not even walk in a man's tracks. In the Torres Straits Islands investigators have found an "intense fear of the deleterious and infective powers of the menstrual fluid," and various taboos are imposed on the menstruant, who must live in seclusion, shun the daylight, and abstain from sea-food. Her Marshall Island sister dwells in a special menstrual hut, is limited to a prescribed diet, and is believed to exert an inauspicious influence.[7]

However, for no other region is the evidence so convincing as for America. One of the most illuminating reports is that of an eighteenth century observer among the Choctaw of Louisiana. Here the women at once left the house, hid from the sight of men, were not permitted to use the family fire lest the household be polluted, and under no condition were supposed to cook for other people. The French narrator, having once stumbled upon a menstruant, prevailed upon her to make him "some porridge of little grain," and after the arrival of the husband invited him to partake of the meal. At first the Choctaw unwittingly fell to eating, but suddenly grew suspicious and inquired for the cook.

. . . When I replied that it was his wife who had been my cook, he was at once seized with sickness and went to the door to vomit. Then, reëntering and looking into the dish, he noticed some red things in the porridge, which were nothing else than the skin of the corn, some grains of which are red. He said to me: "How have you the courage to eat of this stew? Do you not see the blood in it?" Then be began vomiting again and continued until he had vomited up all that he had eaten; and his imagination was so strongly affected that he was sick on account of it for some days afterward.

In intensity of reaction the Menomini of Wisconsin rival the Choctaw. A woman must use her own culinary utensils during her illness, and she must not touch a tree, a dog, or a child lest it die. She is not supposed to scratch herself with her fingers but with a special stick. As Mr. Skinner reports:

To this day many pagan Menomini positively refuse to eat in Christian houses for fear of losing their powers through partaking of food prepared by a woman undergoing her monthly terms.

The Winnebago go so far as to assert that sacred objects lose their power through contact with a menstruating woman.

If the Winnebago can be said to be afraid of any one thing it may be said it is this—the menstrual flow of women—for even the spirits die of its effects.[8]

In the Far West the same psychological attitude appears practically unchanged. A Blackfoot menstruant must keep away from sacred articles and from sick people: something would strike the patient "like a bullet and make him worse." What is particularly noteworthy is the diffusion of corresponding beliefs throughout the area of rudest culture. As late as 1906 I myself was able to observe the seclusion of Shoshoni women in Idaho, where abstention from meat was likewise imperative during the period. The same food taboo was observed by their kinsmen, the Paviotso of Nevada, who gave as a justification that if the women ate antelope flesh the game impounded in a drive would break through the enclosure. In north-central California the Shasta impose a special hut, the scratching-stick, strict food taboos, and the rule that the woman must not look at people or the sun or the moon. Should a woman be taken unexpectedly ill while at home,

all men leave at once, taking with them their bows, spears and nets, lest they become contaminated and thus all luck desert them.

Among the Chinook of the lower Columbia the adolescent girl is under rigorous restrictions.

She must not warm herself. She must never look at the people. She must not look at the sky, she must not pick berries. It is forbidden. When she looks at the sky it becomes bad weather. When she picks berries it will rain. She hangs up her towel of cedar bark on a certain spruce tree. The tree dries up at once. After one hundred days she may eat fresh food, she may pick berries and warm herself.

In subsequent catamenial periods she must not be seen by a sick person, nor must berries picked by her be eaten by the sick. Finally (though the list could be greatly enlarged),

there are the Northern Athabaskans. According to Father
Morice, "hardly any other being was the object of so much
dread as a menstruating woman," who ate only dried fish,
drank water through a tube, and was not allowed to live with
her male kin nor to touch anything belonging to men or related to the chase "lest she would thereby pollute the same,
and condemn the hunters to failure, owing to the anger of
the game thus slighted." More than a century ago Samuel
Hearne made corresponding observations among the related
Chipewyan: women in question lived apart in a hovel and
were not permitted to walk near a net or to eat the head of
an animal or cross the track where a deer head had lately been
carried,—and all this to ward off bad hunting luck. Quite
similar notions prevail among their fellow-Athabaskans, the
Anvik, of Alaska.[9]

It is not so easy to trace the distribution of such a trait in
the southern half of the New World, yet, thanks mainly to
Father Schmidt's indefatigable industry, we are in a position
to state positively that in one form or another the usage
extends all the way to Tierra del Fuego, being found in
southern Central America, Colombia, Guiana, Peru, Brazil,
Patagonia, and around Cape Horn. The descriptions are
not always so circumstantial as for North America. Thus,
from a Fuegian report I glean merely the imposition of a
puberty fast on girls. The Mundrucú added exposure to
smoke, the Paravilhana corporal punishment. Among the
Siusi the girl was under dietary restrictions, her hair was
cut, and her back was daubed with paint. The Arawak of
Guiana present the typical complex of seclusion, fire and food
taboos.[10] To what extent fuller knowledge of all these tribes
would bring ampler accounts, remains obscure. We should
like to know especially whether later menstruation is likewise
linked with definite regulations. But even in our present

state of ignorance it is proper to advance the hypothesis that some sort of menstrual taboo is a deep-rooted, an archaic element of American culture.

Let us now survey the remainder of the world. I have already pointed out that the sentiment underlying menstrual prohibitions exists in Oceania, Australia, and Africa. In the rudest tribes for which I can get evidence it likewise occurs, but not in the extreme form typical of, say, the Choctaw. The Andamanese do not insist on departure from the camp, but proscribe certain kinds of food for their alleged evil effects *on the woman*. Bushman practice, at least at the time of adolescence, conforms more closely to type: the adolescent is segregated in a tiny hut with a door closed upon her by her mother; she must not walk about freely nor look at the springbok lest they become wild; and when going out she must look down at the ground. On rules of subsequent periods I cannot find any data. Of the Paleo-Siberians, the Maritime Chukchi do not allow a menstruating woman to approach her husband; even her breath is impure and might contaminate him, destroying his luck as sea-hunter, nay, causing him to be drowned. Under similar circumstances, her Koryak sister must not tamper with her husband's hunting and fishing apparatus or sit on his sledge, while among the Yukaghir she is forbidden to touch the sacred drum.[11]

From the occurrence of the custom among the rudest peoples of the Old World—the Paleo-Siberians, Andamanese, Bushmen—and the rudest peoples of America, and its wide distribution on somewhat higher levels, we can draw the conclusion that menstrual restrictions are of great antiquity in the history of human culture, though probably not in the extreme form distinctive of many Indian tribes of Canada and the United States. Reverting now to my hypothesis that disabilities are correlated with the awe inspired by men-

struation, I should like to cite several facts by way of corroboration. Where the relevant taboos exist in mild form
or are lacking, sex discrimination seems to be likewise moderate. The Bagobo let women share in ceremonial life on a
footing of virtual equality and I cannot find evidence of menstrual restrictions. In the Andamans women do not ordinarily join in the dancing but attend, forming the chorus; and
quite similarly the Bushman women beat the drum and clap
their hands for the male dancers.[12] Still more interesting,
where the discrimination is intense, it is relaxed in old age:
old women enjoy privileges in Australia and New Guinea that
are denied to their younger sisters. The reason is not difficult to divine and is explicitly stated by a Winnebago informant:

At a feast . . . the old women, who have passed their climac-
teric, sit right next to the men, because they are considered the
same as men as they have no menstrual flow any more.

That is to say, before the menopause women are weird creatures, after the menopause they become ordinary human beings, though in many cases, no doubt, their former uncanni-
ness still in some measure clings to them. A fact otherwise
obscure can be explained from this angle. Why do the Chukchi, who close the highest grade of shamanism to women,
fail to bar male inverts who in every way dress and act as
women? Obviously because in their case the sentiments produced by the thought of menstruation are eliminated.

In closing the discussion of this topic I am painfully conscious of having contributed very little to a highly important
subject. But I hope the attempt to treat it as a distinct set
of problems will lead to more systematic research,—especially
in the field.

This is perhaps as good a place as any to express what little I have to say about a theory broached rather vociferously in some quarters, to wit, the view that religion is at bottom nothing but misunderstood erotic emotion. It must be obvious that two phenomena that exert so profound an influence on so many phases of human conduct must have certain points of contact. The simplest kind of interrelationship occurs where the gratification of erotic desire is merely one of the life-values, which accordingly like other life-values can be secured by an appropriate intercourse with the Extraordinary. Following the traditional technique of his tribe, a Crow will seek a vision, where a Bukaua mutters a spell and uses some magical charm. But these procedures, employed for a hundred other purposes, can obviously not be derived from a single, arbitrarily selected motive for their application.

There are, however, a group of other facts adduced by the adherents of the theory to prove the dependence of religious feeling on the sex instinct. I will follow the convenient summary provided by Mr. Thouless. It is asserted that adolescence is preëminently the period of religious conversion, hence religious experience is functionally related with the instinct that comes to maturity at this period. Secondly, religion employs the language characteristic of the expression of erotic passion. Finally, the theory assumes a special concern of religion with the suppression of normal sexual activity, and a compensatory reaction against such asceticism.

Viewing the question primarily from the ethnological angle, I find myself in substantial agreement with James and Thouless in rejecting the evidence as ludicrously inconclusive for the attempted demonstration.[13] Mystic experiences are indeed commonly sought and secured at the age of puberty but by no means exclusively so. Indeed, as Dr. R. F. Benedict has proved, several of the Plains Indian tribes regularly permitted the obtaining of a revelation in mature middle age, sometimes to the exclusion of the puberty fast.[14]   On the other hand, among the tribes of the Great Lakes the experience considerably antedated what could by the wildest stretch of the imagination be called adolescence.   Here, as everywhere, the psychological problem is complicated by the influence of cultural environment.   It is evidently a matter of social tradition whether the religious thrill is looked for and obtained at seven, at fifteen, or at forty.   Hence, it might be argued that these conventions artificially defer or accelerate the advent of religious emotion that "naturally" comes with the approach of adolescence.   But this would be an arbitrary assertion pending empirical confirmation.

The argument from religious phraseology seems weaker still.   It is true that a Crow visionary is greeted by his patron with the words "I adopt you as my son," and the associated ideas are undoubtedly those of the aid and protection the "son" is henceforth to receive from his "father."   But I am quite unable to see in this any adumbration of an occult "father-complex."   As James wisely remarks, religious sentiment simply utilizes "such poor symbols as our life affords," and he amply proves that digestive and respiratory concepts serve the same purpose of vivid representation as directly or indirectly amatory ones.   If we attach undue importance to the words used by man in his groping for an adequate expression of his thoughts and feelings, we may be driven to reduce the sex instinct to that of nutrition when a lover "hungers" for the sight of his sweetheart and charge him with a latent cannibalistic inclination which is at least improbable.

As for the repression and compensatory over-indulgence of the sex appetite, neither can be said to be characteristic of primitive religion. Special phenomena, appearing in restricted points of space and time, are here confounded with the universal essence of religion. The same applies to the orgies that are sometimes spectacular accompaniments of ceremonialism; interesting specimens of the ideas that *may* become associated with religious phenomena, they do not as a rule touch the core of religion. *That* must be sought where James looked for it, in "the immediate content of the religious consciousness," and I quite agree that "few conceptions are less instructive than this re-interpretation of religion as perverted sexuality."

REFERENCES

[1] Lowie, 1919: 119 sq.; id., 1922: 339 sq.

[2] Talbot: 21, 23, 25, 95, 225, 284. Shooter: 174-183. Junod: II, 377, 438, 444, 456, 466.

[3] Bogoras: 415. Brown: 129, 131, 176. Malo: 50-53, 112. Mariner: 262.

[4] Parker: 6, 8, 42-49, 59.

[5] Parsons, 1922: 337 sq.

[6] L. W. Benedict: 10, 76 sq., 193 sq.

[7] Smith and Dale: II, 26 f. Spencer and Gillen, 1904: 601. Roth, 1897: 184. Reports of the Cambridge Expedition: v, 196,, 201 sq. Erdland: 135.

[8] Swanton, 1918: 59. Skinner, 1913: 52. Radin, 1923: 136 f.

[9] Wissler, 1911, 29. Dixon, 1907: 457 sq. Boas, 1894: 246. Morice: 218. Hearne: 313 sq. Parsons, 1922: 344.

[10] Schmidt, 1913. Martius: I, 390, 631. Koch-Grünberg: 181. Roth, 1915: 312 f. Buschan: 217, 360.

[11] Brown: 94. Bleek and Lloyd: 76 f. Bogoras: 492. Jochelson, 1905-1908: 54; id., 1910: 104.

[12] Brown: 131. Bleek and Lloyd: 355.

[13] James: II. Thouless: 130 sq.

[14] R. F. Benedict: 49 sq.

CHAPTER XI

INDIVIDUAL VARIABILITY

USEFUL, nay indispensable, as is the historico-sociological point of view for an understanding of the individual's religious life, there are limits to its potency. The individual is not merged *completely* in his social milieu,—he reacts to it *as* an individual, that is, differently from every other group member. The cultural tradition of his people dominates him, but it is reflected in a distinctive fashion by each psyche. Were it otherwise, novel conceptions could never arise. It is reckoned one of the most epoch-making steps in the history of psychology that Galton investigated mind not in the abstract but in its varying manifestations among different personalities. For too long a time it has been customary to ignore corresponding differences in primitive peoples on the familiar principle that "all Chinamen look alike." Only in quite recent years men like Dr. R. R. Marett in England, Dr. W. D. Wallis in America, Fathers Wilhelm Schmidt and W. Koppers in Austria, have insisted that what holds among us also holds in ruder levels of culture.

In the following pages I make an unpretentious effort to furnish some illustrative material. The question involved is at bottom that of the *relation* of the individual to society. Sometimes no doubt personal idiosyncrasies seem to produce no effect on the life of the community; but they do not, for that reason, remain free from social entanglements. The extent to which they are free to assert themselves is itself a function of the social system in which they appear.

Even when we are bent on determining the individual mentality, we are thus obliged to examine constantly the social concomitants. It might appear at first blush that a basic phenomenon such as that direct communion with the supernatural which underlies all religion could be comprehended in purely psychological terms, that is, without reference to any social norms. The very fact, however, that a given individual shall be eligible for converse with supernatural powers is socially determined. The differences obtaining in this respect within a single continent have been clearly summarized by Mrs. Benedict. In the Plains area, as typified by the Crow, there is free access to the powers of the universe: "die Geisterwelt ist nicht verschlossen" to any one, hence all have at least potential personal contact with the divine; here, then, innate differences may correspond closely to the observed differences in religious behavior. But it is quite otherwise where, as in California, the prerogative of a guardian spirit or of vision-seeking is confined to a small group of shamans, who acquire their status by some such means as inheritance. Here, the majority are socially precluded from competition with "the vested interests," so to speak, and no sound conclusions could be drawn as to their inborn religious deficiencies by comparison with the shamanistic class.[1]

Even where the direct communion with superior beings is unrestricted, special cultural conditions complicate the individual's behavior. We found this to be true among the Crow, where such accepted notions as the mystic potency of the number four spontaneously affect the character of an experience, whatever may be the individual's mental characteristics. This automatic influence of the surrounding culture is all the more noteworthy because here there is no conscious attempt on any one's part to influence the would-be visionary's experiences. We are thus dealing with an a fortiori case. Among the Great Lakes Indians, such as the Ojibwa and Winnebago, the social factor plays so dominant a rôle as almost wholly to obscure and eliminate the individual nature of the experience.

The Winnebago youth's fasting experience is carefully tested by the elders, and if found wanting in any respect the youth has either to try again or give up.

We constantly read of how parents exhort boys to fast and fast long in order to acquire a blessing, how offerings of power deemed unsuitable by the elders are rejected at their behest in the hope of more favorable revelations, yet among the Menomini even this veto privilege is conventionally regulated and when an evil spirit has appeared a fixed number of times his blessing *must* be accepted. When we read how the Ojibwa Forever-bird was sent out to fast at the age of *five* and thereafter constantly urged to repeat the experience at intervals, it is obvious that no spontaneous psychological reaction can be expected under such external prompting and surveillance.

This is positively proved by Forever-bird's description of what happened to him after the powers had addressed him as their grandchild and expressed their good-will:

Everywhere roundabout was I conveyed; roundabout was I shown what the earth everywhere was like, and likewise the great deep. And when I was able to go without food for eight days, then was the time that I truly learned everything about how the sky looked.

Taken by itself, this might be accepted as a purely psychological experience. But when we turn to another man's fasting narrative, the following sentence strikes our eye:

Concerning all sorts of things did I dream,—about what was everywhere on earth did I dream; and about the sea, the suns, and the stars; and about all things in the circle of the heavens from whence blew the winds, did I dream. . . . By a great throng of the sky-people was I blessed; everywhere over the earth and on high was I conveyed by them, how it (all) looked I was shown, how it was everywhere in the circle of the heavens that I had dreamed about.

This, however, is not the only parallel. In a tale about a youth who over-dreamed he is represented as thus speaking to his father:

Already now have I really dreamed of everything. About how the whole earth looks, about how the winds repose from whence they blow, have I learned. And all kinds of doings have I dreamed of. And also about everything that is in the sky have I dreamed.

In short, cosmic exploration is an integral part of the conventional revelation pattern and is a recurrent feature simply because the tribal standard molds the suggestible tribesman's psychic experiences.[2]

The only possible meaning of an attempt to study individual differences should now be clear. We can never hope to see the individual displaying his inborn religious capacities in independence of his milieu. Nevertheless we can determine individual peculiarities by comparing the behavior of those exposed to like cultural norms: where the same environment provokes a different response, the reason may safely be sought in the respective individuals' original nature.

Sensory Types

When discussing Crow visions I briefly alluded to differences in the content of the supernatural revelation that seemed correlated with mental differences on the part of the recipients. Galton's relevant investigations of psychological variability among Britons are too well known to require detailed exposition here. Suffice it to say, that according to the latest authorities differences in intensity of memory images are fully established, while the theory of quite distinct sensory types has been practically abandoned.

In fact, it is now known to be very unusual for an individual to be confined to images of a single sense. Nearly every one gets visual images more easily and frequently than those of any other sense, but nearly every one has, from time to time, auditory, kinesthetic, tactile and olfactory images. So that the "mixed type" is the only real type, the extreme visualist or audile, etc., being exceptional and not typical.[3]

I know of no anthropologist who has made definite studies in this field among primitive tribes, with the solitary exception of Professor Brown, who found that the majority of Andamanese dreams were visual or motor or both. He does not give the details of the dreams themselves and makes the significant remark that their study "is made very difficult by the fact that it is never possible to tell how far the original dream has been arranged and altered by the waking imagination."[4] My own attempts to secure accounts of Crow dreams suffered from the corresponding difficulty that there was an overpowering tendency to present them in conventionalized form. The Indians generally recounted seeing a particular type of landscape symbolic of a supernatural promise that they and their kin should live in safety until the season in question. For example, a man who saw the berries ripening—probably the most frequent formula—would feel confident of living until the next summer; and so, *mutatis mu-*

tandis, with those who saw the leaves turning yellow or the ice floating down-stream.

This inclination to standardize in conformity with a preconceived norm has been pointed out in the preceding section. Indeed among the Great Lakes Indians this tendency has been carried so far that from the samples available I doubt whether appreciable mental variations could be found in the narratives of visions from that region, leveled as they have been by the roller of conventionality. But in my fairly large series of Crow visions matters have not been carried so far, and while I have myself stressed the rôle played there by the preëxisting social norms, certain individual differences are in my opinion still clearly perceivable.

But before indicating such variants I should like to point out that the Crow data seem to agree very well with the findings of modern psychology. Visual imagery certainly seems to preponderate, and what frequently impresses us is its vividness as evidenced by the great particularity of the descriptive detail. One-blue-bead not merely sees a person on a horse, but a rider with face and forehead painted red, wearing a buckskin shirt with a chicken-hawk feather tied to one shoulder, while the horse is a buckskin with a white mane. Lone-tree is visited by a white bird, big as a Mission building, with his face turned south, the lightning issuing from his eyes and the smoke rising from where he sat down; when a hailstorm approaches, it leaves a circle free round visitant and visionary. So the couple who come to bless Medicine-crow hold each in one hand a hoop ornamented with feathers, in the other a hoop with strawberries; and various objects, including the entire body of a red-headed woodpecker, are tied to the back of their heads; further, half of the young woman's face is painted red. Again, Soretail's eagle patron shows him a tent with four main poles, eleven lateral poles, and two on each side of the doorway; and the tipi is decorated with differently colored streamers.[5]

Such details, apparently quite trivial, are not so to the native: the Eagle chapter of the Tobacco society originated in the last-mentioned vision, while Medicine-crow's revelation led to the institution of the Strawberry chapter. The detail is significant because it is associated with the basic psychic experience of Crow religious life, but without a certain keenness of visualization it could never have assumed definite shape and become the starting-point of religious innovations.

Moreover, our Crow material falls in line with the recent psychological views not only in illustrating the prevalence of visual imagery but also in exemplifying the frequency of the "mixed type." One of the most common elements in the revelations made to Indians of this tribe is the song imparted by the visitant. True, this is an integral part of the tribal pattern and in so far is socially determined. But how regularly could such a union of auditory with visual images be suggested by social tradition if there were not a frequent combination of the corresponding native dispositions? From this angle we can understand the character of the Tobacco songs: people used to lie at or near the Tobacco garden with the hope of a revelation, and if they simultaneously saw an animal and heard a song there would be a synthesis of the two, that is, the animal would come to be mentioned in the song. This auditory susceptibility, it should be noted, may be significant in other ways. It may lead to the definite recognition of the supernatural visitor, whose identity might otherwise remain obscure. Thus, Lone-tree on a fast was visited by a man, who offered him food. "I did not know it was the Dipper, but something at the back of my head was whispering to me, 'The man giving you food is the Dipper.'" It was only after this audition that my witness, looking at his patron's long hair, *saw* the Seven Stars hanging there: the auditory had evoked the relevant visual hallucination. Those who, like the present writer, are subject to auditory hallucinations, both in presomnic and full waking condition, will appreciate the convincing character of such experiences.

To cite another illustration of the mixed type, we find Medicine-crow on the same occasion hearing a shout and a whistling sound, then a warning of the approaching visitant, who turned out to be a handsome young white man with a sweet-smelling strawberry pinned to his clothes. Again Hillside saw a gray-haired buffalo, heard him snorting, and felt his licking.

Nevertheless, though the mixed type with visualistic hegemony seems prevalent in the Crow tribe as well as among Caucasians, certain individuals represent, to all appearances, extreme types. Thus, Scratches-face is evidently an audile. On a single occasion he experienced a variety of auditory impressions such as is not recorded for any other tribesman: intermittently he would hear footsteps of an approaching person, then a man clearing his throat, then the snorting of a horse, then a person asking him what he was doing and announcing the arrival of a spirit. Next the heralded visitant was heard, also the tinkling of bells, the main visitant's speech, promiscuous talk, yelling, and whistling. Arm-round-the-neck, on the other hand, gives an account that in spite of its brevity bristles with references to falling, jumping, kicking, driving,—presumptive evidence of a motor type.

Finally, a very interesting group of cases merits consideration. A minority—but an appreciable one—of the Crow visionaries display the peculiarity of having an animal or, more rarely, an object enter their bodies. This tenant has a tendency to come out in part or wholly on special provocation, such as the singing of a certain tune or the transgression of a taboo; and, owing to the otherwise fatal consequences to the host, the parasite must be coaxed back again. The clearest exposition was given by Muskrat, who pretended to have both a weasel and a horse inside of her. Whenever the Bear Song dance is performed, some mysterious power drives her to the site, where she goes into a trance. On one of these occasions the tail of the horse protruded from her mouth, but people took some warts from a horse's leg, made incense therefrom, and smoked her with it, thus making the tail reënter her body. Whenever a person bumps into her, either the horse tail or the weasel will come out, so people take care to avoid doing so, and she keeps a horse wart about her for an antidote. On the other hand, Crane-head had a frog within him, and in the winter people could hear it croaking in his throat. Again, the Egg chapter of the Tobacco society originated in the vision of a man who discovered a nest of eggs, one of which entered his mouth and would regularly come out when a certain song was sung in the Tobacco ceremony.

This conception is not confined to the Crow. Almost ninety years ago Prince Maximilian of Wied-Neuwied noted it among the Hidatsa and Mandan of North Dakota, where one man would often feel a buffalo calf kicking about inside of him, while the Prince himself saw a woman produce a corncob that was later conjured back into her body with incense. Somewhat similar notions have been reported from the Blackfoot, Arapaho, and Menomini.

So far, then, we are merely dealing with a historical phenomenon: the idea arose, so far as our present data go, somewhere between Wisconsin and western Montana and was disseminated from its center of origin. But at once the query arises, why only certain persons in the tribe are directly affected by a traditional belief accessible to all members of their group. The combination of auditory and visual sensations involved in the simultaneous acceptance of a song and, say, certain ceremonial designs is practically universal among the Crow; not so the belief in a mysterious parasite of the type described. I infer that this latter is due to an individual peculiarity,—to an excessive sensitiveness to tactile, kinesthetic and visceral impressions. Given such idiosyncracy, the traditional conception—itself ultimately intelligible as a product of this phenomenon— strikes a responsive chord, while the normal "mixed type" fails to react.

Lest it be supposed that such phenomena as I have cited have a restricted distribution in the world, reference may here be made to the "Bushman presentiments." Among these South Africans there was general reliance on the inferences to be drawn from a distinctive "tapping" in the body, which was interpreted according to a traditional system. Thus, when a man felt a tapping in the lower part of the back of his neck, it meant that an ostrich was coming and was scratching himself in a corresponding spot; "when a woman who had gone away is returning to the house, the man who is sitting there feels on his shoulders the thong with which the woman's child is slung over her shoulders;" again, to quote Dr. Bleek's witness, "I feel a sensation in the calves of my legs when the springbok's blood is going to run down them." [6]

Psychologically these manifestations are evidently equivalent to the kinesthetic and visceral sensations of the Hidatsa or Crow, and when we are told that the stupid Bushmen who do not understand the presentiments get into trouble and

may even be killed by lions we have fair evidence of the
recognition of individual differences : the "stupid" ones are
obviously those who either have no such sensations or experience them to so moderate a degree as to attach little
significance to them.

Suggestibility and Independence

Important as may be the individual differences noted
above in determining the details of a psychic experience, a
far greater importance in the religious life of the individual
must be ascribed to the degree of his suggestibility. Does
he automatically bow to the ideas presented by an elder
wielding authority? Is he susceptible to the more insidi-
ous influence of an impersonal social atmosphere? Is he
willing to set at naught the traditional heritage of belief
and place reliance mainly on his own experiences? The
measure in which he corresponds to the several categories
implied in these questions will make him a member of the
rank and file, a veritable pillar of society, or a doubting
Thomas threatening to sap its foundation by his very existence. The older ethnology took little conscious interest in
such differences of outlook, yet it is not difficult to glean
some evidence of their existence from the descriptive
records. Only we must make due allowance for the extraneous pressure under which the individual acts : a Winnebago
boy under the unremitting surveillance of his parents is not
the relatively free agent represented by a young Crow.
Deviation from the traditional norm argues a far greater
strength of mind in the former than in the latter. But in
appraising the subjective phenomena involved, considerable
caution is imperative. "Suggestibility" is not by any means
a uniform thing : psychologists tell us that there are "various

tests of suggestibility, and an individual who succumbs to one does not necessarily succumb to another, so that it may be doubted whether we should baldly speak of one individual as more suggestible than another." [7]   It is obvious that an incapacity to receive ideas from without may have quite another cause than intellectual independence; nothing more may be involved than dullness or lack of interest.   Again, the very exuberance of the novice's imagination, the exalted anticipations aroused in him, may build up a fantasy by the side of which *any* possible real experience is so disappointing as to be ruled out.

The relevant problems are, I think, neatly illustrated in a human document rescued for science by Dr. Paul Radin. [8] His Winnebago hero, "S. B.," recounts the typical puberty experiences,—the preparatory abstinence from food, the detailed instructions by his elders when he was definitely sent out to fast for a blessing, the visits and further admonitions of his father during the fast itself.   But "in spite of it all, I experienced nothing unusual."   Dreading, however, a prolongation of the fast, S. B. pretended to have had a revelation and received food.   Subsequently, in obedience to the craving for social recognition or the prompting of eminent men, he repeatedly fasted but through it all "I was not in the least conscious of any dreams or blessings." This the narrator retrospectively imputes to his lack of religious fervor at the time,—his failure to concentrate on anything but outward glory and the favor of women: "I was never lowly at heart and never really desired the blessing of the spirits."   Subsequently he is trained for initiation into the secret Medicine Dance and learns that instead of being actually shot and revived by the old-stagers he is merely to feign death and resuscitation at their hands.   An intense shock of disappointment comes over him and he

becomes skeptical of all the things held sacred by the Winnebago.   Later he becomes a toper and frequently boasts
of his alleged blessings.   On one occasion he promises to
intercede with four female spirits on behalf of a woman
big with child, and the ease with which she for the first
time gives birth demonstrates his pretensions not only to
the mother and her kin, but even to himself: "I was sur-
prised.   Perhaps I am really a holy man, I thought."   After
a while S. B.'s parents came under the sway of the new
Peyote cult that menaced the very existence of the older
faith since the votaries "insisted that all the other ceremonies were wrong and must be abandoned and because
they destroyed war-bundles, medicine-bags, etc., everything
dear to the hearts of the conservative Winnebago."   S. B.
resented this iconoclasm as much as the average tribesman, but after joining his converted kin and receiving
manifold favors at their hands he consented to partake of
the new medicine.   For a time he maintained an expectant
and even negative attitude, as of old toward the ancient religion of his people.   But when he beheld some of the gorge-
ous color visions induced by the drug, his skepticism was
swept aside in the twinkling of an eye, and he became a
full-fledged peyote-worshiper.

Now, as Dr. Radin points out, what S. B. had striven for
in all his previous religious experiences was a distinctive
thrill, an inward change.   He had been keyed up to expect
it from the normal puberty rite and fasting generally, but
it never came.   From this we can hardly conclude that he
was less suggestible than other boys, but he was certainly
not suggestible in the same way.   I hazard the guess from
the evidence presented that he was like Ibsen's Brand an
"all or nothing" spirit of *excessive* suggestibility.   Other
boys were willing to present any image that appeared dur-

ing their vigil as answering to the experience depicted by
their elders; *his* expectations had been raised so high that
they acted as a *counter*-suggestion, so that he could retrospectively declare that "I experienced nothing unusual"
where a normal youth would have been quite content to
regard himself as visited by a mysterious agency. But,
whether this be or be not a valid interpretation, there can be
no doubt that some real individual difference of psychology
is involved and that it had a most important effect on S. B.'s
religious life. Apart from this particular case, it is clear from
the parental admonitions reproduced by Dr. Radin that "not
every one was able to enter into communication with the
spirits" and that in view of this contingency a vicarious
reliance on medicinal herbs was enjoined by a father when
lecturing his adolescent son. In other words, different persons behave differently under similar circumstances and
after subjection to similar exhortations.

The degree of suggestibility is of course inversely pro-
portional to the subject's willingness to rely on his direct
experience, but it is again necessary to take into account the
amount of pressure exerted from without. It is easy
enough for a Crow, free as he is from the superintendence
of elders and shamans, to accept whatever communication
may be granted by the spirits he invokes. Hence when
we find occasional instances of men who dare not avail
themselves of their blessings without a previous conference
with the sages of the tribe, they may well be reproached for
timidity. But the case of the Ojibwa or Winnebago boy,
incessantly drilled and harried by his parents as to what
he ought and ought not to get in the way of a revelation,
is not comparable; and here it would require unusual audacity to break away from the fetters of social and family
tradition.

Again, when we find an abundance of versions regarding the hereafter in tribes of such differing cultural level as the Andamanese, the Shoshoni, or the Polynesians, this should not be taken to prove an extraordinary prevalence of latitudinarianism. It may mean nothing more than that there is an absence of obligatory sentiment on the subject, and where there is no orthodoxy there cannot be any heterodoxy. Why *shouldn't* Red-shirt accept the evidence of his senses to the effect that the dead live underground rather than in the sky, as he had supposed, if that notion, however popular, was not sanctioned by any authority, formal or informal?

The matter is further complicated by the purely personal factor, by those temperamental differences that make it possible for the same man to resent the leadership of one hero and blindly to trust himself to another. Whatever we may think of the formal schemes broached in recent and former times for the division of mankind into psychological categories, the commonsense experience of the ages supports the existence of distinct types, however hard it may be to define them. Sometimes, but by no means always, the leader is merely a magnified edition of the follower. In other cases, adherence seems to rest precisely on a sense of difference in a complementary sense. Again, the peculiar circumstances of the situation may lead to the acceptance of a prophet as "true" or his rejection as "false." We must therefore again proceed with caution before translating into direct and even quasi-quantitative psychological terms a concrete observation apparently illustrating greater or lesser suggestibility. For instance, among the Crow Tobacco Dancers of the Lodge Grass district the prestige of Medicine-Crow succeeded in substituting a crane for the traditional otter-skin carried in a procession. But I have heard an

Indian more or less sneeringly refer to the substitution as a *mere* novelty introduced by Medicine-Crow. The critic, however, was not a rationalist: he was not challenging the value of the sacred object carried on the occasion, he did not consider that the otter had, in principle, precisely the same sanction as the crane, to wit, an individual's revelation. He merely had not for some reason or other come under the spell of Medicine-crow's personality and accordingly displayed the natural enough predilection for an old rather than a new ritual device.

But there are not lacking instances of genuine independence and perhaps the most interesting are those of the two Tongan kings described by Mariner. Finau I, with characteristic cunning, utilized the prevalent beliefs in executing his own purposes, but seems to have been singularly free from their sway. He went so far as to confess to Mariner that he doubted the very existence of the gods; and when met with the argument that he had professed himself to be possessed by the spirit of one of his predecessors, he replied: "True! there may be gods; but what the priests tell us about their power over mankind, I believe to be all false." When his daughter died, he planned to execute the priest of one of his patron deities, a design only thwarted by his own death. His sacrilegious impiety constantly scandalized the people, who marveled at his continued prosperity when he was so audaciously throwing down the gauntlet to the gods. On one occasion, when he was about to proceed against the enemy, one of the chiefs sneezed,—an evil omen. But Finau wrathfully clenched his fists and uttered this cry of defiance: "Crowd, all ye gods, to the protection of these people, nevertheless I will wreak my vengeance on them tenfold!" Finau II, notwithstanding his intelligence (see below), was not wholly free from the last-mentioned super-

stition, for on a solemn occasion he came near slaying
Mariner for an untimely sneeze, and the subsequent explanation, that he merely feared its effect on his attendants,
hardly rings true. However, as might be expected, he also
showed great independence and abolished two deep-rooted
customs, the sacrifice of the Tuitonga's chief wife on her
husband's death, as well as the Tuitonga's office itself,
though among his subjects "it was whispered about that
some great misfortune would happen to the country." [9]

The greatest men never wholly succeed in escaping the
impress of their time, and it is not difficult to point out all
manner of inconsistencies in the notions of the two Tongan
rulers. The elder, his infidelity notwithstanding, evidently
expected succor from the family god during his daughter's
illness; the son was not above conceiving a compass as inspired by a god. Nevertheless, the two Finaus doubtless
stand out as extraordinarily free-thinking in their mental
habits.

This negative activity of theirs, however, again reminds
us of the subtle relation between individual character and
the culture of a group. A person endowed with Finau II's
ability and outlook could not possibly have exerted any
noticeable effect on Tongan faith and ritual if he had happened to belong to the plebeian ranks. It was the peculiar
culture of Tonga at that time, involving as it did the concentration of temporal power in Finau's hands, that enabled
him to abrogate the time-honored pontificate of the Tuitonga. Without so enlightened a ruler that dignity might
have long survived, but enlightenment and sovereign power
were *both* prerequisite to bring about the result.

Intellectual Powers

In one of his books on the Thonga M. Junod points out how much his informants vary in narrative skill: where one contents himself with a bald summary of events, another will give the most vivid detail, even to the point of pantomimically representing the actions of his characters. Every field-worker is able to provide corroboration from his own experience. What is so conspicuously true of the literary sphere holds in equal measure for the intellectual as a whole, and the differences in question cannot be ignored in the present context. For though I have insisted again and again that the essence of religion is to be sought elsewhere, this implies a lesser weighting, not an elimination, of the intellect, which of course continues to operate somehow in association with every mental state. Moreover, what begins as a predominantly intellectual theory may become secondarily an object of emotion. Views as to the nature of the soul, cosmogony, and a host of other subjects may conceivably be divorced from religion at the start, yet subsequently become indissolubly linked with it. Such elaborate systems as have been concocted by the Polynesians or the Dakota are clearly not random expressions of the "folk-soul" but the joint product of a number of comparatively refined intellects who have grappled with the riddles of the universe.

That savage society verily produces intelligences with a definitely speculative bent, can no longer be doubted. Thus, Mariner was struck by the mental operations of the Tongan ruler whom, for convenience' sake, we have called Finau II. His father, Finau I, had been a man of ambition and Machiavellian cunning; his uncle, Finau Fiji, was a man of sound enough judgment, based on stability of temperament and considerable experience. But neither displayed a tithe of the younger sovereign's intellectual parts. He was constantly visiting the workshops of the skilled artisans. He delighted in poetry and restored the concerts by professional minstrels which had been abolished by his father. Novel ideas were readily absorbed by him and combined with unusual alertness. Best of all, he took pleasure in gratifying his reasoning faculty:

He had learnt the mechanism of a gun-lock by his own pure investigation: one day on taking off the lock of a pistol to clean it, he was astonished to find it somewhat differently contrived, and a little more complicated than the common lock, which he had thought so clever and perfect that he could not conceive anything better; on seeing this, however, he was somewhat puzzled, at first with the mechanism, and afterwards with its superiority to the common lock, but he would not have it explained to him; it was an interesting puzzle, which he wished to have the pleasure of solving himself: at length he succeeded, and was as pleased as if he had found a treasure, and in the afternoon at kava he was not contented till he had made all his chiefs and matabooles understand it also.

Similarly, a practical demonstration of the correctness of Mariner's lectures on the pulse put the ruler into such good humor that he dispensed with the corporal punishment about to be inflicted on one of his servants.[10]

Junod has given his impressions of an equivalent Bantu personality, Rangane. While the majority of his tribesmen never troubled themselves about the creation of the world, Rangane from a boy sought an answer to the riddle, rejecting the curt folk-explanations of his mother and older Thonga men, and finally embracing the circumstantial account of the Bible. M. Junod writes:

I remember his face beaming with joy when he told his story. But such earnest, philosophical natures are very rare amongst Natives, and Rangane was an exception. He died when still at the beginning of his course of study; and he was vastly superior to most of his comrades as regards religious perception.[11]

Our informant refers to men of this type as "religious geniuses": I should rather term them philosophical ones. But there can be no question that where the religious emotion is joined with such speculative interests and a dominant personality to boot, that type of leadership resulting from the combination may well be ascribed to a "religious genius." For example, had the younger Finau taken a definitely spiritual attitude towards life, his powerful intellect might have reshaped and elevated the traditional faith of his people and would have made him a positive rather than a mainly destructive agency in the history of Polynesian religion.

Various Idiosyncrasies

Suggestibility, it has been found, is far from being a simple psychological phenomenon. Accordingly, in segregating it I do not mean to assert that some of the features there discussed do not correspond to or at least overlap phenomena that can be conveniently regarded from another angle. Thus, when one Crow youth, privation and torture notwithstanding, fails to obtain a vision in trial after trial, while another repeatedly succeeds, nay, may acquire a revelation without a deliberate quest, the difference *can* be put in terms of suggestibility. But we have already seen that the result may have such antithetical causes as hyper-sensitiveness and insusceptibility. It is therefore imperative to in-

quire with what temperamental or other qualities a given
form of "the religious impulse" is correlated. That differences in its intensity are largely recognized by the primitive
folk themselves, is proved by some cases in which religious
activity is inherited. For often there is no automatic transmission of authority to, say, the eldest-born: a Thonga
physician, for example, passed on his art to that one of his
sons or nephews who was most strongly "induced by his
heart" to devote himself to the profession.[12] The question
is, What are these inducements and their accompaniments?

In many cases, no doubt, a definitely religious attitude is
quite consistent with a normal mentality, heightened in certain of its phases. The Andamanese believe that certain men
can communicate with spirits in their dreams, and this is
one source of shamanism among them.

If a man or boy experiences dreams that are in any way extraordinary, particularly if in his dreams he sees spirits, either
the spirits of dead persons known to him when alive or spirits
of the forest or the sea, he may acquire in time the reputation
of a medicine-man.

To be sure, his claims must be submitted to the test of experience before he is generally recognized; nothing succeeds like success in primitive society, and the variation that
may be subjectively significant must conform to chance corroboration in the world of reality before it can become a
cultural factor. Psychologically, we may say that while
all normal Andamanese have dreams, and may even have
dreams of spirits, constant and vivid dreaming would pre-
dispose a man to shamanism.[13]

However, it is a remarkable fact that the shaman or
priest—in other words, the preëminently religious person—

so frequently represents a clear deviation from the psychic norm. That is to say, whatever else may be implied, the protagonist of religion is often a pathological case, a "neurotic" in the modern psychiatric vernacular. Thus, Bogoras writes of the Chukchi:

> Nervous and highly excitable temperaments are most susceptible to the shamanistic call. The shamans among the Chuckchi with whom I conversed were as a rule extremely excitable, almost hysterical, and not a few of them were half crazy. Their cunning in the use of deceit in their art closely resembled the cunning of a lunatic.[14]

One of Bogoras's acquaintances, whose grandfather had likewise communed with the spirits and was not improbably tainted with a hereditary tendency to hysteria, would fly into a rage on the slightest provocation and attempt to assault even a Russian cossack. Another shaman, Scratching-woman, was so excitable that he could not sit still for any length of time but would leap up with violent gestures; and when he was in drink, all knives had to be placed out of his reach to prevent a brawl. Other shamans were conspicuous for an incessant nervous twitching of the face, and a female practitioner had actually been insane for three years, "during which time her household had taken such precautions, that she could do no harm to the people or to herself." These nervous idiosyncrasies are not without importance when we remember that one of the characteristic performances of the Chukchi shaman, especially when going in search of a patient's missing soul, consists in violent singing and drumming, followed by a trance, during which the doctor's soul is supposed to visit his guardian spirits and secure their advice. Regarding the psychology of these states, I need merely refer to the explanation already offered for the inspirational ecstasy of Polynesian priests.

Among the Thonga corresponding peculiarities are not less important. Here spectacular nervous afflictions lead to the theory that the patient is possessed by a spirit,— oddly enough, not one of the ancestors of his own tribe, but by a Zulu spirit. A man will come home trembling, attack his fellow-villagers, fall unconscious, suffer abnormal pains in the chest, become emaciated, yawn and hiccough to an unusual extent. As another instance of how the individual is inevitably dependent on the culture of his community, we find that the diagnosis of possession must be established by the customary throwing of the divinatory bones. The possessed puts himself into the hands of an exorcist and, when cured, himself advances to the status of an exorcist, diviner, prophet or wonder-worker. Sometimes he becomes the originator of a new school, developing novel rites of exorcism and applying hitherto unknown drugs. The spirits who once tormented him are now his benefactors, and he will show his gratitude by daily acts of devotion that eclipse the piety with which the ordinary Thonga worships his ancestral gods.[15]

In this connection it is impossible wholly to ignore sexual anomalies already mentioned in connection with historical problems, for in some primitive communities what we should regard as pathological phenomena in the sexual sphere are intimately related with religious activity. The berdache (French Canadian, *bardache*) or " hermaphrodite" of popular speech was a familiar figure in not a few American Indian tribes. According to all accounts anatomically a genuine male, he nevertheless affected the garb of a woman, mastered feminine accomplishments, in which he often excelled, and indulged in homosexual intercourse. The Crow at one time had relatively many of these psychiatric cases and insisted that it was their nature to dress and act as they did; to them belonged the definite task of chopping down the sacred tree of the Sun Dance. I saw presumably the last representative of the species. The Omaha believed that berdaches became such as a result of their first puberty quest of a vision. The Moon would appear, holding in one hand the bow and arrows symbolic of the warrior's life and in the other the pack-strap used by women. By quickly crossing his hands, the visitant might deceive the visionary into grasping the badge of womanhood. "In such a case he could not help acting the woman, speaking, dressing, and working just as Indian women used to do." Miss Fletcher tells of a case in which a man tried to resist the implications of his experience but found the conflict unbearable and committed suicide.[16]

The psychological interpretation of these cases is not especially difficult. The fact that not every person in the community, that only a small percentage had the berdache vision proves a predisposition to perversity on the part of the exceptional individual. But the idiosyncrasy is no doubt sincerely interpreted in accordance with the vision pattern, as though it were the creature and not the author of the vision seen.

Very similar transformations have been recorded among the Chukchi, where in addition some women likewise assumed the character of men, though this case was of rarer occurrence and eluded Mr. Bogoras's personal observation. The Chukchi berdaches marry men, but they are believed to be wedded to spirit husbands, who act as their special protectors and issue orders through them, so that the human spouse is degraded to a rather humble status in the household. It is remarkable that the "transformed shamans" enjoy a position of special prestige : they are supposed to excel in all shamanistic practices, even in that of ventriloquism, which is barred to normal women; even other shamans dread the berdache because of the power of his supernatural patrons.[17]

It is interesting to find similar conceptions in the southeastern corner of Asia, to wit, in Borneo. The highest grade of shaman, *manang,* among the Sea Dyak is that of the *manang bali* or "changed shaman," that is, one who has changed his sex, assumed feminine dress and occupies himself with female pursuits. The transformation is said to be due to a supernatural command conveyed on three distinct occasions in dreams. Disobedience would mean death. Owing to his higher rank, the *manang bali* naturally receives much higher fees than ordinary doctors and is summoned when others have failed to effect a cure. The wealth thus accumulated leads men to marry a *manang bali,* but the rôle of these husbands seems as unenviable as that of their Chukchi equivalents.[18]

It may not be superfluous at this point to revert to a subject broached in the last chapter. If such phenomena as have been described in the preceding paragraphs occur, have I not been over-confident in my repudiation of the theory that religion is founded in the sex instinct? Such an objection would be the result of a confusion of the issues involved. As I have already explicitly stated, sex and religion are bound to come into contact at times. It may even be admitted without hesitation that such association may be of great importance to the individual, nay, to the tribe, as in Siberia and Borneo. But what is the nature of the bond? The Plains Indian berdache does not have a vision *because* he is an invert, for of all the men in a generation who have visions only a handful are inverts. What he does is to justify his innate propensities by an unconscious rationalization that shall make his conduct fit into the scheme of tribal convention. His spirit is that of any person who cites divine support and prompting for what he craves to do. The tribesmen who accept the rationalization as a legitimate explanation would not do so except for their preëxisting idea of the Sacred, that is, the idea that a visionary experience imposes an obligation which cannot be safely ignored. The berdache phenomena are not the root of Plains Indian religion, they pre-suppose its existence. Even where the invert plays a dominant part in religion, as in Borneo, similar reasoning can be applied. For whence comes the notion of supernatural commands in dreams that ostensibly underlies the *manang bali* institution? The sense of the Supernatural cannot be created by the perverse longings of the shaman; it is already present in the minds of his audience or his plea would fail to be even intelligible. On the other hand, so far as the very abnormality of his case makes upon them a profound impression, it is evidently not because of their own sex cravings but because the Extraordinary *qua* Extraordinary is of basic significance. Nothing in these data thus justifies the derivation of the religious impulse from sex: there is a conjunction, not a genetic connection with sex as the cause and religion as the effect.

LEADERSHIP

Leadership in religion, as elsewhere, is psychologically a very complex and anything but uniform phenomenon. As the musical genius is not necessarily the man who possesses to the highest degree the specifically musical talents, so the religious creator, that is, the producer of new religious values for his group, is not necessarily the one who spontaneously displays the most intense or readiest religious emotion; and the same holds for him who, instead of enriching the cultural content of his people, merely transmits the social heritage in unaltered form. That *certain* qualities of mind are prerequisite to leadership in religion as in politics, requires no special affirmation. Apart from the a priori certainty of the proposition, we can point to the frequent transmission of authority from one member of a family to another, which, as has been pointed out, by no means follows a mechanical law of succession but doubtless exemplifies the hereditary character of certain innate qualities. The prophet of the Ghost Dance had for his predecessor a close kinsman reputed to be his father; Medicine-crow, one of the eminent Crow Indians of recent decades, had a paternal uncle (his step-father) renowned for his supernatural powers.[10] Something, of course, must be credited to the direct influence of nurture, and wherever the specific details coincide the resemblance is best explained from that angle. Thus, it is hardly accident that both Medicine-crow and his "father" had a vision of the crane, a bird otherwise far from conspicuous in that context. But the general tendency to communion with the supernatural is probably to a far greater extent transmissible by education in so far as there is an hereditary predisposition; and where such intercourse depends on abnormalities, epilepsy, for example, the hereditary character of the trait can be inferred with certainty from our knowledge of psychiatry.

It was natural for older writers to make the assumption still current among educated laymen, that on primitive levels no individuality can assert itself sufficiently to rise definitely above the rank and file and impress its own stamp upon the whole community. We have already seen numerous indications destructive of this hoary fallacy. It remains to examine a few typical examples from the psychological point of view. Once more we shall be driven to regard the phenomenon sociologically as well, for the concept of leadership demands as its logical correlate that of the group. What is more, this will involve to a certain degree a retracing of our steps; for whatever may be the constituents that jointly produce "leadership," those who are led must illustrate in greater or lesser degree the "suggestibility" of an earlier section.

In the first place, let us consider a case that exemplifies leadership in its less spectacular forms. Among the Crow of the Lodge Grass district Medicine-crow had at the time of my visits risen to a position of preëminence. His ignorance of English and consequent difficulty in directly dealing with Government officials somewhat diminished his influence with the very young "educated" Indians but could not shake it among the people at large, who were duly impressed by his war record, itself on native theory the consequence of supernatural favor. I found Medicine-crow a very dignified, courteous but elusive personality. He was perfectly willing to give information when not otherwise engaged, and in fact he himself took the initiative in introducing me into the delights of a sweat-lodge, but it was hard to find him unoccupied. He had a very distinct sense of responsibility as a result of his status in the community and was constantly visiting back and forth. When a newborn infant was to be named, Medicine-crow was naturally in demand as a name-giver; when a delegation was to be sent to Washington, it was a foregone conclusion that he should be a member of the party; and of course any public assemblage gave him an opportunity to recite his achievements as a warrior. Turning now to his strictly religious activities, he owned a sacred pipe and an especially sacred rock, and was by far

the most prominent figure of the district in the greatest surviving ceremony, the Tobacco Dance. He had not only
founded a distinct chapter of the Tobacco society as a result of a vision, but had enough authority to alter a symbol
carried in the procession of all the chapters,—again, of
course, through another specific revelation. His fame was
by no means restricted to Lodge Grass: I remember meeting
him at Pryor as the guest of a man he had adopted into the
rite of the Sacred Pipe, and in the same district, some eight
or nine years ago, a case of serious illness led to the idea
that Medicine-crow should revive the Sun Dance, which here
had invariably been a ceremony of vengeance, as a curative
ritual.

From the subjective point of view, there was undoubtedly
about the man an impressive high-seriousness. He was
known for the meticulous care with which every ritualistic
detail was carried out in conformity with tradition, as when
he slowly unwrapped his sacred shield for me, smoking it
with incense, then four times raising it, each time a little
higher, till he had lifted it aloft, high above his head. The
same occasion brought out another aspect of his character.
I asked him whether he would sell the shield for a hundred
dollars. He politely but firmly refused. Without my sanction, my interpreter then asked him whether he would take
two hundred dollars for it. Medicine-crow replied that he
would not accept a thousand, for he wanted to be buried with
it. In order to appreciate this attitude, it is necessary to recall that before my visit Dr. Dorsey and Mr. Simms had
bought up nearly every shield on the Reservation for the
Field Museum in Chicago, and that I myself had succeeded
in buying two of the small remaining number, one of them
without any difficulty, the other after some cajolery.

Psychologically, then, Medicine-crow was a devout man,

loyal to the received creed. In a subordinate way, of course, he was able to add to that creed because his personality was sufficiently powerful to gain cultural acceptance of his individual visions. At the same time he evidently was not the type to produce revolutionary changes: such modifications as he introduced—that is, variants in ritual detail suggested in abnormal psychic states—belong, indeed, to the very warp and woof of Crow religion. As he must then be reckoned a minor rather than a major prophet with reference to the scope of his mission, so as a social figure, too, he does not loom as a really dominant personality sweeping everything before him. Gray-bull, for example, a resident of the same district, whom I knew well, never gave me the slightest indication of an inferiority complex with reference to Medicine-crow. It was not that he suffered from delusions of grandeur: indeed, he was very humble when he spoke of Bell-rock, his one-time leader in war. But, comparing his own record and his own reputation in the community with Medicine-crow's, Gray-bull felt no such difference as he was conscious of when he thought of this famous captain of yore. Technically he might not rank as a "chief" because he lacked one particular deed of valor, but the totality of his exploits did not seem to him appreciably less than Medicine-crow's, and his bravery was as little challenged among his tribesmen. He had had visions of his own and had played his part in the ceremonies of the Crow; Medicine-crow's corresponding activities could not make the impression they did on others. Naturally Gray-bull was too intelligent not to know that there *was* a difference in social status, that Medicine-crow was constantly in the limelight and was surrounded by a group of satellites, but the fact did not seem, in Gray-bull's mind, to have a bearing on intrinsic worth.

When we inquire next what made Medicine-crow a religious leader in contrast to Gray-Bull, we must look to both subjective and external determinants. Medicine-crow was clearly by nature and nurture the more religious, while Gray-bull represented what Dr. Radin has called the "intermittently religious" type. But this initial difference alone would have been wholly inadequate to raise Medicine-crow to his actual status as in a measure a molder of Crow belief if he had not enjoyed the conspicuous success characteristic of his career as a warrior, which tribal thought invariably linked with supernatural sanction. Without these tangible tokens of divine favor the utmost possible religiosity would not have availed him in the least.

This coöperation of subjective and objective factors is not less marked in the more spectacular instances of primitive leadership. Let us consider a few representative cases.

The sudden contact of an aboriginal and a Caucasian population in South Africa produced results there roughly comparable to the Messiah cults of the North American Indians, and a series of remarkable characters came to the foreground. Of these, Makanna, who led the attack on a British fort in 1818, was one of the most interesting. His intellectual abilities strongly recall Finau II, but in the case of the Bantu they were coupled with a definitely mystical disposition. When visiting the British headquarters, he

evinced an insatiable curiosity and an acute intellect on such subjects as fell under his observation. With the military officers he talked of war, or of such of the mechanical arts as fell under his notice; but his great delight was to converse with the chaplain, to elicit information in regard to the doctrines of Christianity; and to puzzle him with metaphysical subtleties or mystical ravings.

He combined the native faith with some notions derived from the whites and professed to be a brother of Christ. Further, he taught a stricter morality and was not afraid to play the part of a Savonarola in denouncing the chiefs, all of whom with one exception came to bow to his influence. Makanna often sought seclusion, yet when he addressed a crowd his eloquence carried everything before him. He announced that he had been sent by the great spirit Uhlanga to avenge the wrongs of the Xosa, "that he had power to call up from the grave the spirits of their ancestors to assist them in battle against the English, whom they should drive before they stopped across the Zwartkops river and into the ocean." When he summoned his warriors for the assault on Graham's Town, he declared that supernatural aid would turn the hailstorm of British firearms into water. As a matter of fact, he all but succeeded in capturing the fort, when at the critical moment the soldiers were relieved by a friendly Hottentot captain. Makanna was obliged to surrender and was imprisoned by the authorities.

Soon, however, another prophet, Umlanjeni, arose, who likewise counseled the chiefs to attack the foreign invaders. He was something of an ascetic, refused the gifts offered by his adherents, and would fast for hours, standing up to his chin in a pool of water. He directed the people to prepare by slaying their cattle and gorging themselves with meat. Despite the failure of his project, he was succeeded in 1856 by another seer with a similar message. Umhlakaza proclaimed a great change: men and cattle were to be resuscitated, while the foreigners were to be swept from the land as though by a whirlwind. This result, however, could only be achieved by a summary destruction of the natives' cattle, goats, and corn. In consequence thousands of heads of cattle were slain,—an extraordinary tribute to the prophet's personality, considering the idolatrous regard of the South Africans for their herds. A definite date was set for the resurrection of dead men and beasts, and the failure of the prophecy was interpreted as due to the umbrage taken by the rising spirits at the reluctance of some chiefs to obey Umhlakaza's orders.[29]

Even from the meager accounts available it is clear that some of these Bantu prophets were men distinguished for character, intensity of faith, and intellectual powers. But it is equally certain that the effectiveness of their propaganda was co-determined by the highly special circumstances of the South African aborigines at the time.

Reverting once more to the Ghost Dance, we find a whole group of interesting personalities and we are also able to glean some faint ideas as to the manner in which they impressed their contemporaries. Wovoka is commonly described as the source and center of the cult, but I am strongly of the opinion that in this, as in so many other historical cases, circumstances lent a purely accidental halo to an essentially commonplace figure. Doubtless Wovoka differed sufficiently from other Paviotso to have normally qualified for the position of a tribal shaman, but there is no evidence that he manifested any unusual ability or any strikingly novel conceptions even in a strictly religious sense. His notions were borrowed in part from his kinsman and forerunner Tävibo, while in part they were derived through contact with the Wilson family. In strength of character, in audacity of imagination, he does not even remotely approach some of the Plains Indian leaders who were content to act as his apostles and to treasure as sacred every object that came from his country. What made Wovoka an intertribal, nay, national, character, was not his native capacity for guiding the destinies of his race but the purely accidental plight in which the vigorous and pugnacious Plains Indians—particularly the Western Dakota—found themselves when he first attracted their notice. His example is all the more instructive as a contribution to the growth of religious thought.

It is extremely suggestive to trace the individual reactions of different Indians to this professed leader of their race. Porcupine, a Cheyenne, who visited Wovoka in November, 1889, forthwith identified him with Christ, nay, even saw the scars left on his hands by the crucifixion. He also reported that Wovoka had addressed all the delegates in their respective tongues. Yet it is an established fact that Wovoka spoke nothing but his native Paviotso and a little English. On his return Porcupine repeatedly saw Wovoka in his sleep: now the Prophet warned him of troubles to be expected with the soldiers, then again he reassured the dreamer, telling him that all would be well. Yet where Porcupine found omniscience and the marks of crucifixion a Kiowa pilgrim experienced nothing but disillusionment: he was forced to use an interpreter to the man who supposedly knew everything, and he could find no evidence of scars on Wovoka's hands. He returned, denouncing the "Messiah" as an impostor. That the different versions brought back by different delegates were in part due to Wovoka's own vacillation, is almost certain. As Mr. Mooney writes,

there can be little doubt that Wovoka made claims and prophecies, supported by hypnotic performances, from which he afterward receded when he found that the excitement had gone beyond his control and resulted in an Indian outbreak.

Nevertheless, the discrepancies are largely accounted for by the disparity in initial attitude, in other words, by individual variation.

From this point of view the report of the Western Dakota delegates merits attention. When they arrived at Wovoka's camp, smoke descended from heaven and when it had vanished the Prophet became visible. He ordered the Dakota pilgrims to kill a buffalo on their way home, to cut off the head, tail and four feet, and to leave them; he declared that the buffalo would come to life again. He also told them to call upon him if they were fatigued when traveling home, and he would shorten their trip. In evident good faith the delegates reported that the words of Wovoka had been fulfilled on their journey: they had killed a buffalo and it was restored to life; they had prayed to Wovoka when tired of a night "and in the morning we found ourselves at a great distance from where we stopped." Suggestion surely could not go much further.

Sometimes members of the same delegation were affected quite differently by the Prophet's practices. On one occasion he had a mixed group of Arapaho and Cheyenne seated on the ground facing him as he was holding a hat and some eagle feathers in his hand.

Then with a quick movement he had put his hand into the empty hat and drawn out from it "something black."

One of the Cheyenne present, Tall-bull, was not much impressed, merely accepting the performance as one comparable with the legerdemain of the shamans of his own people. But Black-coyote looked into the hat and there "saw the whole world,"—a phrase, incidentally, characteristic of certain Plains Indian visions and reminiscent of the cosmic visions of the Ojibwa. This difference in reaction is satisfactorily explained by Mr. Mooney. Tall-bull was a lighthearted, skeptical person untinged with "other-worldliness."

Black-coyote was a mystic and aspirant to shamanistic honors, a man who had cut off seventy pieces of his flesh as an offering to the Sun because it had been prescribed in a vision. He was predisposed to see marvelous things, and in consequence he saw them. No wonder he became one of the chief apostles of the new cult among the Arapaho.

However, he was eclipsed by a fellow-tribesman, Sitting-bull, who at the early age of about thirty-six developed into the principal propagandist of the Ghost Dance in the southern Plains area, teaching the faith to the Caddo, Wichita, and Kiowa by means of the elaborate gesture language of the area. Sitting-bull made a deep impression on General (then Lieutenant) Hugh L. Scott, who, prepared to meet a charlatan, found a sincere, unpretentious, and disinterested believer, who was inculcating in his people "precepts which if faithfully carried out will bring them into better accord with their white neighbors, and has prepared the way for their final Christianization." His influence on his followers was remarkable: "All sorts of people wanted to touch him, men and women would come in, rub their hands on him, and cry."

Not less interesting than these Arapaho leaders is the figure of the Kiowa seer dubbed "The Messenger." Long before the rise of the Ghost Dance he had been conspicuous for his revelations. He would frequently go up into the mountains to fast, especially to secure aid in doctoring the sick and to convey messages from the departed to their surviving kin. According to Mr. Mooney, he was a man of great intellectual endowments: he devised a wholly novel system of ideographic writing based on the gesture language, and by means of his invention was able to correspond with his sons.[21]

Compared with Sitting-bull and the Messenger, Wovoka

cuts a rather sorry figure; he had neither the humility and altruism of the one, nor the intellectual capacities of the other. How, then, did this mediocre, weak-spined member of one of the rudest Western tribes succeed in enlisting as disciples men coming from richer aboriginal cultures and unequivocally superior to him in every respect as personalities? The answer is not difficult if we admit that psychology, like history, is not logical. Why did a highly intelligent and open-minded man like John Morley follow a pompous and dogmatic leader like Gladstone? Endowed with an extremely moderate equipment beyond that of the ordinary Paviotso, Wovoka was placed in a position where he could absorb some of the ideas of Christianity and unite them with those of his predecessor and kinsman Tävibo. It is almost certain that he did not start with an exalted conception of his mission, that had his teachings never reached the Plains Indians he would never have risen to more than local fame. It was the character of Plains Indian culture and the character of some of its individual bearers that transformed Wovoka into a national figure. Paradoxical as it may seem, the most spectacular of recent Indian religious movements had its origin in the least interesting and powerful of its personalities.

REFERENCES

[1] R. F. Benedict: 67 f.

[2] Radin, 1923: 290 sq. Jones: II, 295 f., 307, 311. Skinner, 1913: 42 sq.

[3] Woodworth: 368 sq.

[4] Brown: 167.

[5] Lowie, 1922: 325, 330; id., 1919: 117, 129.

[6] Bleek and Lloyd; 331 sq.

[7] Woodworth: 548.

[8] Radin, 1920: 390, 397, 402, 410 f., 440, 461.

[9] Mariner: 113, 139, 235, 298, 332, 338, 353, 388.

[10] Mariner: 295; chap. XIV.

[11] Junod: II, 280.

[12] Junod: II, 414.

[13] Brown: 167, 177.

[14] Bogoras: 415, 426 sq., 441.

[15] Junod: II, 435-460.

[16] Lowie, 1912: 226; id., 1915: 31. J. O. Dorsey: 387 f.

[17] Bogoras: 450 sq.

[18] Gomes: 179. H. L. Roth: II, 270.

[19] Lowie, 1919: 164; id., 1922: 389, 422.

[20] Shooter: 195-212; Wallis: 255-263.

[21] Mooney: 797, 821, 896 f., 909 sq., 918.

CHAPTER XII

RELIGION AND ART

THE relationship of religion and art has often been discussed and indeed could hardly fail to attract notice. They are closely intertwined in many cultures, and in that ancient civilization which has exerted the most profound influence on our own the connection was a peculiarly intimate one. Psychologically, both involve above all an appeal to the emotional side of man, though of course not to the exclusion of the intellectual element. Small wonder, then, that we find the morbidly devout genius of Kierkegaard pathetically bent on marking off the field of religion from that of esthetics; small wonder, too, that they have sometimes been brought into a simple genetic sequence. Miss Jane Harrison, for example, has written a suggestive book, in which she attempts to show, through parallels with simpler peoples, how Greek drama sprang from ritualistic dances and that Greek sculpture was merely "a rite frozen to a monument." She suggests that while ritual does not uniformly develop into art "in all probability dramatic art has always to go through the stage of ritual." [1]

Without entering into a detailed examination of this thesis, we may observe that its very simplicity should militate against its acceptance, for the phenomena of culture do not so readily lend themselves to a short-hand description of their sequences. A priori it is better to assume with Wundt that primitive man no less than ourselves is actuated by a variety of motives and that among this number those of

259

genuinely esthetic character, i. e., those quite divorced from ulterior or correlated ends, must have exerted their influence even at a very early period. If, he contends, dancing has developed into a source of recreation and enjoyment, the reason lies in the sensations and affective accompaniments of the dance, irrespective of any other associated purposes. Indeed, we shall go further than Wundt, or rather shall adhere more consistently to the view here propounded by him. For, notwithstanding the passage just paraphrased, this writer tends to obliterate its effect by constantly harping on the concomitance of religio-magical factors; thus, contrary to some of our descriptive statements, he shrinks from interpreting the Australian corroborees as forms of social entertainment pure and simple.[2] Frankly casting aside such timidity, I will postulate the esthetic impulse as one of the irreducible components of the human mind, as a potent agency from the very beginnings of human existence. In other words, I hold with Jochelson that "the esthetic taste is as strong and spontaneous a longing of primitive man as are beliefs." Accordingly, its interaction with other such elements rather than its derivation from qualitatively distinct phenomena will form the subject of this chapter; nay, I shall not be afraid to suggest that sometimes the ostensibly religious is rather to be traced to an esthetic source than vice versa.

INFLUENCE OF RELIGION ON ART

It is obvious that religion provides art with subjects for pictorial, plastic, and literary representation. This appears very clearly in typical Plains Indian decorations of tentcovers, robes, or shields. For example, when we survey the Southern Siouan designs published by J. O. Dorsey, we find that they are, in aboriginal theory, replicas of things revealed in visionary experiences.

Should a man wear such a decorated robe without having had a vision of the mystery object, he was in danger (if the object was connected with the Thunder-being, etc.) of being killed by lightning. Every Omaha feared to decorate his robe, tent, or blanket with an object seen by another person in a dream or vision. For instance, George Miller would not dare to have bears' claws, horses' hoofs, etc., on his robe, because neither he nor his father ever saw a bear or horse mysteriously.

The prerogative was transmitted to the next descending generation, but unless the son repeated his father's mystic experience he might not in turn bequeath it to his issue.[3]

Whenever the relation of religion to art is discussed, it is necessary to inquire first into the technical equipment, the stock of artistic ideas, characteristic of the people in question. In their secular paintings on, say, wind-screens or robes the Plains Indians are capable of vivid representations of military exploits: here the owner is depicted driving off a herd of the enemy's horses, there he is holding his own against a hostile group and striking one foeman with a feathered spear. Let us recall that such scenes are indeed taken from actual life but are theoretically often mere fulfillments of the visions that lent sanction to the war expeditions delineated. It is accordingly not a little noteworthy that in the avowedly sacred paintings no such composition occurs. An Omaha has a vision of deer and he paints one of these animals on either side of his lodge door; he sees two stars and the new moon, and a crescent flanked by two four-pointed figures appears on his robe; and when he has a vision of horses he represents on his tent cover horsetracks and horse tails. It is not that human figures are lacking,—a red circle symbolizing the sun may harbor a man shaking a dewclaw rattle; it is not that all sacred decorations are equally simple, —on one Omaha lodge a row of bear-paw prints is topped by a quartette of differently colored lightning lines, above which a circle stands for the bear's cave. However, adventures that are quite within the native craftsman's capacity are not reproduced but merely suggested in the religious art of these tribes. The ideas may be identical, but their expression differs: on a Crow robe devoid of religious value the enemy is shown shooting at the hero, but is struck by him; on a sacred shield from the same tribe the glancing off of bullets is *symbolized* by a series of lines.

It would certainly be rash to deny that the Plains Indians *ever* applied principles of composition current among them to the religious domain, yet the fact that in several dozen samples examined at random not one exemplifies the assimilation of the realistic style cannot be without significance. In his treatise on the Ghost Dance Mr. Mooney, it is true, reproduces two specimens that apparently contradict my observations,[4] but a closer scrutiny disposes of the difficulty. One of them purports to depict a Kiowa seer's experience and really goes much further in the direction of pictorial composition than the Omaha illustrations described above. Yet the entire upper third of the picture consists in a mass of strokes wholly unintelligible without a special interpretation, which connects them with the prairie and buffalo. The remainder is, indeed, almost self-explanatory, yet there is a total want of that spirited realism distinctive of the better Plains Indian paintings. Now this charge cannot be leveled against the second painting, which delineates faithfully and graphically a group of Cheyenne and Arapaho Ghost Dancers. But here another point enters. In what sense are we dealing with a genuinely *religious* picture?

There is of course the representation of a religious scene, but interestingly enough it is not the work of a votary of the tribes in question, but that of a Ute captive. There is not the slightest suggestion that the painting had any religious value for its maker, who may well be supposed to have merely exercised an observant foreigner's curiosity and to have given rein to a purely artistic impulse.

Perhaps we can safely go a step further and offer a plausible suggestion for the difference between the secular and the religious art of these people. The overpowering sense of communion with the supernatural may evoke a desire for outward representation without requiring more than a suggestive memento of the wonderful experience. In other words, it is not necessary to draw the supernatural patron in the act of addressing his suppliant and conferring upon him some longed-for boon. Just as a chicken-hawk feather becomes sacred not because it is identical with the object of the vision, let alone with the giver of the blessing, but because of its *association* with the ultimate fount of the religious emotion felt, so the merest outline commemorating the great event acquires a derivative holiness as a symbol that may or may not merge in the total memory image of the mystic exaltation.

A parallel difference in secular and sacred art style has been noted by Mr. Jochelson.[5] As producers of miniature carvings in wood, ivory, or whalebone, the Koryak of eastern Siberia stand perhaps supreme among the unlettered peoples of the globe. Even complicated tasks, such as the representation of a pair of wrestlers or of a sledge with driver and dogs, are successfully executed by the native sculptor. One striking illustration furnished by the Russian investigator veritably has some connection with the religious sphere: the artist exhibits a shaman beating the drum emblematic of his office and even reproduces the gleam of ecstasy on his subject's face.   But, as in the case of the Ute painting of an alien ceremony, the work of art is a work of *art* devoid of sacred meaning.   If, now, we turn to objects of definitely religious value among the Koryak, we receive a rude shock: the makers of these charms and idols and holy fire-making apparatus seem to belong to a realm of artistic endeavor utterly and hopelessly inferior to that of their fellow-tribesmen when intent on solving a purely esthetic problem.   For example, the wooden bear carved for the occasion of the Bear festival is of a crudity that simply beggars description when placed side by side with what is done for the sheer love of carving.

Mr. Jochelson is inclined to explain the disparity by the vagueness of primitive man's conception of his supernatural anthropomorphic beings, but I am not convinced that the whole or even the main solution is to be sought in this direction.   For one thing, some of these beings are made sufficiently definite in tribal mythologies; again, the manufacturer of sacred carvings, as indicated by the case of the bear, may fail no less as an artist when he attempts the well-known animal form, even among so skillful a people as the Koryak. It seems simpler and more plausible to assume that the native, in certain moods, ignores the ideals of art for the plain reason that his attention is riveted to other ends.   Take, for example, the birch-bark records associated with the Mystic Rite of the Ojibwa about Lake Superior.   The drawings, incised upon bark with a pointed piece of bone, are often exceedingly crude, but it is hardly because of the vague conceptions of the supernatural beings, since the like deficiency is noticeable in the pictures of such familiar creatures as the wolf or bear.   As a matter of fact, when we compare the several records published, it becomes clear that each artist has consistently attacked as a whole the problem confronting him; he does not discriminate between supernatural beings and phenomena of every-day existence: everything seems, as it were, cast in a single mold. Thus, the Red Lake chart reproduced by Hoffman is throughout characterized by a neatness that, despite its schematism, sets it off favorably from the uniform slovenliness of the Mille Lacs record, while a third specimen displays a distinct effort towards not merely symbolic but pictorial delineation and succeeds in conveying a sense of movement no less in the drawing of the drumming Great Spirit than in that of a similarly occupied priest. If even in the last-mentioned sample the execution falls manifestly below the draftsman's technical capacity, it is presumably because the primary purpose of the charts is mnemonic, so that artistic finish would be a work of supererogation, perhaps the veriest preciosity. It is none the less interesting to observe how, presumably without set purpose, native talent or the esthetic conscience may assert itself in individual instances.[6]

In connection with these charts and similar phenomena of other regions their esoteric character should not be overlooked; they are not exposed to the public gaze, and "there does not appear to be a recognized system by which the work of any one person is fully intelligible to another." It may well be that the lack of definition in the products of religious art is often co-determined by deliberate shrouding in mystery. In some instances, other motives may operate in the same direction: as Professor Boas once suggested, "the very sacredness of the idea represented might induce the artist to obscure his meaning intentionally, in order to keep the significance of the design from profane eyes." [7]

Have we, then, hit upon one of those general laws which modern ethnology, to the disgust of outsiders, is so reluctant to proclaim? Does religion by some inherent necessity exert a deleterious influence on art or, at least, on realism? A glance at the history of Egypt demonstrates the shallowness of such a formulation. It is true that, in the words of the late Professor W. Max Müller, "adherence to tradition constituted an especially grave barrier to artistic development," that "the figures of the gods always preserved, more or less, the stiff and—in some details—childishly imperfect style of the early period." But on the other side may be cited "the marvelous portrait sculpture of the Pyramid Age," intimately correlated with religious conceptions and plausibly adduced by Wundt to demonstrate the effectiveness, nay, possibly omnipotence, of religious factors in leading to a higher stage of individualistic representation.[8] Religion and art are both too intricate to admit of an "either-or" type of interaction: even in the same society and at the same time contradictory currents may well be seen according to the phase of the phenomena envisaged.

To return to lowlier planes of culture, there is an additional way of accounting for the slovenliness of pictorial or plastic art when associated with the sacred. Besides these arts there are other means of esthetic expression,— those corresponding to our drama. The Menomini, who had been blessed by supernatural buffalo, would assemble twice a year, and execute a dance with a buffalo headdress, "imitating the pawing, bellowing, and hooking, of the buffalo." [9] Such dramatic performances will engage our attention a little later. In the present context the point to note is that they are a potentially stronger means of emotional attachment to the Sacred than the feather or painted figure symbolic of a vision, for while the latter, when once put on or executed, respectively, may leave the owner in a quite passive state the animal dance involves an active identification with the object of religious veneration. But to what extent such a means for the expression of the religious idea may have been previously established and may serve adequately to fulfill the esthetic urge is a question that can only be answered by viewing *all* the phases of a tribal culture in unison; and apart from such synthetic surveys any generalization is almost sure to miss the mark.

Retroactive Influence of Art

If art derives much of its subject-matter from religion and may even in some instances draw technical advantages from the association, it is not the less true that religion in turn may draw sustenance from art. Nor is it difficult to determine the general character of this retroactive influence. Let any one attempt to draw, let alone model a house, from no matter how good a verbal description: there will be innumerable details that *must* be defined yet remain indeterminate in the directions. All the more will this apply to the case of human physiognomy. Hence an artist who should wish to depict with precision the popular conception of a given supernatural being is bound to rely upon his individual fancy to fill in the lacking details. That there is no necessity for his conceiving his task from this angle at all, that he may be content with mere sketchiness or symbolism, has already been demonstrated. But as soon as an esthetic impulse goads him into different paths, he may come to create a type that at once synthesizes the essentials of current belief, without contravening them in any particular, and yet at the same time adds a series of strokes that may not merely shade but materially alter the pre-existing picture. So long as things go no further, the new image is no more than an individual version of the general norm. But as soon as that variant, whether through its maker's prestige or through priestly patronage, is elevated to the position of a standard representation, it becomes itself thenceforward a determinant of the popular conception.

To take a simple example, there is a widespread belief in North America that thunder is caused by a large bird. So long as this notion is merely transmitted by oral tradition it may remain quite vague. But when a native attempts to incise his conception on birch-bark or to carve it in a wooden mask, he will naturally add distinctive features that make of the Thunderbird an eagle, or a hawk, or a nondescript product of fancy. Now such identification may have far-reaching consequences, for it would naturally tend to raise, say, the eagle to a level of sanctity that did not originally belong to it and cannot well belong to it where, as among the Nootka of Vancouver Island, the Thunderbird does not correspond to any actual species. Moreover, if two or more distinct representations are both accepted, a dual or multiple conception of the being is fostered, as when the Menomini now picture the Thunderers in human form, now again as birds, and arrive at the notion that the eagles are *related* to the Thunderers.[10]

The reaction of pictorial representation on mythology is strikingly exemplified by the story of the Egyptian deity Qeb (Geb). Artists depicting him in erect posture showed a goose perched on his head, and later theologians accordingly construed this earth-god into a huge gander, who, with divine indifference to sexual disabilities, laid the solar egg. As a matter of fact, the goose was primarily nothing but the hieroglyph forming an abbreviation of Qeb's name.[11]

Fetichism furnishes one of the most instructive examples of the interrelationship under discussion. At least in one of the regions regarded as preëminently characterized by fetichism—in the Congo, including Loango—the connection differs fundamentally from what might be expected. That is to say, a fetich is not the execution of the craftsman's conception of some divine being; but among the legion of human effigies produced in this region of carvers some specimens are selected for sanctification: the representation of a human figure "is not an effective fetich until it has been through the hands of the medicine-man and received its power from him." What confers upon the object its supernatural potency is solely the mysterious spell sung over it or the substance, wonder-working in its own right like the *ngula* paint, thrust into a ventral cavity. Hence, only a moderate percentage of the human or animal figurines are in reality fetiches. On the other hand, the sanctifying technique can manifestly be applied to quite different objects,— to artifacts not suggesting the human form or to inanimate phenomena of the surrounding world, a stone, a tree, a crossroad. Any object can become a "fetich" if only it has been ritualistically consecrated.

By dint of the wizard's incantations an inert mass comes to acquire an altogether remarkable but specialized potency: it may ward off a fever or grant invulnerability, render its owner invisible or banish a plague of grasshoppers.

Now it is a matter of considerable interest to find a close correlation between the development of wood-carving and the occurrence of anthropomorphic and theromorphic figures. If for convenience' sake we restrict the term "fetich" to such effigies as these and call other objects of generically similar sacred character "amulets," we find that amulets predominate markedly in the Uele and Ubangi districts, while the Lower Congo, the Kasai and Kwango districts display an incomparably greater abundance of fetiches. Thus, the Tervueren Museum near Brussels has 73 fetiches from the Maritime Region but not a solitary amulet; while from the Uele there are 27 amulets and no fetiches, from the Ubangi 16 amulets and a single fetich. The distribution of the two is clearly one of mutual exclusiveness; and it coincides definitely with the efflorescence and the decay of woodwork in the Congo. In other words, the prevalence of an artistic technique determines the outward form of religious objects.

But we can perhaps safely go a step further. It is all very well for our anonymous authority to say that amulet and fetich "sont deux expressions matérielles d'un sentiment uniforme." Generically, no doubt they are; and perhaps they may be even more specifically in special cases. But as we turn the plates illustrating the Tervueren collections, the thought inevitably obtrudes itself that in a strict sense this cannot always be true. A whistle, a bit of horn, or a pebble in the nature of the case is incapable of arousing the set of ideas evoked by the image of a woman nursing an infant, of a man bending over a drum, or of the grotesqueries connected with the representation of sex organs. When what mere artistic fancy has created is hallowed by the fetich-monger's chant or pigment, the craftsman's fantasies adhere to and aid in molding the popular conception of the mysterious. Take a concrete case from the Kwango, for which a series of obviously related figures have been pictured, the extremes representing, respectively, a physiognomy with slightly tilted nose and a full-fledged recurved proboscis. Assuming that the more realistic effigy is the earliest, we can readily imagine how esthetic playing with the motive of the up-turned nose led to the ludicrous exaggeration of this feature, which by consecration and personification might become one of the attributes of a nascent deity.[12]

However, the art that has probably contributed in by far the greatest measure to the conceptual tenor of religion is literature,—in that unwritten form, of course, represented by orally transmitted folk-tales. For, though the outward shape of folklore heroes may remain inadequately defined without the aid of plastic and pictorial delineation, their intellectual and moral characters can be determined with incomparably greater precision through the medium of narrative.

As we have seen in a previous chapter, the influence of literary fancy on religion is also championed by Andrew Lang and Father Schmidt, but in a sense rather different from the one I should here suggest. Assuming an archaic concept of an ethically pure Creator, they assert that this noble ideal has been covered with a debasing veneer of anthropomorphic simplicity and drollery, nay, ribaldry. It is not easy for me to understand how a sharply defined replica of our own monotheistic ideal can fail to withstand whatever lure there may be in folkloristic fantasies. On the other hand, it seems entirely possible that in fulfillment of distinct human demands there should develop in mutual independence the comic episodes of a trickster cycle and the *shadowy* character of a creative being; that the origin of specific phenomena in society or the universe should be ascribed to the well-known trickster; and that this common element of creativeness should lead to a fusion and confusion of the two characters till not even the most devout Crow can state with assurance that the earth was made by the Sun rather than by Old-Man-Coyote. My point is that such amalgamation and consequent obscurity would be inconceivable if the primary notion of the Sun were that of an ethically immaculate Supreme Being; but that a vaguely and only incidentally beneficent creator can well be credited with even the more grotesquely offensive exploits of a trickster.

Irrespective of this moot-problem, it is easy to illustrate how literature may color the aspect of religious figures by comparing two versions of a Shoshonean solar myth recorded by me among the Lemhi Shoshoni of Idaho and their congeners, the Southern Ute of Colorado, respectively.

According to the Shoshoni, the sun was at one time so close to the earth as to burn people to death. A council was summoned, and the Indians delegated Cottontail to shoot the Sun. He concealed himself, and as the Sun rose Cottontail let fly arrow after arrow, but without avail, for they were all consumed by the Sun's heat. At last he used his fire-drill and with it killed the Sun, who in falling burnt yellow spots on his enemy's neck and legs. The corpse was cut open, the gall was extracted, and then another tribesman raised the sun to his present height.

It is clear that the narrator's conception of the solar being fluctuates between that of a mortal with human organs, and a material body with the characteristic store of heat; and also that the Sun plays throughout a purely passive part. Now contrast the Ute myth:

Cottontail was wandering about, slaying people. He lay in ambush for the Sun. When the arrows shot against his enemy were burnt up, he took a club and with it knocked off a piece of him, which caused a conflagration. Fleeing from the fire, he sought refuge under a certain fireproof weed, which protected him, so that only a little yellow spot was made on his neck. But as Cottontail walked on the hot ground, his legs burned off. Finally Sun caused a snowfall that put out the fire. Now, however, Sun punished his enemy by transforming him into a rabbit and decreeing that thenceforth it should be easy for any one to track him in the snow.

First of all, it is of course clear that we are dealing with variants of a single Shoshonean myth centering in the antagonism of Sun and Cottontail. Now, whether we assume the Ute or the Shoshoni version as approximating more closely the archetype of the tale, an effect of the story on the religious notion of the Sun can be plausibly argued. Let us postulate, in conformity with Lang's scheme, the greater antiquity of the Ute myth, in which the Sun appears as a comparatively dignified, active, powerful, and avenging transformer. Then the Shoshoni, by modifying the incidents and the motivation of the conflict, have appreciably debased the earlier picture of the solar god. If the alternative hypothesis is entertained, the Ute have secondarily embellished it.

I am not at all disposed to deny that the facts admit of a somewhat different formulation. It may very well be that unless the Ute had entertained a preëxisting conception of the Sun as a powerful deity they would not have developed the tale in their distinctive way; and that the absence of a like conception paved the way for the Shoshoni variant. Such intricate inter-relations are precisely what I contend for; and my point at present is merely that the mythopeic imagination working with the traditional religious stock-in-trade *may* sensibly affect the core of the religious sentiment, may tend to a shifting of the center of gravity, so to speak. If a story-teller has adequate authority to establish his individual version as the standard, then it may appreciably modify the reactions to traditional sacred figures, adding to the sanctity of some, detracting from that of others by the definiteness of the picture thus impressed on the auditors. To exemplify the power of the literary fancy in this direction we may once more revert to the Crow. For some Crow Indians the legendary Old-Woman's-Grandson, slayer of monsters, is a deity prayed to for help on the vision-quest. Some, in other words, have become more deeply impressed than others by this literary figure and ascribe to him definite divine powers. It might be said that this is merely due to his being conceived as the child of the Sun. But what is this notion itself, of solar offspring, if not the result of literary fancy?

CEREMONIAL DRAMA

The naïve way of interpreting the festivals of primitive peoples is to accept as authentic the explanations of the participant. Thus, the pledger of a Crow Sun Dance desires the death of an enemy; hence the ceremony must be a prayer for revenge. The Cheyenne pledger wishes to insure a sick relative's recovery; hence the ceremony is a prayer for health. Correspondingly simple views might be advanced with regard to the Hawaiian Luakini or the Tongan Harvest ceremony and a host of other equally elaborate performances in other parts of the world.

Interesting as aboriginal theories as to aboriginal conduct invariably are, they are no more to be accepted unmodified in matters of psychology than in matters of history: the native does not know his motives and those of his collaborators any more than other folk do, and they are only revealed by a critical analysis of his and their behavior. The subject is a large one, and at present I am merely concerned to prove the co-existence of latent esthetic factors where many recognize only the patent religious ones.

Take the case of the Crow Sun Dance, on which information is relatively full.[18]   According to native theory, the essence of the ritual lies in the vision-quest of a mourner thirsting for revenge. Instead of relying on a revelation to be secured by his own efforts, he resorts to the possessor of a sacred doll, whose power is expected to grant his prayer. So far the conception corresponds entirely to a familiar Crow procedure; the only varying feature lies in the specific character of the holy object, but that would differ in any case according to the shaman's personal "medicine." Why, however, all the pother? Why do not this pair of main performers, the shaman and the mourner, go about their business along the lines of the ordinary routine of a war expedition? Why is it necessary to involve the whole tribe for a period of months? Why must a special lodge be erected with the assistance of all the men? Why do dozens of young men fast and torture themselves *not* in order to help the mourner gain his desired end but to achieve their own longing for a vision craved for purposes strictly their own? Why do noted warriors recite and represent their deeds and receive cooked buffalo tongues as a reward of past bravery?

It is perfectly obvious that to characterize this composite performance as a prayer for revenge is to fall prey to a rationalistic simplification of the facts. Doubtless that motive is a powerful one for the supplicant, yet even for him it is not the only one. It is obviously different for the fellow-fasters, though their participation still bears a definitely religious stamp. But what of the hundreds of onlookers, now hurrying to bring and raise the lodge-poles, now philandering with their sweethearts during a period of privileged license, now boasting of their prowess or engaging in a sham combat? Part of the time, no doubt, they are held awe-struck and spellbound in the presence of a prospective communion with the supernatural. But for the rest they are thrilled as onlookers or supernumeraries of a spectacular play on the grandest scale within the tribal comprehension; and if all the complex machinery hinted at rather than described above is set in motion, it is because the alleged cause of the vast undertaking is in a sense nothing but its occasion. Even the main performers are not of course unaffected by the display of general activity: whatever else they may be doing, they are unconsciously playing a part for the approval of an audience. Thus, each and every one participating in the Sun Dance is partly affected by esthetic, extra-religious motives. To assert from this point of view that "ceremonialism exists for ceremonialism's sake" is not to forgo a psychological formulation, as an otherwise friendly critic oddly imagines,[14] but to penetrate beyond the obvious interpretation of religious behaviorism.

REFERENCES

[1] Harrison.
[2] Wundt: 103, 221, 230, 484, 504.
[3] J. O. Dorsey: 394-409.
[4] Mooney: plates CVII, CIX.
[5] Jochelson, 1905-1908: 33, 88, 646 sq., 668.
[6] Hoffman: plates III, IV, VIII.
[7] Boas, 1903.
[8] Müller: 12. Breasted: 179. Wundt: 215 f.
[9] Skinner, 1915 (a): 202.
[10] Skinner, 1913: 74-78, 99, 102, 104 sq.
[11] Müller: 42, 368.
[12] Notes analytiques: 149 sq., 161, 212, 219, 239, 248; plates XXX, XLVII. Weeks, 1913: 254; id., 1914: 232 sq. Pechuel-Loesche.
[13] Lowie, 1914; id., 1915.
[14] Bartlett: 202.

CHAPTER XIII

ASSOCIATION

INDIVIDUAL AND SOCIAL ASSOCIATIONS

IN a previous chapter I have pointed out how largely the thoughts and the behavior of individuals are determined by factors arising not from the inborn characteristics of the thinker or actor but from the cultural conditions affecting all the members of his group jointly. This principle can be amply illustrated by the associations of ideas that appear in different societies, for though such associations have been commonly studied only from the point of view of individual psychology it is not difficult to prove that exclusive attention to this aspect of the phenomenon fails to bring adequate illumination. This, indeed, is fully recognized by Professor Höffding, the Danish psychologist, who expresses himself as follows:

> Associations of ideas may . . . be so firm and constant that it is forgotten out of what elements they have arisen. Some of the greatest mysteries in the province of psychology owe their origin to such deeply rooted associations of ideas, the beginning and history of which have been forgotten . . . that which presents itself to us as a unity and as necessarily coherent, may yet have arisen from the fusing of different elements. It demands therefore a deeper and more extensive psychological analysis than the dogmatizing psychology enters into. Such an analysis finds an especial application in the associations which have not been formed in the actual consciousness of the individual, but are the bequest of earlier generations. . . .[1]

The fusion of originally distinct elements alluded to by the Scandinavian scholar will be considered in a later section of this chapter. What concerns us at present is the extent to which the association of ideas presented by a given person can be accepted as a genuinely individual mental product or as one functionally dependent on his social heritage. Perhaps we can most profitably approach the question by considering Kent and Rosanoff's studies in word association, which by many of their colleagues are regarded as classical. After preliminary experimentation these authors hit upon a list of one hundred words and recorded the ideas associated with those of the list by a thousand normal subjects. Thus 191 individuals thought of "table" in response to "chair," while only a single one gave as his reaction "office." Treating the results secured as a standard for testing other subjects, the investigators distinguish as "common" those reactions represented in their tables, while those not found there are called "individual," though not necessarily abnormal.[2] To what extent is it possible to apply a similar technique to anthropological material? Scanning Kent and Rosanoff's list, we are first of all impressed with the necessity of restricting its use to persons living under similar cultural conditions. Apart from the fact that certain abstract ideas, such as "music," might not have equivalents in other cultures, the reactions to the concept would inevitably differ in other civilizations. For instance, "piano," "violin," "harmony," "Merry Widow" would be excluded. It might be easy to suggest plausible equivalents in the second culture, but their precise value would be highly problematical. The utility of mass investigations of this sort rests on the exposure of all individuals to a comparable educational environment. This may be illustrated from another angle. Of the American subjects studied by Kent and Rosanoff only one responded to the stimulus "tobacco" with "stars"; among the Crow, who identify their sacred tobacco with the stars, it is safe to assume that considerably more than one-tenth of one per cent would have had this reaction. Similarly, with the word "eagle"; not a single American associated it with "thunder" but in any Crow list the two ideas would certainly be coupled with a relatively great frequency. Probably some reactions would coincide in the two tests: there is no good reason why some Crow subjects should not offer as the second member of the pair such words as "beak," "clouds," "feathers," or "mountains." But evidently individuality in our psychologists' sense could not be established by the Crow list for Caucasian subjects or vice versa: the coupling of "eagle" and "thunder" would be "common" for a Crow, "individual" for an American, though the investigators' wise precaution in their Appendix, that anything should be reckoned a normal response if symbolized by the eagle, must not be overlooked.

Another word of warning must be added: the psychological appraisal of a given association is impossible without a consideration of linguistic data. For example, in Kent and Rosanoff's list the "eagle" is linked 568 times with "bird." This would be impossible for the Crow for the simple reason that the eagle as the bird par excellence is commonly designated by the same term as the whole zoölogical class. Again, the constellation of the Dipper is preëminently associated by the Crow with the number seven. Thus, the Dipper appears to Lone-tree in a vision as a man but is identified when he rises, exposing the seven stars on his queue; and so, when Lone-tree subsequently goes through a rite to aid a woman he summons six other men, "for with them I should make seven, and there are seven stars in the Dipper." Again, Hillside's brother sees the constellation

as seven persons singing songs for him. Still another visionary infers that *four* visitants are the Dipper because they
sing seven songs for him; and when he organizes a ceremony
on the basis of his revelation, he assembles seven married
couples. The last two instances are especially interesting,
for they show that so long as the number seven appears in
some fashion no incongruity is felt in the representation
of the Dipper.[3]

Now, plausible as this association may seem, there is no
obvious reason for the exceptional emphasis on the numerical
aspect of the constellation until we find that the Dipper in
Crow is simply called "Seven Stars," so that we are not
dealing with an ordinary association of distinct ideas at all.

These examples show how important it is to take into
account the linguistic data involved. This is indeed obvious when we recall that in Dr. Jung's experiments with Swiss
subjects such external factors as similarity in sound (green-
greed) or the conventional coupling of terms in set phrases
(assault-battery) played an important part.[4]

The systematic study of individual associations among
illiterate peoples is hardly even in its infancy, but an un-
published series collected by Dr. Spier among the Havasupai
of Arizona strongly impresses one with the psychic unity
of mankind as regards the principles at work in producing
responses from cue words. Thus, there is "coördination"
in uniting concepts both of which belong to the same general
head, but also "contrast," "predication," and, as might be
expected, some residual instances remain obscure. At all
events, there is every reason to look for an explanation of
the associations of primitive folk towards the same psychological principles operative among ourselves.

A fruitful line of research lies in the study of variants of
myths and prayers. Sometimes these may be so stereotyped

that for generations not the slightest alteration has been permitted. This, for example, is reported for some Hawaiian hymns, a phenomenon in harmony with Polynesian formalism. But elsewhere some latitude is allowed, and the resulting substitutions may repay study from more than one angle. We can thus examine the versions of the same myth told by two different narrators. We can also profitably examine the variations in the same individual's account at different times, for that will indicate the range of ideas evoked in one person by a fixed stimulus. At a certain stage of the Crow Tobacco ceremony a warrior is supposed to come running and to report what he has seen on a raid and on the return journey. At three different times Gray-bull dictated to me in his own language the actor's speech. There is of course far-reaching similarity, yet enough difference to prove that the form was not standardized. Thus, in all three versions the speaker stresses the abundance of the Tobacco crop and of the wild cherries, but only once uses a superlative in that connection, which accordingly is a dispensable element. In all three variants an enemy is killed, but while the narrator twice reports how he captured a gun the third account substitutes the striking of a blow: these were both conventional deeds of valor and evidently reckoned as equivalent. That is, the cue "victorious exploit" might arouse in Gray-bull's mind either "gun-capture" or "blow."

Such individual interpretations are significant even for a purely cultural inquiry because the traditional associations described by Höffding have not always been traditional, and whenever we observe a deviation from the norm we have before us a possible starting-point for a cultural innovation. Unfortunately, when a given traditional association confronts us, it is often wholly enigmatic from a psychological point of view, that is to say, no hint remains of the principle on which the underlying ideas were ever linked by any individual mind. It is easy enough to proceed from cue to reaction, but to work backwards is more difficult, just as it is harder to extract a cube root than to raise a number to the third power. Still there are degrees of obscurity, and at all events a brief discussion of some instances may illuminate the nature of the problem.

To begin with a difficult case, Dr. Spier tells me that among the Havasupai of northern Arizona a woman will not scratch her head with her fingers during either menstrual seclusion or the period preceding and following childbirth; instead she uses a special head-scratching stick. Evidently there is here a firm association between certain important periods in a woman's life and the desirable mode of scratching her head; and since it is not a sporadic habit but a general observance, it would be vain to seek for the origin of the custom in the mental reactions of individual tribesmen. As a matter of fact, we should have to go much further back than tribal history, for comparison with other peoples proves that the practice is found among the Pima of southern Arizona, in California, British Columbia, and, indeed, among the Menomini of Wisconsin and the Yuchi of South Carolina.[5] Evidently the usage is of fair antiquity and has spread from tribe to tribe over a wide area. At some time and place the association must have sprung into existence in some individual brain and struck a responsive chord in the social environment; but what may have produced this original association eludes our scrutiny.

The psychology of associations is not always equally opaque. The Jagga of East Africa view multiple births with alarm as portending bad luck: triplets are accordingly killed, their mother being despised as though guilty of a heinous crime, while in case of twins one of the infants is regularly strangled. Obviously the same qualification holds here as in the preceding case: we are dealing not with an idiosyncrasy but with a rule imposed by tradition. Nevertheless, here the motive does not lie wholly shrouded in mystery, and we can apply with some show of plausibility the explanation given for a similar custom in Central Australia, to wit, that twins "are usually destroyed at once as something uncanny." In other words, the Negroes, like the Australians, may have reached the conclusion that what was out of the ordinary was necessarily weird and pregnant with evil potency. However, further study would show that even among fellow-Bantu tribes the interpretation does not conform to that of the Jagga, is indeed antithetical inasmuch as twins are viewed as omens of good fortune. Yet a modification of our hypothesis would bring the new facts into line with a generic interpretative principle: we may assume that the Extraordinary is potentially ambivalent, that it may be credited with either a mysterious power to confer benefits or a weird tendency to destroy, and which of the alternatives prevails is a matter of chance according to the specific circumstances surrounding the origin of the custom. Of course, such a general interpretation not only leaves undetermined the path actually followed but also fails to account for specific ideas reported, such as the Nootka notion that twins are intimately connected with the salmon, which Mrs. Spier informs me also occurs among the Klallam.[6]

There are, however, still other cases in which the processes seem so transparent that it requires hyper-skepticism to doubt the patent cause of an association. Thus, granting that the hands are brought into juxtaposition with the idea of sex differentiation, we understand at once why a Thonga connects the left hand with the female sex and the right with males.[7] Traditional though the association may be, we see at once its aptness, the motive for its currency and for its invention.

Among the constantly recurring associations may be noted those by which a specific value is attached to certain numbers. It has been pointed out that the Crow, for example, like the majority of North American tribes, regard four as the mystic number, while the Paviotso ascribe similar significance to five. While it is of course impossible to give an ultimate explanation of numerical associations found in a given tribe, we are in a position to range these phenomena with comparable psychological manifestations of educated Europeans. In his well-known *Inquiries into Human Faculty and its Development* Francis Galton records that he himself associated even numbers with the male sex, while his informants frequently invested numbers with definite personalities,—one of them described Three as a good old friend, another as a treacherous sneak, and so forth. As a boy I myself had a special fondness for both Three and Four, but felt that somehow Three was closer to me so that I rather resented its inferiority to Four.

In correlating the ethnographic data with the Galtonian phenomena it is necessary to define exactly what is meant. There is not the slightest reason to suppose that an individual Crow has a greater inborn tendency to view four as sacred than a random Caucasian: if he so regards it, it is because his reaction is predetermined by the cultural tradition that he has shared from early childhood. The psychological explanation of a particular Crow's attitude towards four has probably nothing to do with his individual mental reactions to the number, but solely with his individual reaction to any social norm whatsoever. But at some time some one must have had a differential feeling for four as compared with other numbers and created the present standard by his personal prestige; and it is that pre-normative individual reaction which we can with some show of reason connect with the data gathered by Galton. A subsidiary and perhaps even equally important source of mystic numbers has been suggested by Boas, to wit, the esthetic satisfaction derived from rhythmic repetition, so that the difference in sacred numbers would correspond to a difference in favorite rhythms.[8]

In this context it may be well to point out that modern psychology notes a variety of associations as more or less commonplace in our own society that are not one whit less fanciful than some of those recorded among illiterate peoples. The late Miss Josephine Meyer, reader of the Theater Guild in New York, told me that she associated all manner of ideas with the letters of our alphabet: "P" appeared to her as the most gentlemanly, "m" as the mother of "n," and so forth. Under this heading, of course, comes the phenomenon latterly described as "synesthesia," of which colored audition is the commonest form. One of Galton's correspondents associated letters of the alphabet with definite colors and conversely read words into color patterns, another always associated Tuesday with a gray sky color, and Friday with a dull yellow smudge. It is an undecided question whether such associations represent an innate idiosyncrasy: Woodworth suggests as the likelier guess "that the extra sensations are images that have become firmly attached to their substitute stimuli during early childhood."[9]

SYMBOLISM

The types of association last considered naturally lead to a discussion of symbolism. If, say, a certain object or idea invariably appears in connection with a certain color, the color can come to acquire symbolic value and will evoke the image or concept of its regular concomitant. Sometimes an association of this character is indirect, that is, the symbol is not immediately associated with the basic emotional value but only through a series of intervening links. Thus, a species of snake among the Andamanese is an emblem of well-being not in its own right, as it were, but because it is associated with honey, which besides its intrinsic attractiveness is again associated with the season of fine weather. Similarly, the Western Dakota may represent the whirlwind by narrow upright figures that directly stand for the chrysalis of a moth from which the whirlwind is derived.[10]

It would be worth while to determine by an extensive survey of the world to what extent certain of the simpler forms of symbolism are rooted in the general mental constitution of mankind. For example, is red, as A. R. Brown suggests, a general emblem of activity and force because of its dynamogenic potency? The idea is attractive, yet we must be on our guard against assuming that even in the simplest cases the interpretation is fully determined. Thus, there is for *us* a natural fitness in the Omaha custom of representing a vision of the Night by blackening part of the lodge-cover; and similarly *we* understand at once why a Menomini boy on his puberty fast should blacken his face to indicate sadness and thus arouse the compassion of the powers he is supplicating. But the very fact that black is so readily connected with death makes it possible to convert it from a symbol of grief into one of joy; and accordingly we find that the Crow warriors who had slain an enemy returned with blackened faces as a sign of victory.

Interesting as such reflections are from a psychological point of view, for our present purpose they must yield precedence to another, to wit, the religious value of the symbol.

The significance of the cross in Christianity or the lotus-flower in Buddhism is too well-known to require more than a passing reference. That there are parallel instances in primitive life is clear from the example, several times quoted, of the significance attached to a feather revealed in a Crow vision. This case is a favorable one for elucidating the source of the symbol's value. It is too readily assumed that since the symbol stands for something else, its potency is derivative from that something, and the overshadowing influence exerted by an apparently secondary phenomenon remains rather enigmatic. Thus, the spontaneous emotion evoked by the flag of one's country is not easily explicable on this view, nor the Crow's appraisal of his feather as "the greatest thing in the world." In both cases the difficulty lies in the assumption of an inapplicable psychological attitude. Only in an intellectualistic sense does the flag or feather represent an ulterior entity of higher order; on the affective plane, either represents *nothing* apart from itself but forms an integral part of an invaluable indivisible emotional experience that immediately asserts itself with all the force of an unanalysable manifestation of the Extraordinary in the special form of the Sacred. This reaction appears clearly in a statement made by an Hidatsa woman to the effect that Indian corn and the wild geese were one and the same thing. It was not that she was of pre-logical mentality in Lévy-Bruhl's sense, that is, incapable in ordinary life of separating the idea of the plant from that of the birds, but that in the given context both were associated in the same sacred complex and stood for that complex: whether one or the other cue was used to evoke the essential emotional state, was a matter of complete indifference.

Rationalization

Whatever sins may have been committed in the name of psycho-analysis, it has the great merit of having clearly brought out and duly stressed the concept of "rationalization," than which few principles are more important for an understanding of human behavior. It is a fact of constant observation in daily life, in the psychiatric clinic, and, we may add, among primitive peoples, that man is not so much a rational as a rationalizing creature. That is, he does not act or work towards conclusions by the careful sifting of evidence but acquires them by some irrational process, subsequently glossing over the logical delinquency by secondary apologetic argumentation. Religion, with its predominantly emotional basis, is naturally a favorite haunt of rationalizers; but in turn it supplies some of the basic schemes for rationalizing conduct of a primarily nonreligious nature. Let us consider the latter case first.

Where, as among the Crow and their neighbors, the vision assumes a dominant position in religion, its scope may easily be extended so as to embrace potentially any and every phase of human existence. Not only does the vision become the theoretical origin of every ceremonial, nay, of every deviation in ritualistic detail, or of such markedly abnormal behavior as that of the berdache, but success and failure are interpreted in terms of the basic concept and, consistently enough, every war-raid may require the sanction of a supernatural urging. "White men," says the Indian, "have ideas; the Indians have visions;" or he may even go so far as the Blackfoot who told Dr. Wissler that the inventor of the phonograph must have had a vision of the instrument and received a circumstantial description of its mechanism. Among the Western Dakota the mythical Double Woman as a culture-heroine is supposed to have instructed a woman through dreams in the art of decorative design composition: sometimes the entire piece of work is exhibited in finished condition, sometimes the design appears on a rock or cliff. By a transparent association twin sisters are believed to dream similar designs, though sometimes other Indian women may get like dreams also derived from the same mythic source. "Such designs are copied by other women, and thus become a part of the art common to all." But an examination of putative dream designs convinced Wissler that they did not differ in principle from other designs, and it is perfectly obvious that certain mystically inclined individuals ascribe a supernatural origin to esthetic notions derived from the traditional stock of art patterns and modified by such minor variations as their own taste and fancy suggested:

A dream design is . . . not so much a distinct type of design as an illustration of the manner in which Dakota philosophy accounts for the origin of the present styles of decorative art.[11]

Among the most delicious rationalizations on record is that by which the Masai of East Africa justify their contempt for the blacksmiths' guild,—the pariah caste of their society. The blacksmiths, it is alleged, tempt the Masai to commit bloodshed by the implements they manufacture, hence they merit ethical condemnation. In order to appreciate the full extent to which this is mere mockery of a genuine reason, it is necessary to recall that the Masai are one of the most warlike peoples of Africa and that successful preying on their neighbors is a prerequisite to social prestige in their community. Of the same piece is the warrant alleged by them for the undertaking of these hostile raids: God, they say, gave all the cattle in the world to the

Masai; if their Bantu neighbors would not exhibit such reluctance in giving up the livestock in their possession, the Masai would not be driven to recover their property by force. Here cupidity is plainly rationalized by an appeal to the Divine Will.[12]

In many mythologies of primitive peoples there figures a character generally described as the culture-hero, that is, the inventor or discoverer of useful arts and other cultural phenomena. It is by no means certain that this personality always bears a "religious" character in the sense adopted in this book, but in many instances this is undoubtedly the case. Now the type of explanation offered by the natives to explain the origin of, say, fire-making or pottery is readily extended to other elements of social life, such as social rules and prohibitions. A Crow will thus naturally refer to Old-Man-Coyote the institution of the "joking-relationship," by which a man may play practical jokes on certain specially defined persons in the tribe.

Psychologically, all such cases do not of course differ from those in which the phenomenon that is accounted for in religious terms belongs itself to the religious category. Thus, the Crow justifies even so trivial a matter as the use of a specific type of facial paint in a rite by a corresponding revelation. Sometimes the generic motive of finding a rationalization in accordance with the current type of explanation is skillfully wielded on behalf of egotistic motives. When a Plains Indian or a Menomini shaman cannot conceive the possibility of giving away his ceremonial prerogatives even to his own children because his supernatural patron prescribed that he *must* receive compensation therefor, the case is obvious. For it is greed that would subconsciously project such a stipulation into the subjective experience, no matter how honestly the native may plead a supernatural decree. Probably some of the specific taboos so commonly recorded among these Indians permit of a somewhat similar interpretation. Thus, One-blue-bead remarked to me:

My medicine forbids me to make myself bleed, for example, to cut off my fingers; and if meat has blood on it, I won't eat it. At the time of my vision I was told not to eat blood and not to make myself bleed.

I think we can plausibly assume that the Crow witness had a personal idiosyncrasy relating to blood and, especially, a repugnance to the self-torture so prominent in his tribe. Auto-suggestion was perhaps strong enough to conjure up the coveted vision without the hateful laceration or finger-cutting, and rationalization would provide an excellent warrant from the aboriginal point of view for avoidance of the customary usage.

The rationalizing tendencies are especially conspicuous in the alleged origin and purpose of ceremonial, a subdivision of the subject sufficiently important to merit separate treatment.

RITUALISTIC MYTHS AND RITUALISTIC ENDS

The ceremonials of primitive peoples often receive an etiological and a teleological justification: they are avowedly performed because of events set forth in an explanatory origin myth and for a definite, plausible purpose,—say, as a thanksgiving for past favors or as a prayer for the public welfare. However, it can be proved beyond the possibility of doubt that many of these explanations are rationalizations which have nothing to do with the real history of the case. This is obvious where the entire ceremonial is simply projected into the past as the ritual taught by a supernatural being or clandestinely observed by the founder as it is performed by supernatural beings. Furthermore, as Ehrenreich among others has pointed out, we find again and again that like rituals of neighboring peoples are linked with utterly distinct myths: the similarity of the procedure is so great that it cannot have been evolved more than once, hence it must have spread from one tribe to another so that except in the center of dissemination the explanatory myths *must* by logical necessity be afterthoughts; "and, with the possibility of such explanation established, it becomes psychologically justifiable to treat the residual case as falling under the same category." [13]

The mode of reasoning applied here coincides absolutely with that which holds for the interpretation of other explanatory myths, of which the ritualistic legends under discussion form only a special subdivision. For instance, the Navaho of Arizona tell a quaint story ostensibly accounting for the color of the coyote's eyes. The Coyote of their traditions learnt the trick of sending his eyes out of their sockets and recalling them, but was warned not to try the performance too frequently. Casting prudence to the winds, he disobeyed and lost his power of recovery, but after wandering about in blindness he secured orbs of pine gum, *whence his yellow eyes to-day.* If this were the only version of the story, we might accept the naïve assumption that the natives, struck with the coyote's appearance, excogitated a series of episodes to account for it. But the Arapaho of Wyoming tell the same story with a different ending: *their* blind hero dupes Mole into lending him his eyes, *whence the mole's blindness to-day.*[14] The stable elements of the two variants cannot possibly be derived from these two utterly diverse points of departure; and when still other versions are discovered without *any* explanatory feature, the case is clear: the plot alone has been diffused from a common center, and in several instances distinct explanatory afterthoughts have been added.

Now, as hinted above, the situation is precisely similar when we are dealing with ritualistic myths: the persistent element corresponding to the stable plot of the "Eye-juggler" story is the fixed procedure, while the legendary justification is the equivalent of the explanatory frill at the end. Having stated the proposition in general terms, it remains to furnish some illustrations from the well-nigh inexhaustible material at hand. In this connection it would be artificial to separate the mythical and the teleological justification of ceremonial since both frequently belong to the same type of psychological manifestations.

Among some of the Australian tribes the rite of knocking out teeth is an integral part of the boys' initiation, which here as in New Guinea constitutes a festival of the first order of importance. But in Central Australia the usage appears without this context and at least two wholly different justifications are offered. The Kaitish nowadays merely practice the custom in order to improve their personal appearance, but explain that in the mythical period teeth were knocked out because the water tasted better without one of them. On the other hand, the Tjingilli knock out teeth towards the close of the rainy season and throw the tooth into a water-hole so that it may drive the rain and clouds away. The Gnanji not only expect the cessation of rain but an increase of water-lilies to follow a similar procedure.[15]

To take an equally simple case from America, the sacrifice of a finger-joint to propitiate the beings from whom a revelation is sought figures as a fairly widespread Plains Indian custom, being found among the Crow, Mandan, Ari-

kara, and Hidatsa. But the same practice occurs in this
area as a token of mourning. Indeed, among the Crow the
women usually cut off their fingers in connection with mortu-
ary rites while the men go through the performance when
fasting for a vision. Whichever of the objects is the older,
a re-adaptation of the purpose has occurred.

To turn to more pretentious rituals, the Crow share
with their Blackfoot neighbors a ceremonial planting of
sacred Tobacco sufficiently similar to exclude independent
invention. According to the most popular Crow version, the
discovery of the Tobacco dates back to the separation from
the Hidatsa, when one of two brothers was adopted by the
stars, with which the Tobacco is somehow identified, and received instructions as to the ceremony. But with the Blackfoot the Tobacco is part and parcel of the Beaver ritual,
transmitted originally by a Beaver who after abducting a
married woman indemnified her husband by sending her
back with the Beaver bundle.[16]

Again, Tozzer and Haeberlin have proved that the Navaho
and the Hopi of Arizona go through an extraordinarily similar series of ritualistic details, such as the use of prayer-
sticks, a specific type of mask, the swinging of a bull-roarer.
To doubt that these identities are due to borrowing would be
madness; yet the motive is quite distinct. "While the great
Navaho ceremonies are all focused on the healing of the
sick, those of the Hopi are obviously directed on the produc-
tion of fertility for the fields." The Hopi bull-roarer, for
example, is twirled as a magical instrument for procuring
rain; the Navaho shaman applies the same object to the patient's body by way of curing him. Haeberlin has further
illustrated his point by the ceremonial associations of a
widespread game,—that of hurling a dart at a rolling hoop.
The hunting tribes of the Plains play the game for the pur-

pose of magically calling buffalo, the hoop sometimes representing the animal, which is symbolically slain by the dart touching it. But with a similar ceremonial pastime the Hopi connect their favorite concept: the act of shooting the dart typifies lightning striking in a cornfield, "an event which is regarded as the acme of fertilization." [17]

One of the most striking illustrations of the principle here expounded is provided by the Sun Dance, as has been convincingly demonstrated by Spier.[18] Performed by about twenty Plains Indian tribes, this festival displays a remarkable stability as to objective traits. For example, in most instances the participants engage in spectacular self-torture; a tree designed for use in the ceremonial structure is commonly scouted for, felled, and struck as though it were an enemy; more than half of the tribes erect an altar of which a buffalo skull forms the most conspicuous object; and so forth. Contrasted with such similarity of behavior, there is a striking disparity as to avowed purpose. A Crow, as we have seen, pledged a performance exclusively to secure a vision promising him revenge for the slaying of a kinsman. An Arapaho did so normally to gain aid in sickness or danger threatening his family. Among the Ponca, individual vows did not figure at all; the dance was executed annually by a fraternity of Thunder men at the chief's behest. Perhaps the best possible example is provided by a comparison of the Arapaho and Cheyenne performances, which are so similar that "members of one tribe find no difficulty in participating in the dance of the other, for even the larger differences relate only to details." Yet neither the etiological myths nor the teleological explanations show like agreement. The Cheyenne explain that the culture hero entered a mountain resembling the Sun Dance structure and was there instructed in the ceremony, which on his return rescued the people from starvation; while the Arapaho account is merged in their general origin myth with emphasis on the flat-pipe that figures as their great sacred object. As for the end sought, it is true that in both instances the initiative is taken by an individual vowing a dance to avert danger; but with the Cheyenne the main point is to reanimate the earth and its life, for example, to call the buffalo. This is of course the main point only from the angle of priestly officialdom; for we saw in the preceding chapter how varying are the motives in a large ceremony of this type, and that among them purely or preponderantly esthetic factors play a large part.

Some tribes manifest an interesting tendency to use for purposes of etiological rationalization folk-tales that are otherwise devoid of ritualistic meaning. For example, the Heiltsuk of British Columbia explain the establishment of the Cannibal society by reciting the story of the woman who gave birth to dogs,—a plot told by the Eskimo, the Northern Athabaskans, and even other Northwest Coast tribes without thought of ceremony. In the Plains area the Blackfoot and the Hidatsa exhibit the same inclination. Thus, the Hidatsa do not content themselves with ascribing certain offerings planted by the bank of the Missouri to the dictates of a local snake-deity, but connect the rite with the tradition of a young man who burnt his way through a gigantic snake lying in his path, ate of the flesh thus cooked, and in consequence was himself transformed into a serpent. Fully half a dozen of the neighboring groups have the same narrative as a mere folk-tale.

Similarly, the Hidatsa Bird ceremony is not merely traced to the favor of supernatural birds but is connected with one of the most widespread mythological motives on the continent,—the unremitting warfare between the Thunderbirds and a water-monster. The method of fitting this conception into a ceremonial context will repay analysis. To tell the myth as it is known to the participants in the ceremony: the Thunderbirds once carried a good Hidatsa hunter, Packs-antelope, to their mountain in order to get his assistance against a water-snake destroying their young. He succeeded in slaying the monster for them, was transformed into one of their number, and killed various powerful beings until a supernatural denizen of the Missouri seized him, changed him back into human shape, and dismissed him with the command to make a ceremony in honor of the Thunderers but to put his captor in a place of distinction therein. All the deities came the following year and gave Packs-antelope detailed ceremonial instructions, as well as the Bird bundle with the correlated chants. The proper performance of the ritual of course ensures good crops, plenty of game, and victory.

Now, obviously, it is exclusively the circumstantial speeches of the divine visitants telling Packs-antelope how to paint the sacred contents of the bundle, what articles to combine, what chants to sing, that in any real sense account for the Bird ceremonial. The plot of the familiar story explains nothing in the ceremony but is prefixed to the essential part of the explanation. The Hidatsa might just as well whittle down the lengthy narrative to a report of the directions supplied to the founder. But this is looking at it from the outsider's point of view. However tenuous may be the thread connecting tale and ritual, the owner of the bundle regards both as an inseparable unit to be transmitted only as the prerogative of initiates; and accordingly the tale of the Thunderbirds and the water-monster is lifted to a level of esoteric sanctity by its association with the ceremony.

It is thus possible that priestly adaptation can convert fiction into a sacred myth. The plot, it should be noted, is sometimes not merely found in non-ritualistic setting in other tribes but may appear in an esoteric and an exoteric form within the same group. Thus, the Menomini of Wisconsin tell of their hero Ma'nabus and explain how the gods destroyed his brother Wolf by dragging him below the ice. Turning into a tree, the hero shoots two of the slayers, who flee wounded and cause a deluge. He finds safety in flight, and, disguising himself in a flayed old woman's skin, he succeeds in killing his wounded enemies and, despite a second flood, manages to escape. However, when a novice is adopted into the great secret society of the tribe, a different twist is given to the narrative: the hero bulldozes the gods into teaching him the sacred cult as a peace-offering.[19]

In the cases cited the ritualistic association rather tends to spoil good fiction by a great deal of prosy recital of ceremonial trivialities (from our point of view). This esthetically unfavorable development, however, is not the only possible one. As Boas has indicated, the priest may act as a creative artist and weld into a unified whole the hitherto disjointed narratives current among his people. That such systematization occurred among the Polynesians, has already been shown. To what extent such intellectual feats remain on the plane of artistic virtuosity or acquire genuinely religious value, will naturally vary in different cases,—nay, possibly even for different individuals.[20]

Enough has been said to elucidate the character of the rationalistic tendency in connection with ritual. Its spontaneous self-assertiveness is perhaps most amusingly exhibited when the zest of justification makes the same people offer quite distinct reasons for the same behavior. Thus, in the Scalp Ceremonial of the Zuñi in New Mexico, men offer prayer-sticks to the ants as well as to the war gods. A triple motive is alleged: the ants are constantly fighting; they help people by removing their tracks; they make many people attend the ceremony,—as many people as there are ants.[21] Evidently, any and every path of association can be used as a warrant for what one wants to do or is used to doing. This leads us to our next topic.

SECONDARY ASSOCIATION AND GROWTH OF CEREMONIAL

The process of rationalization forms part of a still wider psychological category, that of secondary association. This is best explained by setting it over against its opposite. If an individual child spontaneously connects, say, the number four with the notion of benevolence or intimacy, the association may be illogical but it is psychologically primary. Similarly, when an artist attempts to represent a specific religious conception in a given technique, the association, so far as the finished product is concerned, must be reckoned primary. For though the concept and the technique can and do exist separately, this particular work flows directly from and is primarily determined by the preëxisting idea. This is not true where, as in Congolese fetiches, the effigy is executed independently of religious motives and only acquires sacred character by subsequent consecration. Again, if the Eye-juggler story in its Navaho version really sprang from the craving for a causal interpretation of the coyote's eyes, we should have a primary connection of plot and explanatory close.

Thanks to Professor Boas, the overshadowing importance of secondary association in art, in ritual, and in mythology is no longer ignored. Of the fact of its constant occurrence in every realm of culture there can be no question, and the preceding pages furnish abundant illustrative material, for example, in the sections devoted to the growth of the Peyote and the Ghost Dance cults. At present we are less interested in proving what has been amply demonstrated than in offering some suggestions as to why specific associations develop secondarily, and what are the psychological implications of such syncretism.

Since the association must invariably go back to processes in a single mind, the mental operations observed will naturally be those described in textbooks of psychology, even though certain social determinants must be taken into account if the phenomenon is to be described in its totality.

In this connection may be cited a suggestive instance of ceremonial borrowing. Most of the northern Plains tribes have a well-developed series of military associations, which in some cases are almost wholly secular, while in others they clearly bear a religious character. In investigating the societies of the Oglala, a branch of the Western Dakota, Dr. Wissler discovered that according to native tradition the Badger dance society was modeled on its Crow namesake. This statement was very puzzling to me since no such performance had been noted among the Crow. But examination of the native word for badger showed that it was practically identical with the Hidatsa and Crow word for the kit-fox, from which one of the best-known organizations of the area gets its designation. Comparison of the regalia and modes of ceremonial organization indicates that the Oglala borrowed the Kit-fox dance of the Hidatsa or Crow and naïvely interpreted the alien name as though it were a vocable of their own tongue.[22]

Here, then, the similarity in sound between two words of different meaning in their respective vocabularies led to the association of the name "Badger" with a combination of ceremonial features originally linked with a quite distinct name. This association in turn had interesting results, for from the primitive point of view there is a good deal in a name. The borrowed complex was *ipso facto* distinguished from an older Dakota dance of essentially similar nature, and still another association was added: the members were exhorted to imitate their eponym in putting up a strenuous fight! One can easily conceive additional rationalizations developing in the most spontaneous fashion: how some Oglala who had forgotten the alien derivation of the dance might ascribe its origin to a revelation granted by a supernatural badger, how members would come to carry badger skins, and what not. As a matter of fact, the name was actually interpreted to refer "to the characteristic grimaces and growlings of the badger when attacked."

The case cited suggests, then, a ready mode for the elaboration of a ceremonial complex. We can understand why some of the dozen tribes of the same region practicing the Kit-fox dance should wear necklaces of the animal's skin, why some should put on headbands set with kit-fox jaws. There is a similar fitness in the wearing of horned buffalo-skin headdresses or masks by the Bull dancers of the area, in their imitating buffalo in their sounds and movements; and again it is obvious why the Mosquito society of the Blackfoot should buzz and scratch. The association is not only one that may automatically arise in an individual member's mind by the principles of similarity and contiguity but will commend itself to his fellow-members by its simplicity and plausibility even if he should not happen to exercise any unusual influence.

An irrational juxtaposition can be quite as effective in welding disparate features into a firm unit. I am not al-

luding here to such cases as the union of maize and the wild
geese by the Hidatsa Goose association, for here the common relationship to a deity they both symbolize adequately
accounts for the phenomenon. I am referring rather to the
strange hodgepodge of songs, material objects, and practices that are associated with the typical American Indian
medicine-bundle. Wherever the vision concept is conspicuous, as among the Crow, the integration is easily effected
through its instrumentality. For example, between the
sacred Tobacco planted by the Crow and the strawberry there
is no logical relation: but the two became connected because Medicine-crow, a member of the Tobacco society,
saw the Tobacco in human form wearing crowns of strawberries.

Again, the Menomini of Wisconsin have an official theory
to the effect that their composite bundles are each the indivisible gift of a benevolent deity. But Mr. Skinner has
rendered it at least highly probable that the observed complexity is the result of secondary association, and he has
shown how this can quite naturally come about. A little
boy, on the assumption of a mystic bond with the Thunder,
often receives from his parents a small club as a symbol of
that tie; when he fasts for a vision at puberty, additional
charms may be prescribed by his guardian spirit, and still
others can be acquired in later life. "What is to hinder these
various charms, when they become too numerous for convenience in carrying, from being made into one large package
or bundle combining the power of all?" Such piecemeal accretion through a sequence of revelations is admitted by the
Sauk and Fox, neighbors and fellow-Algonkians of the
Menomini. Nay, among the latter themselves Mr. Skinner
once bought the mingled remains of what had been three distinct bundles. The contents had become mixed by accident,

and since nice assortment was impracticable the whole was preserved as a unit.

If the bundle had been handed down for several generations more, until the accident of the confusion had been forgotten, who can doubt but that its final owner would have looked upon it as a universal bundle of great power? And what more natural than to ascribe its origin, as a whole, to one of the great beneficent powers, Ma'nabus, for instance? [23]

In other words, by the legerdemain of a rationalizing origin myth elements of the utmost heterogeneity can be welded into an inseparable whole.

Such a secondary combination of originally disparate features is particularly likely where the idea holds sway that a given ceremonial prerogative can be bought and sold. According to Maximilian Prince of Wied-Neuwied, the Hidatsa Stone Hammer organization purchased the Hot Dance from a neighboring tribe, the Arikara. Now the Stone Hammers formed a group of young men carrying lances stuck through a perforated stone bearing designs emblematic of celestial beings; they were expected to be brave in battle and were licensed to steal food from their fellow-tribesmen, —if not caught. The Hot Dance, on the other hand, has for its most characteristic feature the trick of thrusting one's bare arm into a kettle of boiling water.[24] Thus, a purely external bond came to unite two separate groups of ideas and activities, which nevertheless might in course of time have fused inextricably and been combined through the rationalizing process.

Under certain conditions secondary association is the result of substitution. It is quite true that the primitive mind in general resents a departure from the traditional norm, but even among so conservative a people as the Polynesians the overshadowing influence of a strong will-power in a man of authority was shown capable of wiping out a custom of hoary antiquity; and in the Plains the vision of a leader was sufficient sanction for a change in routine. However, I am not so much concerned now to illustrate substitutions due to great prestige as rather the changes inevitably arising through novel conditions. Assuredly there is a healthy preference for the good old way, but even where departure from it appears a venturesome enterprise the conflict, whether to perform with some modification or not at all, will often be decided in favor of the former alternative. Thus, in the summer of 1916 I witnessed the Hopi of Oraibi village perform the Snake Dance without any of the Antelope priests traditionally expected to go through certain activities. A schism dividing the villagers had left the victorious party in possession of their habitations but without one of the two sacred brotherhoods that ought to coöperate in the ceremony: accordingly, some of the Snake priests took over functions not "properly" belonging to them. The case is doubtless typical of much ritualistic history. A still more instructive example has been discussed by Dr. Spier. Among the Arapaho a "flat-pipe" represents the most highly venerated object, and its keeper naturally acts as the master of ceremonies in the Sun Dance. But in the Oklahoma branch of this people the tribal palladium was lacking, and a sacred wheel, such as played only a subordinate part in Wyoming, rose to ascendancy and "acquired an enhanced value, until it is to-day, *in the eyes of the southern Arapaho,* next to the tribal pipe the most sacred possession of the tribe." [25]

As an accompaniment of diffusion secondary associations may develop not only without arousing antagonism but even without entering consciousness. A tribe borrowing an alien dance does not and cannot copy it with photographic exactness. For one thing, the learners may not have been initiated into the esoteric or subjective aspects of the performance. For another, even if they were, certain features could not possibly be transplanted. Thus, the Plains Indian tribes have in part military societies graded in a series, in part coordinate societies of otherwise similar character. But if a people lacking the hierarchical grading patterned a rite no matter how closely upon that performed by one of the graded associations, essential elements would *have* to be omitted, to wit, the relations of the society to its neighboring grades. But what is true negatively also holds in a positive way: a native observer not merely eliminates what he cannot assimilate, he also amplifies what he borrows in harmony with his received notions of ritualistic propriety, never dreaming perhaps that he is adding to the borrowed feature something alien to the borrowers, nay, conceivably militating against *their* ceremonial ideals. Thus, the military societies of the Hidatsa and Mandan were all entered by purchase of membership rights. Hence if any addition was to be made to the system, it was possible only by making purchase a *sine qua non:* a dance borrowed from, say, the Crow, where no such idea was in vogue for performances of this category, was perforce altered by a sort of analogic leveling to the Hidatsa pattern.

Now it is a significant observation that the ritualistic pattern of a tribe may embrace not merely the characteristics of observances but the very purposes for which the ceremonial is performed; or, to be more precise, for which it is *avowedly* performed. Thus, the Arapaho have eight major ceremonies, each and every one of which is initiated only as the result of a pledge made to avert danger or death. In short, because of the standardization of rationalizing about ceremonial aims, ceremonial activity has become firmly linked with one particular type of explanation. The inevitable consequence will be that when any new set of comparable observances is introduced *its* rationalization will follow the path of least resistance, that is, will fall into the accustomed groove. In principle, this of course exactly parallels the etiological pattern characteristic of the region, the inclination, so often emphasized above, to derive anything and everything from a visionary experience. When my Hidatsa informants did not know of a vision-myth to account for a given ritual, they quite automatically inferred that the ceremony was not of native origin. I encountered an instructive case among the Crow. These people had within recent times adopted a Pipe ritual from the Hidatsa and had discovered that the sister tribe lacked the Crow Tobacco ceremony. These facts were introduced into the legend accounting for the separation of the two groups by the assumption that when the division occurred the founder of the Crow tribe was blessed with a revelation of the Tobacco, the founder of the Hidatsa tribe with that of the sacred Pipe. The assurance with which this rationalization was advanced is rather amusing because the Hidatsa themselves, far from claiming authorship of the Pipe ritual, say that they obtained it from the Arikara. That was a possibility the Crow rationalizer had not considered: his craving for a causal explanation for certain differences in religious behavior between two branches of a once undivided people was adequately satisfied when he had applied the approved formula.

Can we define the phenomena described above in more definitely psychological terms? Always with the understanding that an association occurring in the individual psyche does not forthwith become a cultural fact but can only be converted into one where the relations of the individual mind to its social environment are favorable, we can proceed to an analysis of the initial association. To take a concrete example, all the Arapaho military organizations performed ceremonies to ward off danger, but some of these are demonstrably of alien origin. Now what happened when one of these foreign ceremonial complexes was adopted into the Arapaho scheme? There was evidently what psychologists generally call association by similarity and contiguity: the complex was at once put into the same category as certain well-established ceremonies and whatever general features were linked with these were thus automatically joined to the newcomer. This implies a partial blindness—doubtless only in the rarest cases a *willful* blindness—as to the phenomenon assimilated. Attention is concentrated on *likeness* to familiar performances, specific differences are of course noticed but merely as constituting a pleasing variation in detail: the new ceremony is merely a novel embodiment of the current "idea" of ceremonialism in a Platonic sense. Hence there is what Professor Woodworth has called the "response by analogy," based on the neglect of everything in the borrowed elements that cannot be forthwith adapted to the norm.

Now the perception of such similarity provides the cue for secondary association in many circumstances that do not involve contact of separate groups; and here lies in my opinion one of the most effective instrumentalities for the elaboration of ceremonial routine. This may be illustrated by a series of otherwise widely divergent cases.

It was a rule among the Hidatsa that in the collective purchase of membership in a military society each purchaser should select an individual "father" who was to be feasted and presented with special gifts during the period of preliminary instruction; and this "father" was chosen from among the kinsmen of the novice's real father. Why this connection between acquiring a particular group of ceremonial rights and the special favoring of patrilineal relatives? For the simple reason that, quite apart from any ritualistic activity, these paternal kinsfolk were according to Hidatsa (as well as Crow) usage preëminently those tribesmen whom it was proper to honor, entertain, and present with gifts when a warrior returned with booty. When, therefore, a Hidatsa found himself in a situation in which entertainment and donations were called for, he naturally singled out for such differential treatment some one who in the normal events of life would be so distinguished. The bond between a particular military society complex and the honoring of the father's kinsman was a wholly adventitious one: the situation, however, happened to furnish the cue for a typical response by analogy.

Let us change the scene and revert to the Papuan initiation festivals described in an earlier chapter. How comes it that a performance purporting to admit youths to the advantages of full-fledged citizenship and to strike terror into the hearts of the women should be combined, of all things, with a pig-market? As a matter of fact, there is more than one *tertium quid comparationis*. Pigs are fattened in any event for the initiation feast, hence why not sell some of them and draw profit as well as amusement and edification from the affair? Again, initiation is an occasion that unites all neighboring tribes, and the same holds for a market; what then more natural than to hit two birds with one stone? The apparently strange association of athletic games with the most sacred Polynesian festivals is probably amenable to an analogous explanation.

It should never be forgotten that when a feature is thus brought into a new context it may thereby assume a character very different from that borne in isolation. For example, the games played by some Plains Indian tribes in the Ghost Dance became holy not because they were such in themselves but because they suggested and symbolized the old life that had become hallowed in the reaction against Caucasian aggressiveness.

In North America, where information is relatively ample, the growth of elaborate festivals by successive accretion through response by analogy can often be traced step by step. Thus, there is no logical connection between initiation into a society devoting itself to the planting of sacred Tobacco and the formal recital of an individual brave's war record; yet when an adoption occurs among the Crow, the entrance into the lodge is uniformly preceded by such a narrative. "The reason is fairly clear. At every festive gathering of the Crow there is a recital of war deeds; the Tobacco initiation produces such a gathering, which elicits the customary concomitant; and thus the coup-recital becomes a feature of the Tobacco adoption ceremony."

The at first bewildering complexity of, say, the Sun Dance becomes intelligible when we apply this principle of interpretation, as has been done by Dr. Spier,[26] whose examples can easily be multiplied. Thus, at a certain stage in the Crow performance distinguished young men point sharpened poles at the cooks of the buffalo tongues prepared during the festival. This is obviously because of the license widely granted to braves on the Plains of appropriating whatever food took their fancy. The interminable recital of war exploits at various stages of the Crow and Dakota ceremonies simply represents the usual procedure on a public occasion. If the first tree felled for the dance structure is shot at and formally struck by the bystanders, nothing is more obvious considering that it symbolizes the enemy, hence evokes the traditional formal charge. The Arapaho share with a few other tribes the notion that a ceremonial superior may be conciliated by the surrender of one's wife, and since the typical relation-ship of ceremonial hierarchy obtains between the Sun Dance pledger and his "grandfather" the offering is made in this connection also. As Spier clearly shows, such amplification implies merely a greater or lesser drawing on the tribal stock of procedure, and it is not difficult to understand why inno-vation along such familiar lines does not evoke resentment but is readily converted from the momentary promptings of a cue supplied to an individual mind into a part of the estab-lished procedure. Why should any one voice objections if a pipe hitherto handled in silence at a certain stage is suddenly offered with traditional prayers to the Four Quarters? And if four is the mystic number, what limit is there to the un-opposed quadrupling—and consequent impressive lengthen-ing—of any integral feature?

The processes of association are of course the same when no particular behavior is involved, when we are dealing with the elaboration not of ceremonial but of mythical concepts. So many illustrations are provided by the material cited in this book that a case or two will suffice for explicit discus-sion. To take a hackneyed instance, as soon as a being as-sociated with a natural phenomenon, say, the sun or sky, or a wind, is clearly envisaged as possessing human character-istics, even though in magnified form, there will naturally arise through association a tendency to ascribe to him an-thropomorphic traits. That is why, even according to Mr. Man's report, the Andamanese god Puluga (Biliku) eats, drinks, sleeps, and begets children. Similarly, it is not dif-ficult to understand why the ancient Egyptians evolved di-vinities in triads of father, mother, and son. In some of the visionary experiences recorded among the Crow the

mental operations are quite transparent. Lone-tree's identification of the Dipper by the seven stars in his queue has already been described. Again, an old man is represented as
being visited by four men and since each has a star in front
of him he knows that it is the stars that are blessing him.
But while the first man sings four songs, the others merely
sing one apiece. "This made seven songs in all, accordingly
the visionary believed these men were the Dipper."

It is of course artificial to separate ideation and behavior.
The way in which they are always potentially interdependent
is seen in the last case when the visionary in conformity with
his revelation unites seven persons for a joint ritualistic
enterprise.[27]

A somewhat perplexing category of associations, both in
myth and in ritual, rests on the principle of antithesis rather
than similarity. It is clear from an inspection of the evidence from individual psychology that different ideas have a
very unequal power of evoking their opposites: for instance,
of Kent and Rosanoff's subjects only 37 responded "high"
to stimulus "deep," while fully 365 coupled "hard" with
"soft." In other words, whatever individual differences
may exist in this respect are shrouded by other effective
causes. It is thus anything but easy to work backwards
from an empirically noted linkage of contraries to the conditions favoring such a result. Nevertheless some observations may be made that are not wholly futile.

In the first place, it may be possible to show that the antithesis is more apparent than real. For instance, some
writers have been puzzled by the dual personality of a creator or hero, as in the case of the Crow Indians' Old-Man-
Coyote. I have already expressed the opinion that if the
creator were really conceived as a definitely ethical personality such extravaganzas of unsocial conduct as are constantly

ascribed to him are not intelligible, whatever allowances may be made for primitive inconsistency. But Professor Boas has solved many cases of this sort by demonstrating that the creator's or hero's feats are not, as our preconceptions impel us to believe, prompted by altruism at all.

Even in his heroic achievements he remains a trickster bent upon the satisfaction of his own desires. . . . He liberates the sun, not because he pities mankind, but because he desires it; and the first use he tries to make of it is to compel fishermen to give him part of their catch. He gets the fresh water because he is thirsty, and unwillingly spills it all over the world while he is making his escape. He liberates the fish because he is hungry, and gets the tides in order to be able to gather shell-fish.[28]

More difficult are those instances in which a sacred rite is combined with an exhibition of buffoonery, obscenity, or at least with what seems a logically inconsistent exhibition of levity. Wundt has expressed the theory that burlesque follows in the wake of solemnity. He is willing to concede that this transition is very old; indeed, he contends that it is found among all peoples in no matter how rude a state of culture. Two psychological factors are said to produce the transformation. On the one hand, the sacred performance from the very start harbored an element of pleasure inseparable from song and dance; and this secular feature is strengthened as the primary religious motive fades away. But, secondly, since this does not wholly vanish, the feeling of pleasure is accentuated by the sense of contrast. He gives as an example that of the once awe-inspiring mask, which becomes comical as the belief in its supernatural potency wanes. When the mummer removes his mask and distorts his own features into a grimace, the humorous effect is enhanced because this action dispels whatever fear may linger in connection with the false face. To this antithesis of dread and relaxation a second feeling of contrast is added, viz., that between the real human face and its imitation. Thus, from Wundt's point of view the comic, however widespread and ancient, is a derivative phenemenon that invariably presupposes the serious since it implies the inversion of a preceding serious impression.[29]

It is quite possible to accept the theory that the comic rests on a feeling of contrast without admitting the special conclusion that burlesque is invariably the outgrowth of a sacred rite. An Andamanese shaman known by Professor Brown performed a pantomimic dance patterned on what he had seen when on a visit to the world of spirits. The kind of thing he did that aroused great amusement among the spectators was to feign having hurt his leg by violent dancing or to imitate the step of the women's dance.[30] The humor of the situation clearly consists not in the degradation of a lofty effect but in the transparent contrast of reality and pretense. So in a Hopi dance I have witnessed the spectators bursting into derisive shouts when a woman attempted to shoot an arrow: between archery and the feminine sex there is an incongruity in the native mind, and the real or assumed awkwardness of the female archer precipitates laughter. It may of course be said that the real act of shooting is serious business, which suffers degradation by mock-practice. But that is very different from deriving the buffoonery appearing in ritual from the serious element in ritual by an inherent process of transformation. Wundt ignores the possibility that the humorous element, while of course inseparable from human life as a whole, may very well appear unconnected with any religious ceremony. The question, then, for us is not how the comic may arise from the sacred, but why drollery such as figures in the non-ceremonial life of the people may be injected into situations of such solemnity as apparently to preclude such secondary association.

It may not be out of place to describe one concrete example of such non-ceremonial comic performances. Among the Crow Indians the clowns are not permanently organized but appear when the people are assembled in large numbers,— in recent times during the Fourth of July festivities. They not only make themselves unrecognizable, wearing a blackened mask, but affect the acme of ugliness in their appearance; for instance, mud is used in place of body-paint, their musician beats a torn drum, their horse is the most crooked-legged and swollen-kneed in camp. They walk as if lame, and their feigned clumsiness of movement precipitates general mirth. One of their number dresses like a woman, and his clothes are stuffed so as to simulate pregnancy; this clown rides double with "her husband." All kinds of buffoonery are perpetrated: the actors mock people in the audience irrespective of their distinction; they dance as ridiculously as possible; and the horseman in mounting purposely overleaps so as to fall, whereupon he acts as if seriously injured; and in answering questions as to their home the clowns may indicate that they have journeyed for hundreds of days to get to the camp. In addition, there was formerly a pantomimic representation of sexual intercourse by "husband" and "wife." [31]

A personal observation may help to elucidate our general psychological problem. In 1911 a group of these clowns rode up to the dance house, where the Hot Dance was being performed, dismounted, and to the amusement of all spectators joined in the dance. Now *this* intrusion, though possibly it had never occurred before, is in no sense enigmatic. For the Hot Dance had long lost among the Crow whatever religious significance it once had, so that the clowns were merely adding a special feature to the amusement program. But further, granting that the idea of playing the clown had occurred at this particular time, nothing was more natural than that the clowns should proceed to the dance house, where most of their prospective audience were gathered.

It is otherwise when such clownishness is coupled with behavior of the utmost solemnity, and then we are confronted by the problem under discussion. This does not happen to occur in representative form among the Crow, but examples from elsewhere abound. Whether the Maidu of the Sacramento Valley in central California are holding a spiritistic meeting or celebrating one of their ceremonial dances, the clown has a part officially not less recognized than the shaman's. He apes the shaman's actions and speeches, tries to make his audience laugh, and gives an exhibition of gluttony only checked with great difficulty by the shaman's reproaches. This character is strongly reminiscent of certain functionaries in the ritual of the Pueblo tribes of Arizona and New Mexico. I have myself seen clowns of the Tewa village on the First Hopi Mesa entertaining spectators by their voracity, practical joking, and every other kind of farcical action while a serious masquerade dance was going on, and even mimicking the priests in asperging the mummers with corn meal. But perhaps the most instructive data are supplied by the Zuñi of New Mexico, and a brief description of the relevant data seems desirable.

All Zuñi males enter a rain-making and mask-wearing society, which is ceremonially distinct from a series of medical and magical associations admitting both sexes and without compulsory membership. Buffoonery is intimately connected with both types of religious activity. During the public performances of the Masked Dancers appear a group of annually chosen clowns, the Koyemshi, who mimic the celebrants, deride one another's appearance, indulge in obscene raillery, play games, pretend being frightened at some child in the crowd, fall to loggerheads with one of the fraternities, and otherwise seek to amuse the spectators. Notwithstanding their distinctness from the Koyemshi in point of organization, the doctoring fraternity known as Newekwe (Galaxy) is often connected with the Koyemshi in public pleasantries. This association is plausible enough considering the comic pantomime correlated with both groups. The Newekwe, however, have as a distinctive feature obligatory eating of filth, members vying with one another as to the amount consumed. This is only one of a series of equally repulsive actions, from our point of view, such as the drinking of urine and the biting off of the heads of living mice. Nevertheless, this same organization practices the typical rituals of other sacred fraternities, erects an altar, indulges in ceremonial smoking, and constructs prayer plumes.[32]

Among the Plains Indians the contrast is of a rather different kind. Thus, in the Crazy Dance of the Arapaho the performers "act in as extravagant and foolish a manner as possible, and are allowed full license to do whatever they please": they annoy every one in camp, some impersonate animals which their comrades shoot at, aiming backward over their shoulders; indeed, all do directly the opposite of what would be expected from a rational being. Thus, if a dancer is carrying a heavy load he pretends that it is negligible, while a light one is treated as though it were a terrible burden; and all members "talk backward," that is, say exactly the opposite of what they mean. Further, the Crazy Dancers rush into a fire specially built for the purpose and trample it out. They have a root possessing the virtue of paralyzing man and beast: using it against a rattlesnake, for example, they can make him unable to coil.[33] These features recur in varying combinations among many tribes of the same region, as a few examples will amply demonstrate. The Crow had "Crazy Dogs" who said the reverse of what they meant and were pledged to foolhardiness in battle. In the Dog society of the Hidatsa the officers distinguished from the rank and file as "Real Dogs" also used backward speech, were expected to be particularly brave, and acted contrary to normal ways, for instance, by walking about practically naked in the winter time. They also took out meat from a kettle of boiling water without injury to their arms or hands. This last-mentioned trick was in the highest degree characteristic of the Heyoka organization of the Dakota, whose general motto was to defy natural conduct and normal custom. They would pretend to be cold in summer and hot in winter, would assist women in cooking, might face west instead of east in a Sun Dance, and altogether played the part of buffoons. Nevertheless, the society had a definitely religious setting. The members theoretically modeled themselves on a being or group of beings from whom the organization derived its name, and participation depended on a particular type of vision,—indeed, was compulsory for those having such visions lest they be killed by thunder.[34]

I am of opinion that the phenomena cited proceed from diverse psychological motives and that successful grappling with the question at issue will only begin when we cease to lump together all so-called clownish behavior under a single head. For one thing, the fire-dance of the Arapaho and the kettle-trick of the Dakota and Hidatsa are probably not to be confounded with buffoonery at all. True, they imply an apparently irrational defiance of the laws of nature. In reality, however, the point of these performances lies in the immunity of the actors from the effects that would normally be expected; in other words, they are demonstrating their supernatural powers, a thing very different from clownishness. Secondly, the reckless bravery of certain men in the military societies, such as the Hidatsa Real Dogs, is also in the nature of a demonstration, though of a different sort: the actor proves that he possesses in an exalted degree a trait incumbent on all tribesmen in milder form. Yet in this case we can see how comic elements might easily develop incidentally. Suppose that the name "Crazy Dog" is once applied to a Crow who has undertaken the vow of foolhardiness; then the very name will suggest certain modes of conduct and correlated modes of treatment. "As these dogs act when they see a cow, so he acted in sight of the buffalo. . . . When they went on a hunt, the people regarded him as a dog." The mad ignoring of danger obligatory in sight of the foe might be extended to like conduct in camp: as a Crazy Dog walked straight towards the enemy irrespective of consequences, so he would ride directly into the midst of a group of tribesmen unless shooed away as a dog. The suggestions of the word "crazy" would also account for backward speech and all manner of eccentricity. In this way, some of the farcical proceedings can be interpreted not as the effect of religious degeneration but as casual ramifications of *military* ideas; and they appear in the religious context merely because these military ideas are linked with religious ones.

As for the buffoonery of the Koyemshi, we may fall back upon a principle previously used to account for ceremonial amplification. If some slapstick sort of comedy exists in a tribe independently of sacred connections and is more or less regularly evoked by a specific condition, then the occurrence of the proper cue in the course of some holy ritual may set in motion the machinery of clownishness without any one's resenting the intrusion as anomalous.

All this must be taken as purely tentative and at best covers only a part of the field. It is, however, useful to point out the existence of problems and also that they are at least in principle not altogether insoluble.

REFERENCES

[1] Höffding, 1893: 152.
[2] Kent and Rosanoff.
[3] Lowie, 1922: 334, 391; id., 1915: 41; id., 1919: 185.
[4] Jung: 27 sq.
[5] R. F. Benedict: 79.
[6] Gutmann: 88 sq.; Spencer and Gillen, 1904: 609. Sapir, 1922.
[7] Junod: 11, 376.
[8] Boas, 1914: 409.
[9] Woodworth: 376.
[10] Brown: 316. Wissler, 1904: 236.
[11] Wissler, 1904: 247.
[12] Merker: 196.
[13] Ehrenreich: 84. Lowie, 1914: 608.
[14] Matthews, 1897: 90. Dorsey and Kroeber: 51.
[15] Spencer and Gillen, 1904: 588 sq.
[16] Wissler, 1908: 74 sq., 78 sq.
[17] Haeberlin: 9, 47.
[18] Spier.
[19] Skinner and Satterlee: 253-263.
[20] Boas, 1914: 403.
[21] Parsons, 1924.
[22] Lowie, 1913 (a): 109.
[23] Skinner, 1913: 92.
[24] Lowie, 1913 (c): 232, 252.
[25] Spier: 515 f.

[26] Spier: 513.

[27] Lowie, 1919: 185; id., 1922: 334.

[28] Boas, 1914: 395.

[29] Wundt: 588 sq.

[30] Brown: 164.

[31] Lowie, 1913 (b) : 207.

[32] Dixon, 1905: 271, 315.   Stevenson: 224, 235, 261, 276, 429 sq.

[33] Kroeber, 1902-1907: 188-196.

[34] Lowie, 1922: 193; id., 1913 (c) : 288; id., 1913 (a) : 113; Wissler, 1912: 82.

CHAPTER XIV

CONCLUSION

In the Introduction I offered a tentative definition of religion; and in concluding it seems desirable to reëxamine it and to consider its implications. Let me reaffirm, first of all, my skepticism as to the adequacy of any definition purporting to summarize the totality of phenomena labeled "Religion." Why, indeed, should any one spread over several hundred pages what could be compressed into a single pithy sentence? The student of religion is, in this respect, neither more nor less favorably situated than, say, a biologist whose labors cannot be summarized by definitions of Life. My position from the very start has been a psychological one: in other words, I have tried to bring under a common head phenomena that from a psychological point of view belong together as set over against the rest of the universe. I reject the parochialism of Fielding's parsons because Presbyterianism and Episcopalianism are psychologically more akin to each other than either is to atheism; I exclude Leibnizian logic-chopping because the mental processes it involves are distinct from those predominant in undoubtedly religious manifestations; I include magic and religion under a common head in so far as both display the same or similar attitudes.

My definition, then, is not meant to be an adequate but a minimum definition of the psychological correlates of religion; it merely attempts to disengage the least common denominator in all religious phenomena. Like Durkheim I derive this common element from a dichotomy of the universe; but, following Marett rather than Durkheim, I see this dichotomy not in the arbitrary division of the Sacred from the Profane but in the differential response to normal and abnormal stimuli, in the *spontaneous* distinction thus created between Natural and Supernatural, which does not require any preëxisting abstract formulation of "nature." The response is that of amazement and awe; and its source is the Supernatural, Extraordinary, Weird, Sacred, Holy, Divine. Possibly in contradistinction from Dr. Söderblom, I am inclined to regard the last three adjectives as denoting an exceedingly common special form of the Extraordinary rather than as quite co-extensive with the Extraordinary as a minimum reality corresponding to the religious sentiment. I agree with him, Drs. Marett and Thurnwald, not to mention others, in regarding the recognition of a personal correlate of that sentiment as unessential, though of course it also is very frequent.

It may of course be objected that without the customary concept of divine personality there cannot be any psychological equivalent to Religion. But let the skeptics beware of Parson Adams's fallacy. The question at issue is at bottom one of logical classification on the basis of empirical findings. It is by no means indispensable that we should all classify in precisely the same way, but it is highly desirable that we should understand the basis of one another's classifications. Hence, at the risk of repeating what has already been expressed in one way or another, I will state the grounds for putting into the category of religion some phenomena others are accustomed to exclude.

If I correctly comprehend the facts, the most vital part of Crow religion is independent of the personality of the supernatural beings but consists in the memory of an ineffable experience of an extraordinary character: it is the Extraordinary nature of this subjective experience that hallows its objective correlates, lifting them, too, into the empyrean of the Extraordinary, usually with the affective tinge peculiar to the Sacred. Among the Ekoi I do not find that the impersonal *njomm* inspire generically different emotions from those connected with *njomm* definitely conceived as personal. The mystic power of a set of words evokes reactions in a Polynesian community that cannot be surpassed in point of solemn awe, if they are ever equaled, by the dignity of their major deities; and in ancient Egypt the occult name might rank as greater than the highest gods themselves. Nay, even when we are dealing with the personal supernatural beings there may be evidence that it is not the element of personality that is significant but a specific impersonal attribute. How, for example, shall we interpret Junod's statement that the maximum devotion among the Thonga is shown by those natives who have been freed by exorcism from Zulu spirits possessing them? Why are the normal tribesman's prayers and offerings to his own ancestors mechanical by comparison with the fervor of the neurotic who lacks the goad of filial piety? It is because the latter has had what the other cannot directly experience,—the thrill that here, as in the case of the Crow, apotheosizes its concomitants. Gods are prized as manifestations of the Extraordinary in direct proportion to their extraordinariness from a subjective point of view.

It is certainly a matter worth noting that two distinguished thinkers who start from a concept of religion that does not coincide with mine but who also adhere to a psychological position, arrive at a conclusion generically similar to mine, that is, feel the necessity of setting aside the conventional boundaries of the religious field. For Höffding, religion is the feeling determined by "the fate of values in the struggle for existence," and he concludes his inquiry as follows:

If this be so, we must not ignore the possibility that this underlying element of religion may exist and operate without expressing itself either in myth, dogma, or cult.[1]

Again, James defines religion as a total reaction upon life when involving a solemn, serious and tender attitude; and the divine, according to him, is that primal reality to which the individual thus responds. He not only is willing to acknowledge non-theistic Buddhism as a religion but goes so far as to say that

the more fervent opponents of Christian doctrine have often enough shown a temper which, psychologically considered, is indistinguishable from religious zeal.[2]

In other words, as soon as a psychological position is assumed, it becomes clear that the most divergent objects, nay, the very negation of what is ordinarily felt to be the objective of religious devotion, can become invested with religious value, that is, can evoke responses psychologically indistinguishable from those evoked by universally acknowledged religious objects. This is evidently an opinion shared by Durkheim in what seems to me much the soundest part of his book. Since the implications of this view are not yet fully recognized, a few examples may be cited for purposes of illustration.

With the spread of free-thought many children nowadays learn an evolutionary account in place of the Biblical story of creation. The truth or falsity of either is not under discussion here, merely the psychological attitude engendered. That is identical in the two cases: since the age of the learner precludes an appreciation of the pros and cons, the secularist's child imbibes evolution in the same spirit of docile acceptance with which the fundamentalist's child accepts the Scriptural account. Evolution for him represents a set of dogmas. These belong to the Extraordinary half of the universe of experience because they are acquired in a manner distinct from that of conclusions reached by personal inquiry and critical reasoning. Moreover they are emotionally tinged by the associations of early childhood. When these dogmas are challenged in later life, there is accordingly the same shock that characterizes an affront to orthodoxy or the infraction of a taboo. Nay, the very presentation of *favorable* arguments may produce a feeling of discomfort. So long as Evolution remains an unanalyzed mysterious complex of ideas sanctified from boyhood, it is taboo, set apart from the operations of logical thinking. Attempt to prove it, and the very need for proof is bound to shake confidence: the beliefs are transplanted to the sphere of the workaday world, hence they become *noa*. Besides there always lurks the disagreeable suspicion that what can be proved by ordinary reasoning might also be disproved by the same processes in the light of wider knowledge.

All the mental processes outlined above in the study of primitive religion are traceable in avowedly rationalistic literature. The case of Ernst Haeckel, for many years the leader of German Darwinism, is instructive. An unbiased reader of his popular book on *The Riddles of the Universe* readily perceives that he is not dealing with a colorless presentation of scientific theory. The author has had a mystic thrill from the philosophical extension of an evolutionary point of view. Unification of isolated biological data, such as every scientific research has for its aim, has led to the emotionally gratifying postulate of unity in the whole of the universe, of "monism." But this term does not bear the meaning attached to it in philosophical nomenclature; it is surcharged with affective significance. It becomes a *symbol* of the soul-satisfying vision and a means for gathering under a common head what is independently felt to be valuable,— very much as the Crow Indian secondarily associates *his* life values with a visionary experience. Haeckel's letters to his parents during the years of adolescence [3] prove that no such mutation as superficial observers have indicated ever took place in Haeckel's mental development. His attitude, from first to last, was psychologically identical,—the attitude of an esthetical, sentimental man yearning for some sort of awe-inspiring mystery in the universe. When the Protestant God of early manhood was superseded by the Principle of Causality or the Law of Substance of later years, there was a mere substitution of scientific for theological phraseology, for the scientific terms did not correspond to the concepts of exact science. To align the ardent Haeckel with his dispassionate preceptor Virchow, both when they met as student and professor and in their later tilts in evolutionary debate, is to observe the profound effect of individual variability in men exposed to similar external influences. Further, the phenomenal vogue of Haeckel's teachings illustrates the influence a powerful personality appearing at an opportune juncture can exert on thousands of followers.

The investigation of Socialism, not as a system of economic thought or of social reform, but exclusively as a phenomenon of social psychology, likewise presents many points of interest of which only one need be mentioned here.

In 1877 there appeared a rather technical book devoted to the evolution of forms of marriage and other sociological phenomena,—Lewis H. Morgan's *Ancient Society*. The author certainly would not have subscribed to many doctrines of classical Socialism, but the then leaders of the German movement were attracted by some aspects of the work, had it translated into German, and made it an integral part of Socialistic doctrine. In this way, specific doctrines which in themselves had no connection with the objects of Socialistic propaganda became, by secondary association, sacrosanct in the eyes of Socialistic orthodoxy, for the whole book had become a symbol of the emotional complex that primarily constituted Socialistic psychology. For example, Morgan had insisted that the monogamous family must have developed slowly out of preceding stages, the earliest being one of complete promiscuity, which was followed by group marriage. If some innocent ethnologist pointed out that the rudest peoples were often monogamous, he was fortunate if Socialistic critics did not charge him with deliberate falsification of facts, but merely with an inveterate Philistine prejudice that made him project *bourgeois* morality into primitive social life. I myself once discussed the kinship systems of certain Indian tribes with an intelligent Russian lady and tried to explain that my observations did not bear out Morgan's contentions. The answer was that they must have changed since Morgan's day as a result of modern conditions. To understand the absurdity of this rationalization *ad hoc,* we must recollect that it is of the very essence of Morgan's system that kinship terms are preserved with the utmost tenacity, survive the wreckage of social systems, and can thus be used to reconstruct social usages dating back not centuries but millennia. Orthodoxy does not change in character with a change from ecclesiastical to secular dogmas: its invariable correlate is "a temper which, psychologically considered, is indistinguishable from religious zeal."

The examples considered above happen to belong to the

field of "radical" movements, but secular movements with a deliberately or, at least, predominantly conservative bias display precisely the same psychology. Thus, admirers of a powerful State glorify their ideals with all the fanaticism of religious enthusiasts and evolve a mythology of their own, with its symbols and rationalizations; and eugenics was heralded by its founder himself as a substitute for traditional religion. We are, however, not concerned with appraising these several religions; we are interested merely in registering the fact that there persists, apart from universally recognized forms of religion, a sentiment analogous to that associated with them. This sentiment, then, is independent of a definable object but capable of concentrating on *any* object and by such concentration creating its Supernatural, while by secondary association all manner of other objects may be gathered within the scope of the Supernatural.

This conclusion gives a sufficiently clear answer to the query so often raised in recent decades, whether religion is likely to outlast the apparently triumphant spread of scientific enlightenment. If religion is understood in our sense, then assuredly it will survive, for history shows merely a transfer of the religious sentiment to new manifestations of the Extraordinary or Holy, never an extinction of the sentiment itself. Science itself—not as the *ideal* of the greatest scientists but as the actual phenomenon of culture-history —exhibits the unremitting sloughing off of folk-beliefs and their unremitting regeneration when the thoughts of the bold innovator turn into the sanctified formulæ of his disciples,— when they accept as Extraordinary or taboo what he established by defying the traditional taboos of his time.

But even if religion is conceived in the customary fashion, there is no obvious warrant in history for presaging its extinction. Personal deities have certainly made a powerful

appeal in a variety of distinct societies, and there is no reason for assuming that within any measurable span of time
such concepts will fail to satisfy the religious longings of a
large portion of mankind. What is more, it is likely that in
our own civilization some of the very forces that have been
most active in combating organized religion in the immediate
past will rally to its defense. The excesses of nationalistic
State worshipers, coupled with the charlatanism of race-the-
orists who ignorantly pretend to knowledge no living man
possesses or even deliberately falsify biological data, may
well raise a doubt among humanitarian liberals of the type of
John Morley, whether the perverse adoration of brute force
is a preferable substitute for a faith and a Church never
wholly devoid of spiritual elements.

From a purely intellectual point of view, too, the attitude
towards established religion on the part of professed ration-
alists is likely to acquire a serenity hardly to be anticipated
a generation ago. On the one hand, the traditional time-
honored allegations against organized religion are appreciably reduced in the light of sane historical inquiry: from
Mach we learn that it was, above all, the inveterate spontaneous human adherence to tradition rather than the external pressure of a hostile Church that arrested progress in
the physical sciences. But historical-mindedness cannot stop
at this point. If it is the anthropologist's first duty to study
his Crow or Ekoi with the maximum possible of sympathetic insight; if practices from our point of view judged
absurd or repulsive are examined without an attempt at adverse comment; would it not be strange if he assumed towards the majority sharing his own culture an attitude of
lofty or at best good-natured disdain? The thinker who de-
clines to pass judgment on the Ekoi belief in sorcery or on
Congolese fetichism cannot consistently denounce as "idola-

trous" the observances of fellow-citizens whose conceptions
of the Divine happen not to coincide with his own.

An unbiased view of human history also leads to a re-
vision of the received rationalist program of future progress.
We cannot lay down as a uniformly desirable goal that
purely intellectual enlightenment which so powerfully stirred
the spirits of many worthy thinkers of the last century. As
Cornelius has well said, not the acquisition of intellectual
insight but the unfolding of human individuality into an
harmonious work of art constitutes the supreme and universal human task. Let those whose Divine lies in the pur-
suit of demonstrable truth pursue their way unhindered by
external obstacles, but let them not foist on others an attitude peculiar to themselves. Thus this book closes with a
note often struck in the preceding pages,—with a recognition
of the importance of individual differences.

REFERENCES

[1] Höffding, 1906: 109.
[2] James: 35.
[3] Haeckel.

BIBLIOGRAPHY

NOTE.—This Bibliography includes all the literature cited in this work. The following abbreviations are used to designate serial publications:

A.F.L., Mem.—Memoirs of the American Folk-Lore Society.
Amer. Anth.—American Anthropologist.
Amer. Anth., Mem.—Memoirs of the American Anthropological Association.
A.M.N.H.—Anthropological Papers of the American Museum of Natural History.
A.M.N.H., Bull.—Bulletin of the American Museum of Natural History.
A.M.N.H., Mem.—Memoirs of the American Museum of Natural History.
B.A.E.—Annual Report of the Bureau of (American) Ethnology.
B.A.E., Bull.—Bulletin of the Bureau of (American) Ethnology.
J.A.F.L.—Journal of American Folk-Lore.
U.C.—University of California Publications in American Archæology and Ethnology.
Z.f.E.—Zeitschrift für Ethnologie.

Bamler, G.
    1911. Tami; *in* Neuhauss, III, 489-566.
Bartlett, F. C.
    1923. Psychology and Primitive Culture. New York.
Beckwith, M. W.
    1919. The Hawaiian Romance of Laieikawai. 33 B.A.E., 285-666.

Benedict, Laura Watson.
   1916. A Study of Bagobo Ceremonial, Magic and Myth. Annals of the New York Academy of Sciences, xxv.
Benedict, Ruth Fulton.
   1923. The Concept of the Guardian Spirit in North America. Amer. Anth. Mem., no. 29.
Bleek, W. H. I. *and* Lloyd, L. C.
   1911. Specimens of Bushman Folklore. London.
Boas, Franz.
   1894. Chinook Texts. Washington.
   1903. The Decorative Art of the North American Indians. The Popular Science Monthly, 481-498.
   1914. Mythology and Folk-tales of the North American Indians. J.A.F.L., xxvii, 374-410.
   1916. Tsimshian Mythology. 31 B.A.E. Washington.
Bogoras, W.
   1909. The Chukchee: A.M.N.H., Mem., xi, Leiden.
Breasted, J. H.
   1912. Development of Religion and Thought in Ancient Egypt. New York.
Brown, A. R.
   1922. The Andaman Islanders. Cambridge.
Buschan, Georg.
   1922. Illustrierte Völkerkunde, 2 vols. Stuttgart.
Collocott, E. E. V.
   1921. The Supernatural in Tonga. Amer. Anth., 415 sq.
Czaplicka, M. A.
   1914. Aboriginal Siberia. Oxford.
Densmore, F.
   1922. Northern Ute Music. B.A.E., Bull. 75. Washington.
Dixon, R. B.
   1905. The Northern Maidu. A.M.N.H., Bull. xvii, 119-346.
   1907. The Shasta. A.M.N.H., Bull. xvii, 381-498.

Dorsey, G. A., *and* Kroeber, A. L.

    1903. Traditions of the Arapaho. Field Museum Publications 81. Chicago.

Dorsey, J. O.

    1894. A Study of Siouan Cults. 11 B.A.E., 351-544. Washington.

Dumarest, F.

    1922. Notes of Cochiti, New Mexico. Amer. Anth. Mem., VI, 135-236.

Durkheim, E.

    1912. Les formes élémentaires de la vie réligieuse; le système totémique en Australie. Paris.

Ehrenreich, P.

    1910. Die allgemeine Mythologie und ihre ethnologischen Grundlagen. Leipzig.

Erdland, P. A.

    1914. Die Marshall-Insulaner. Anthropos-Bibliothek. Münster i. W.

Frazer, J. G.

    1922. The Golden Bough. London.

Gill, W. W.

    1876. Myths and Songs from the South Pacific. London.

Goldenweiser, A. A.

    1917. Religion and Society. Journal of Philosophy, Psychology, and Scientific Methods, XIV, 121 sq.

    1922. Early Civilization. New York.

Gomes, Edwin H.

    1911. Seventeen Years Among the Sea Dyaks of Borneo. Philadelphia.

Gutmann, Bruno.

    1909. Dichten und Denken der Dschagganeger; Beiträge zur ostafrikanischen Volkskunde. Leipzig.

Haeberlin, H.

    1916. The Idea of Fertilization in the Culture of the Pueblo Indians. Amer. Anth., Mem., III, 1-55.

Haeckel, Ernst.
1921. Entwicklungsgeschichte einer Jugend; Briefe an die Eltern 1852-1856. Leipzig.

Harrison, Jane.
1913. Ancient Art and Ritual. New York.

Hearne, Samuel.
1795. Journey from Prince of Wales Fort in Hudson's Bay to the Northern Ocean. London.

Höffding, Harald.
1893. Outlines of Psychology. London.
1906. The Philosophy of Religion. London.

Hoffman, W. J.
1891. The Midewiwin or "Grand Medicine Society" of the Ojibwa. 7 B.A.E., 143-300.

Holmes Anniversary Volume.
1916. Anthropological Essays presented to William Henry Holmes. Washington.

Howitt, A. W.
1904. The Native Tribes of South-east Australia. London.

James, William.
1902. The Varieties of Religious Experience. New York.

Jenness, D.
1922. The Life of the Copper Eskimo. Ottawa.

Jochelson, W.
1905-1908. The Koryak. A.M.N.H., Mem., x. Leiden.
1910. The Yukaghir and the Yukaghirized Tungus. A.M.N.H., Mem., xiii, 1-133. Leiden.

Jones, William.
1919. Ojibwa Texts. Publications of the American Ethnological Society, vol. vii, pt. 2. New York.

Jung, C. G.
1919. Studies in Word-Association. New York.

Junod, H. A.
1912. The Life of a South African Tribe. 2 vols. Neuchatel.

Kent, Grace Helen *and* Rosanoff, A. J.
  1910. A Study of Association in Insanity. Reprinted from
    American Journal of Insanity, vol. LXVII, nos. 1 and 2.
    Baltimore.
Koch-Grünberg, Th.
  1909. Zwei Jahre unter den Indianern. Reisen in Nordwest-
    Brasilien. Berlin.
Koppers, Wilhelm.
  1921. Die Anfänge des menschlichen Gemeinschaftslebens.
    Gladbach.
  1924. Unter Feuerland-Indianern. Stuttgart.
Kroeber, A. L.
  1902-1907. The Arapaho. A.M.N.H., Bull. XVIII, 1-229,
    279-454.
  1916. Thoughts on Zuñi Religion; *in* Holmes Anniversary
    Volume, 269-277.
  1922. Elements of Culture in Native California. U.C., vol.
    13, 259-328.
  1923. Anthropology. New York.
Lang, Andrew.
  1901. Magic and Religion. London.
  1909. The Making of Religion. 3rd. edition. London.
Lehner, Stefan.
  1911. Bukaua; *in* Neuhauss, III, 397-485.
Lowie, R. H.
  1909 (a). The Northern Shoshone. A.M.N.H., II, 165-302.
  1909 (b). The Assiniboine. A.M.N.H., IV, 1-270.
  1912. Social Life of the Crow Indians. A.M.N.H., IX, 179-
    247.
  1913 (a). Dance Associations of the Eastern Dakota. A.M.
    N.H., XI, 105-142.
  1913 (b). Military Societies of the Crow Indians. A.M.
    N.H., XI, 145-217.
  1913 (c). Societies of the Hidatsa and Mandan Indians.
    A.M.N.H., XI, 221-358.

1914. Ceremonialism in North America. Amer. Anth., 602-631.

1915. The Sun Dance of the Crow Indians. A.M.N.H., xvi, 1-50.

1919. The Tobacco Society of the Crow Indians. A.M.N.H., xxi, 101-200.

1922. The Religion of the Crow Indians. A.M.N.H., xxv, 309-444.

Lublinski, Ida.
1920-1921. Der Medizinmann bei den Naturvölkern Südamerikas. Z.f.E., 234-263.

Malo, David.
1903. Hawaiian Antiquities. Honolulu.

Marett, R. R.
1914. The Threshold of Religion. 2nd. edition. London.

Mariner, William. *See* Martin, J.

Martin, J.
1820. An Account of the Natives of the Tonga Islands in the South Pacific Ocean, compiled and arranged from the extensive communications of Mr. William Mariner. Boston.

Martius, C. Fr. Ph. von.
1867. Beiträge zur Ethnographie und Sprachenkunde Amerikas zumal Brasiliens. 2 vols. Leipzig.

Matthews, Washington.
1877. Ethnography and Philology of the Hidatsa Indians. Washington.
1897. Navaho Legends A.F.L., Mem., v. Boston.

Merker, M.
1910. Die Masai. Berlin.

Mooney, James.
1896. The Ghost Dance Religion. 14 B.A.E., pt. 2. Washington.

Morice, A. G.
1906. The Canadian Denes. Annual Archæological Report. Toronto.

Müller, W. Max.
1918. The Mythology of All Races, vol. XII, 1-245; Egyptian. Boston.

Neuhauss, R.
1911. Deutsch Neu-Guinea. Berlin. 3 vols.

Notes analytiques sur les collections ethnographiques du Musée du Congo. 1. 1902-1906. Brussels.

Parker, K. Langloh.
1905. The Euahlayi Tribe. London.

Parsons, E. C.
1922. (*Editor.*) American Indian Life. New York.
1924. The Scalp-Dance at Zuñi (in press). Amer. Anth., Mem. no. 31.

Pechuel-Loesche, E.
1907. Volkskunde von Loango. Stuttgart.

Perry, W. J.
1923. The Children of the Sun: a Study in the Early History of Civilization. New York.

Radin, Paul.
1914 (a). A Sketch of the Peyote Cult of the Winnebago; a Study in Borrowing. Journal of Religious Psychology, VII, 1-22.
1914 (b). Religion of the North American Indian. J.A.F.L., XXVII, 335-373.
1920. The Autobiography of a Winnebago Indian. U.C., vol. 16, 381-473.
1923. The Winnebago Tribe. 37 B.A.E. Washington.

Reports of the Cambridge Anthropological Expedition to Torres Straits, vol. V, 1904. Cambridge.

Rivers, W. H. R.
1914. The History of Melanesian Society. 2 vols. Cambridge.

Roth, Henry Ling.

    1896. The Natives of Sarawak and British North Borneo. London.

Roth, W.

    1897. Ethnological Studies Among the North-West-Central Queensland Aborigines. Brisbane.

    1915. An Inquiry into the Animism and Folk-Lore of the Guiana Indians. 30 B.A.E., 117-384.

Russell, Frank.

    1908. The Pima Indians. 26 B.A.E., 3-390. Washington.

Sapir, Edward.

    1907. Religious Ideas of the Takelma Indians. J.A.F.L., xx, 33-49.

    1922. Vancouver Island Indians; in Hastings, Encyclopædia of Religion and Ethics., vol. xii.

Schmidt, Wilhelm.

    1908-1909. L'origine de l'idée de Dieu; in Anthropos, iii, iv.

    1913. Kulturkreise und Kulturschichten in Südamerika. Z.f.E., 1014-1124.

Schmiedel, P. W.

    1906 (a). Das vierte Evangelium gegenüber den drei ersten. Tübingen.

    1906 (b). Evangelium, Briefe und Offenbarung des Johannes. Tübingen.

Scott, E. F.

    1909. The Historical and Religious Value of the Fourth Gospel. Boston.

Shooter, Joseph.

    1857. The Kafirs of Natal and the Zulu Country. London.

Skeat, W. W., and Blagden, C. O.

    1906. Pagan Races of the Malay Peninsula. 2 vols. London.

Skinner, A. B.

    1911. Notes on the Eastern Cree and Northern Saulteaux. A.M.N.H., ix, 1-177.

1913. Social Life and Ceremonial Bundles of the Menomini Indians. A.M.N.H., XIII, 1-165.

1915 (a). Associations and Ceremonies of the Menomini Indians. A.M.N.H., XIII, 167-215.

1915 (b). The Indians of Greater New York. Cedar Rapids, Iowa.

1920. Medicine Ceremony of the Menomini. Indian Notes and Monographs, IV, 15-188.

Skinner, A., *and* Satterlee, J. V.

1915. Folklore of the Menomini Indians. A.M.N.H., XIII, 223-546.

Smith, E. W. *and* Dale, A. M.

1920. The Ila-speaking Peoples of Northern Rhodesia. 2 vols. London.

Söderblom, Nathan.

1916. Das Werden des Gottesglaubens; Untersuchungen über die Anfänge der Religion. Leipzig.

Speck, F. G.

1909. Ethnology of the Yuchi Indians. University of Pennsylvania, Anthropological Publications of the University Museum, I, 1-154. Philadelphia.

Spencer, B., *and* Gillen, F. J.

1899. The Native Tribes of Central Australia. London.

1904. The Northern Tribes of Central Australia. London.

Spier, L.

1921. The Sun Dance of the Plains Indians: Its Development and Diffusion. A.M.N.H., XIV, 451-527.

Stevenson, M. C.

1909. The Zuñi Indians. 23 B.A.E.

Stoll, O.

1904. Suggestion und Hypnotismus in der Völkerpsychologie. Leipzig.

Sumner, W. G.

1919. War and Other Essays. New Haven.

Swanton, J. R.
1908. Social Condition, Beliefs, and Linguistic Relationship of the Tlingit Indians. 26 B.A.E., 391-485. Washington.
1911. Indian Tribes of the Lower Mississippi Valley. B.A.E., Bull. 43.
1918. An Early Account of the Choctaw Indians. Amer. Anth., Mem. v, 53-72.

Talbot, P. Amaury.
1912. In the Shadow of the Bush. London.

Teit, J.
1909. The Shuswap. A.M.N.H., iv, 443-789. Leiden.

Thouless, Robert H.
1923. An Introduction to the Psychology of Religion. New York.

Thurnwald, Richard.
1922 (?). Psychologie des primitiven Menschen. Handbuch der vergleichenden Psychologie, i, 147-320. München.

Tregear, E.
1904. The Maori Race. Wangani, New Zealand.

Tylor, E. B.
1865. Researches into the Early History of Mankind and the Development of Civilization. London.
1881. Anthropology. New York.
1913. Primitive Culture. 2 vols. London.

Walker, J. R.
1917. The Sun Dance and other Ceremonies of the Oglala Division of the Teton Dakota. A.M.N.H., xvi, 51-221.

Wallis, W. D.
1918. Messiahs: Christian and Pagan. Boston.

Weeks, John H.
1913. Among Congo Cannibals. Philadelphia.
1914. Among the Primitive Bakongo. Philadelphia.

Wissler, C.
1904. Decorative Art of the Sioux Indians. A.M.N.H., Bull., xviii, 231-277.

1908. Mythology of the Blackfoot Indians. A.M.N.H., II, 1-164.

1911. The Social Life of the Blackfoot Indians. A.M.N.H., VII, 1-64.

1912. Societies and Ceremonial Associations in the Oglala Division of the Teton-Dakota. A.M.N.H., XI, 1-99.

Woodworth, R. S.

1921. Psychology. New York.

Wundt, Wilhelm

1919. Völkerpsychologie, 3. Band: Die Kunst. Leipzig.